THE CITY OF HERMES

THE CITY OF HERMES
Articles and Essays on Occultism

John Michael Greer

AEON

Aeon Books Ltd
12 New College Parade
Finchley Road
London NW3 5EP

British Library Cataloguing in Publication Data

A C.I.P. for this book is available from the British Library

ISBN-13: 978-1-91280-718-5

Typeset by Medlar Publishing Solutions Pvt Ltd, India
Printed in Great Britain

www.aeonbooks.co.uk

CONTENTS

INTRODUCTION

The essays and articles collected in this volume sum up the first not-quite-decade of my career as a writer on magic and occultism. While they cover a range of subjects, all of them share a common theme and were shaped by certain experiences that remade my spiritual life just before the first of them was written.

Like many young Americans of my generation, I went to college right after high school, when I had only the vaguest notions of what I wanted out of life. Three years of college didn't bring me any closer, and I left college without a degree in 1983, moved to the nearest large city, married, and helped support our little household with a string of low-paying jobs while devoting my spare time to magic and writing. By 1991, I had a much clearer idea of what I wanted from life, and my wife's career as a bookkeeper and office manager brought in enough money that with a little help from the State of Washington, I was able to return to college.

The professors and guidance counselors I met at the University of Washington in Seattle probably never guessed that they were helping to train a wizard, but that's basically what happened. Two years of Latin, followed up with further study on my own time, gave me access to occult literature that had gone untouched for centuries; classes on the history of philosophy and the history of science gave me the background I needed to understand what I was reading. Meanwhile, by way of a chance conversation on the newborn internet, I met my first occult teacher, who gently but relentlessly pushed me to enlarge my understanding of magic and look at its philosophical and historical dimensions.

I came to these experiences as a student of the Golden Dawn tradition, the most widely practiced system of ceremonial magic in today's world. I came out the other side dazzled by the discovery that the Golden Dawn tradition was only one small slice of a much vaster movement of thought and practice, which took the name of Hermeticism after its mythic founder, the fabulous Egyptian sage Hermes Trismegistus. The more I studied the older literature, the more obvious it became that many of the elements of the Golden Dawn system were fragments of that vaster phenomenon, and could be enriched immeasurably by being reconnected with their more ancient context. Adocentyn, the legendary city founded by Hermes, was much on my mind in those days—thus the title of this anthology.

That sense of treasures to be found sent me digging in a dizzying assortment of old books, and while I found no shortage of dead ends, the live options I encountered more than made up for that. A Latin text on geomantic divination, *Modo Judicandi Quaestiones secundum Petrum de Abano Patavinum*, turned out to contain keys to interpreting geomantic charts that had been lost for centuries, and made geomantic divination far more effective and useful; a brief discussion in Joy Hancox' *The Byrom Collection*, a book about eighteenth-century sacred geometry, led me to Gerard Thibault's *Academie de l'Espee*, a textbook of rapier fencing based on Renaissance Pythagorean mysticism; a nineteenth-century book on a nearly forgotten fraternal order, the Odd Fellows, led me to apply for membership, and in the process I discovered the roots of Golden Dawn ritual in eighteenth- and nineteenth-century fraternal lodges—and these were simply the high points in a decade of discoveries that transformed my understanding of the occult traditions I studied and practiced.

That, in turn, was what launched my career as a writer on occultism. Until my second stint at college, the focus of my writing had been science fiction and fantasy fiction, and I had written a flurry of novels in those genres, none of which made it into print. (There was good reason for that, too, but it was a long while before I figured that out.) Fired by the conviction that I'd discovered some of the forgotten secrets of Hermetic occultism, I turned my hand to articles on occult topics—and to my delight, started getting acceptance letters and modest checks in place of the rejection slips I was used to seeing from publishers. On the basis of that experience, I put together my first book on occultism, *Paths of Wisdom*, and promptly placed it with a major occult publisher. I would be lying if I said I never looked back—fiction remains a passionate interest of mine, and in the decades that followed I finally managed to figure out what I was doing wrong and start getting novels into print—but the writing career I'd longed for since childhood was underway at last.

The books and articles that followed were only part of what came out of my discoveries in those years, however. I helped launch a quarterly journal of Hermetic studies, and when that fell apart due to quarrels among the participants, I launched another entirely on my own; I helped found two magical lodges; I studied historical swordsmanship, and plunged into the work of putting Thibault's great manual into English. All this, along with the writing, was in the service of a vision of a renewed Hermeticism that took the Golden Dawn tradition as its foundation but fused it with the riches of Renaissance Hermetic theory and practice.

That was the dream, and by the end of the decade, I was convinced that it had failed, or that I had. My efforts to interest the occult community in what I'd found seemed to go nowhere, and my interests were shifting; in 1994, I was initiated into the Order of Bards Ovates and Druids (OBOD), and over the years that followed, Druidry gradually became more and more central to my personal spirituality. That interest, and a series of improbable events, resulted in my election as Grand Archdruid of the Ancient Order of Druids in America (AODA) in 2003, and during the twelve busy and eventful years I held that office, my involvement in Hermeticism was on hold.

Looking back on the decade of work chronicled in this volume, I'm far less sure than I was that it represents a chronicle of failure. Some of the teachings I dragged out of obscurity eventually found their audience—there is now, for example, a modest but significant number of geomancers who use the classic methods I rediscovered. It may just be that changes of the sort I hoped to accomplish take time.

Whether or not that turns out to be the case, I felt it was time to take these early essays and articles of mine, all of them published in periodicals that no longer exist, and make them available again. I hope they will provide inspiration as well as entertainment to their readers.

—John Michael Greer

The fifty gates of understanding

My first published article, this study of an obscure corner of Cabalistic theory and practice appeared in the Neopagan magazine New Moon Rising *in 1993, and apparently went zooming right over the heads of its audience. Some of it was incorporated in my first published book,* Paths of Wisdom.

Since the teachings of the modern magical tradition began to emerge from secrecy about a hundred years ago, the Thirty-Two Paths of Wisdom—a traditional term for the Sephiroth and Paths of the Tree of Life—have been the dominant model of the magical universe in the Western world. This is quite understandable; as a key to the tradition's teachings, and a practical and philosophical tool for occult work, the Paths have enormous power. It may be worth noting, though, that the Tree of Life as it is presently understood is only one of the models which were used in older versions of the magical tradition.

Another model, and one which has nearly as broad an applicability as the Paths, is a system called the Fifty Gates of Understanding. These are so called, according to the Renaissance Qabalist Athanasius Kircher, "because ... no one can arrive at a perfect understanding of the afore-mentioned Paths, unless he first enters by them." Intended specifically to complement the Paths of Wisdom, the Gates of Understanding offers a different but related view of the universe, one which modern students of the magical arts may find useful.

The fifty gates of understanding

1. Primary matter, Hyle, chaos.
2. Matter in manifestation: formless, empty, and inanimate.
3. Natural forces of attraction and repulsion: the Abyss.
4. Separation and first rudiments of the Elements.
5. Elemental Earth, from which all seed is as yet absent.
6. Elemental Water, acting upon the World.
7. Elemental Air, issuing from the abyss of waters.
8. Elemental Fire, warming and giving life.
9. Elements interacting through the Qualities (hot, cold, dry, wet).
10. Their attraction toward a mixture of all.
11. Emergence of metals through the division of Earth.
12. "Flowers" and "saps" ordered for the generation of metals.
13. Seas, lakes, secret flowers among the cavities of the Earth.
14. Evolution of grasses, trees, and all plant life.
15. Processes of growth and reproduction in the plant kingdom.
16. Evolution of animal life in its most basic forms.
17. Evolution of insects, worms, and other invertebrate animals.
18. Evolution of fish, with their special properties.
19. Evolution of birds, with their special properties.
20. Evolution of the mammals.
21. Emergence of human beings.
22. Human physiology.
23. Human subtle anatomy, etheric structure, soul.
24. Human sexuality and reproduction.
25. The human being as a microcosm of the Universe.
26. Five external powers: hearing, touch, sight, taste, smell.
27. Five internal powers: memory, will, imagination, emotion, thought.
28. Humanity in the nonphysical realms of the Universe.
29. Humanity as an angelic order (*Ishim*).
30. Humanity as image and likeness of the Divine.
31. Sphere and spirits of Levanah, the Moon.
32. Sphere and spirits of Kokab, Mercury.
33. Sphere and spirits of Nogah, Venus.
34. Sphere and spirits of Shemesh, the Sun.

35. Sphere and spirits of Madim, Mars.
36. Sphere and spirits of Tzedek, Jupiter.
37. Sphere and spirits of Shabbathai, Saturn.
38. Sphere and spirits of Mazloth, the outer planets and stars.
39. Sphere and spirits of Rashith ha-Gilgalim, the galaxy.
40. Sphere and spirits of the cosmos as a whole.
41. Kerubim, Mighty Ones.
42. Beni Elohim, Sons of Divinity.
43. Tarshishim, Brilliant Ones (or Elohim, Deities).
44. Malakim, Angelic Kings.
45. Seraphim, Fiery Serpents.
46. Chashmalim, Shining Ones.
47. Aralim, Strong Ones.
48. Auphanim, Wheels or Whirling Forces.
49. Chaioth ha-Qodesh, Holy Living Creatures.
50. AIN SOPH, Divinity Itself.[1]

Commentary

This long and somewhat arcane list may seem baffling at first glance. A few points of explanation, though, may offer some clarity. The Fifty Gates of Understanding make up one variant—a very sophisticated one—of an ancient visionary model of the Universe: the Great Chain of Being. In this model, everything in existence is part of a continuum which extends, unbroken, from the central creative Power down to the densest forms of physical matter. Creative energies emanating from Deity flow along this continuum, sustaining it and connecting all things back to their Source.[2]

It will be seen that this way of thinking about the world is far removed from the more common views of reality in the modern West. In our culture's established religions, the Universe is split down the middle into one world of matter and another of spirit, and any contact between the two is labeled "evil" unless it takes place through official channels. Translate this same dualism into "physical" and "psychological," and the same thing holds true for most modern scientific thought. The model of the Great Chain of Being, on the other hand, expresses far more clearly the dance of interactions between many different levels of existence—from dense matter and physical energies through the subtle energies of life and health, through the many aspects of human consciousness, up into the high reaches of the spiritual realm—which we as human beings actually experience every day.

The Qabalistic version of this model adds certain additional touches to this picture. Fifty items in a list, obviously, do not exhaust the full range of levels in the Universe; they were never intended to do so. In Qabalistic thought, the continuum reaching from the Divine to its furthest creations is not seen as linear, like a chain. Instead, it radiates outward along an infinite array of lines; in much the same way light radiates from a lamp. The Fifty Gates symbolize the course of just one of these lines: specifically, the line that includes human beings along its path. This is why the list of the Gates includes the particular parts of the Universe it does, and why the various elements of the human organism have so much space given to them. A system of Gates intended for jellyfish, dolphins, or disembodied spirits would probably have little in common with this one—but that is hardly our concern!

The human perspective implicit in the Gates determines another, extremely important aspect of the system. A quick glance over the list will show that the Gates divide naturally into five groups of ten each. These correspond to five broad levels of existence: the physical level, consisting of dense matter and energy perceptible by the senses; the etheric level, consisting of the subtle energies of life and form which structure the material world; the astral level, or level of concrete consciousness, which gives shape to the etheric; the mental level, or level of abstract consciousness, which gives shape to the astral; and the spiritual level, reaching beyond definition, which gives shape to all. This is one of many ways of classifying the continuum we've discussed; it has the advantage, though, that all the levels it contains can be directly experienced by human beings, and ordinary human awareness stands at the center of the scheme.

Practical applications

Traditionally, the Fifty Gates are assigned to Binah (Understanding), the third Sephirah on the Tree of Life, while the Thirty-Two Paths are assigned to Chokmah (Wisdom), the second.

This points up an important distinction. Chokmah corresponds to force, Binah to form; while the Paths focus on the forces of the Universe, the Gates focus on the forms through which those forces come into play.

The Gates thus have a particular relationship with the world of everyday experience, and it can be a useful exercise to make a habit of identifying ordinary objects with their corresponding Gates: grass on the roadside with the 14th Gate, for example, a neighbor's dog with the 20th, or romantic feelings with the 33rd.

The Gates come into their own, though, when they are used as a subject for meditation and visionary work. The individual Gates, their order and interrelationships, and their place in the system as a whole are all food for meditation. An extremely valuable practice is to build up a Gate in the imagination, in the form of a great Portal bearing the appropriate number. This then becomes the starting point for a pathworking, or rather a Gateworking, into the corresponding level of the astral. The 6th Gate thus allows visionary access to the realm of elemental Water; the 41st, to the sphere of the Angels of the Ninth Choir.

As always with workings of this type, the usual precautions should be taken; these can be found in the Golden Dawn documents on "scrying in the spirit vision," and in many other sources as well.[3] While I have not been able to find a traditional set of Divine Names governing the Gates, my own experience has been that each of the five groups mentioned above can be related to one of the five Spheres of the Middle Pillar, and thus to the corresponding Divine Name. The physical Gates are therefore related to the Name ADNI, Adonai; the etheric, to ShDI ALChI, Shaddai El Chai; the astral, to YHVH ALVH VDAaTh, Tetragrammaton Eloah va-Daath; the mental to YHVH ALHIM, Tetragrammaton Elohim; and the spiritual to AHIH, Eheieh. These Names may be used to open the Gates, and to test entities encountered on the other side.

The general correspondence between the Gates and the Sephirah Binah has another implication for practice, for Binah as the first origin of form has a special rulership over all works of practical magic. The Fifty Gates will thus be found to have much to teach about this aspect of magical work. These lessons are best learned by way of the methods mentioned above, but one note may not be out of place. Magic may be worked on different levels of the continuum represented by the Gates; some rituals make use of the subtle forces stored in herbs, stones, and metals, while others focus, on planetary or even angelic powers, and still others combine levels in different ways. Each of these approaches has its own character and will be found to produce different results and to be more or less effective in different situations. Work with the Fifty Gates can help to clarify these relationships to a remarkable extent.

Conclusion

These notes are intended as a first, fairly tentative look at a neglected area of Qabalistic tradition—one which has potentials going far beyond the suggestions I've made here. For the time being, despite Kircher's advice, the Fifty Gates of Understanding are probably best suited to those who have already done a good deal of work with the Tree of Life and are comfortable working in areas where few guidelines exist. Nonetheless, the symbolism of the Gates has a great deal to teach, and I hope other students of the magical tradition will find them interesting enough to begin explorations of their own.

Notes

1. This list of the Gates is adapted from the somewhat confused version used by the nineteenth-century French occultist Dr. Gerard Encausse. See Papus, *The Qabalah* (Aquarian, 1977, pp. 230–233).
2. For those who can handle academic writing, the classic book on the Great Chain of Being is still Lovejoy, A.O., *The Great Chain of Being* (Harvard University Press, 1936).
3. See Regardie, I., *The Golden Dawn* (Llewellyn, 1971, Vol. 4, pp. 11–46), and also Kraig, D.M., *Modern Magick* (Llewellyn, 1988, pp. 486–503), for discussions of the methods involved in this type of work.

Bibliography

Kraig, D.M., *Modern Magick* (Llewellyn, 1988, pp. 486–503).
Lovejoy, A.O., *The Great Chain of Being* (Harvard University Press, 1936).
Papus, *The Qabalah* (Aquarian, 1977, pp. 230–233).
Regardie, I., *The Golden Dawn* (Llewellyn, 1971, Vol. 4, pp. 11–46).

Meditation in magical practice

This was my second published article and appeared in New Moon Rising *in 1994. It was my first attempt to explain discursive meditation—the central meditative practice of traditional Western occultism—to modern students of magic.*

For many people in our present culture, the word "meditation" calls up vaguely Oriental images of strange postures, stranger chants, and aspirants "blissing out" into mental states more usually associated with various illegal chemicals. Given our society's monumental ignorance of spirituality, this is not surprising. What is surprising is that these same attitudes can be found to some degree in the magical community. I have heard people who ought to have known better insisting that meditation, and meditative techniques, are Oriental methods with no real place in the Western esoteric tradition.

In fact, the West has had its own systems of meditation since at least classical times, and these form a valuable but too often neglected part of Western magical lore. The most common of these, which will be out-lined here, differs from better-known Eastern methods (such as zazen and mantra meditation) in some important ways. Like them, it involves disciplining the mind, and so teaches the control of consciousness that is so important a part of magical work. Unlike them, it does not seek to "stop" or "empty" the mind, but rather to direct it and focus it on a magical symbol, as a key to open up the symbol's inner meaning. Because of this, it benefits the aspiring magician in two ways: by developing mental clarity and focus, on the one hand, and by deepening understanding of the symbolism of magic on the other. Both of these are vital elements of esoteric training, and there is no better way to learn them.

Time, posture, and surroundings

Meditation should be a daily practice for any serious student of magic. Twenty to thirty minutes a day is enough, but this should be done every day without fail, and it's best to schedule it at the same time. Many people find that the early morning, just before breakfast, is a good time for this practice.

Like its Eastern equivalents, this method of meditation has a traditional posture; fortunately, this is a good deal easier on inflexible Western bodies than, say, lotus posture! You'll need a chair with a straight back and a seat high enough that, when you sit on it, your thighs are parallel to the floor. Sit with your back straight, your hands palms down on your thighs, and your knees, ankles, and feet together. (If you've ever seen an ancient Egyptian picture of a goddess or god seated on a throne, you'll recognize the posture at once.) This posture will seem uncomfortable at first, but with time it will become stable and comfortable—something which is just as true of meditation itself.

Some details of the surroundings will help your practice. Distractions should be minimized; thus, windows and curtains should be closed, music turned off, other people asked not to interrupt. A room of your own, with a door you can lock, is a great help in this work. A clock should be placed where you can see it without moving your head. Lastly, your chair should be facing east; this isn't an absolute necessity, but it aligns you with energy currents in the etheric body of the Earth, and these have a subtle but definite positive effect on this kind of work.

The fourfold breath

Rhythmic breathing has far-reaching effects on many levels of the human organism; in meditation, these are put to use. Once you've arranged time and space for your practice and learned the posture, your next task is to learn the way of breathing.

The rhythm of breath to be used here is a simple one: draw in a breath while mentally counting from one to four, hold the breath for the count of four, let it out to the count of four, and then hold it out, keeping the lungs empty, to the same count. Repeat this cycle, keeping the breathing and the counting steady and even. If you run out of breath during the cycle, you're doing it too slowly; stop, breathe normally for a minute or so, and then start again with a slightly faster rhythm.

This pattern is called the fourfold breath. You'll want to do five minutes of this, by the clock, at the beginning of each session of meditation, and a few more cycles at the end of each session; during the meditation itself you'll be breathing normally.

Invocation of the higher

At the end of the five minutes of fourfold breath, take a moment to invoke the Higher, in whatever form you conceptualize this: a Hermetic magician might call upon the Higher Self or an appropriate Qabalistic Name of God, a Wiccan the Goddess and/or the Horned God, and so forth. An example drawn from traditional Rosicrucian lore, using one of the Qabalistic Names, runs as follows: *Blessed be Thou, Adonai, enlighten me through thy initiation!* As this shows, the invocation can be (in fact, should be) brief, approximating an ordinary prayer.

Short or not, this is a much more important part of the practice of meditation than it will probably seem at first. One of the core ideas of the philosophy of magic teaches that consciousness only seems to be "bottled up" inside the brains of individuals, rather, according to the teaching, all consciousness is a unity, and different nervous systems and personalities serve as its Contact-points with matter, in much the way that different beaches are washed by the waves of one sea. By turning the attention toward the Higher, it becomes possible to open up to this unity; this has effects which, at least potentially, reach upwards to the highest levels of mystical attainment, but the one you'll probably notice first is that your meditations may turn up pieces of information which you can't trace to any known source.

Choosing a topic

At first thought, the idea of having to come up with a topic for meditation every day may be daunting. In practice, though, you'll find that it's not a difficulty; in fact, you're likely to end up with a long waiting list of potential topics in a fairly short time.

Literally any aspect of magical theory, symbolism, or practice can be used in this way. The Tarot is a very common first topic, and runes or any other symbolic system of divination would be an equally good choice. Traditional myths and legends are another source of topics, one which Pagans may find particularly useful, while Hermetic magicians might easily devote several years to the Qabala and its symbolism. Another source of material, one of special importance to the practical magician, is magical ritual itself; when a ceremony has been worked through in meditation, so that each phase is familiar and every nuance open to awareness, the experience of ritual can be deepened to a startling extent.

As you work with your topics, whichever you choose, you'll want to keep track of the directions in which your meditations lead. Ultimately, the best source of topics for your meditative work is meditation itself; your own discoveries will guide you more effectively than any external resource.

Meditation

The word "meditation" comes from a Latin word meaning, simply, "thinking," and you may be surprised to find that unlike the Oriental methods mentioned earlier, the method of meditation described here involves exactly that. However, this thinking is thinking of a very specific kind, and it needs to be done in a very specific way.

When you've finished the breathing and invocation, the real work of meditation is ready to begin. You'll have chosen a topic for meditation beforehand, as discussed above. For a few minutes, think about the topic in general terms. Then, focus on one small facet or portion of the subject, and work your way through its meanings and implications, following these out to their conclusion.

For example, let's imagine that you're meditating on Tarot Trump II, the High Priestess. After a few minutes spent considering the Trump in general, you turn your thoughts to the two pillars that frame the image. These may make you think of the number 2, of duality in general, of parallel lines, of balance and symmetry, or (if you have some exposure to Western esoteric tradition) of the pillars of King Solomon's Temple, or of other things entirely. Whatever ideas cluster around the image, gather them up, consider them, compare them with one another and with what you already know of the High Priestess. One or more of them may set a train of thoughts moving; if this happens, you follow it out to its conclusion. This process continues for the full time you've chosen to spend in your meditation.

The great difficulty, of course, is that your mind will tend to wander off the subject... again, and again, and again. Especially in the first weeks and months of practice, you'll find yourself thinking about dinner, the book you just read, next Friday's party—anything under the sun, in fact, except the topic you've chosen. Change, especially the sort of inward change needed to master meditation, requires that inertia be overcome; in this case, the inertia is that of ordinary, lazy, half-random thoughts, the "internal monologue" that fills most people's heads during every waking hour.

Unfortunately, there's no quick and easy answer to the problem. The solution is simply patience and continuing effort. Whenever you notice that your mind has drifted off the subject, bring it back gently and pick up the meditation at the last point you remember reaching. If your mind drifts off again, bring it back again. There may be times when you'll spend an entire practice session doing nothing more than dragging your mind back to the subject. This is actually a good sign, for increasing resistance is evidence of increasing progress; the faster you're going, so to speak, the more bugs you'll get on your windshield. Given time and regular practice, you'll develop the inner skills necessary to go beyond this state into real meditative clarity.

Finishing steps

When you've meditated for the full amount of time you've set for yourself, take a moment to bring your thoughts back to the original topic. Then, as mentioned earlier, do a few cycles of the fourfold breath in order to clear your mind and bring yourself back to ordinary consciousness.

You may find it useful at this point to rub your palms together for a minute or so, until they feel warm, and then rub the following points on your body: the crown of your head, the base of your neck, your solar plexus, the area around your tailbone, and the soles of both feet. These are the physical anchoring-points for the five energy centers of the Middle Pillar, and rubbing them will help your body's energies make the transition from the stillness of meditation to other activities.

Finally, as with any other magical practice, the results of your meditation should be noted down in a practice journal or magical diary as soon as possible after you finish. In particular, as I've suggested earlier, be sure to write down the ideas and understandings that come up during the practice. You will find that these will become a resource of quite some value both in your meditations and in the whole range of magical work through personal experience of the meaning of magical symbols experience which meditation, of all the magical disciplines, may be best fitted to provide—the rote learning necessary in the early stages of magical training can be replaced with real understanding, and this understanding becomes a guide not only in magical matters but in the whole of life as well.

The magical lodge

My initiation into the Independent Order of Odd Fellows in 1993 marked an unexpected watershed in my magical work. About ten minutes into the Initiatory Degree, the first of the initiations conferred by the Odd Fellows, I realized that there was something very familiar in the ritual I was passing through—though its words and actions were entirely different, the basic structure of the ritual closely echoed that of the Golden Dawn initiations I'd been studying in my magical work. This article was my first attempt to discuss the magical lodge system in print, and was followed later the same year by the essay "The Hall of Thmaa" (included in this volume) and in 1998 by my book Inside a Magical Lodge.

First principles

Up to the 1960s, when the current revival of the magical arts in the Western world got off the ground, most magicians belonged to lodges the way wolves belong to packs or whales to pods. The lodge system was not merely the primary but very nearly the only form of organization within the then-small magical community, and the magicians themselves benefited from several centuries of collected experience in

13

lodge work, both from magical groups and from the fraternal lodges to which many magicians belonged.

Times, obviously, have changed. The renaissance of magic which came surging out of the back closets of our culture three decades ago drew, and continues to draw, on published resources rather than the private lore of the surviving magical orders. Most magicians these days are self-taught, with books as their only instructors. At the same time, the slow decline of the fraternal orders turned into freefall in the 1960s, choking off the other major source of information on lodge technique. The outcome of these two factors is a complete reversal of the earlier situation; not only do most magicians not belong to anything that can be called a lodge, even in the loosest terms, but many of those who do belong have little access to the details of lodge structure and technique.

One of the results of this has been a lot of time spent reinventing the wheel in magical groups. This is by no means an entirely bad thing—there is always the chance that the new wheel will turn out better than the old—but there's also much to be said for examining older attempts at wheel-making as part of the process.

Additionally, some of the more popular magical systems studied at present were set up entirely within a lodge context and have substantial elements which depend on standard lodge technique for their meaning and function. As I am not a member of the OTO, I can't speak to their experience, but certainly the lack of a background in lodge work has been a common (though often unrecognized) problem in groups deriving from the Golden Dawn tradition, among others.

My own background combines some years of magical practice (mostly in the Golden Dawn tradition) with an extensive involvement in one of the surviving non-magical fraternal orders, and access to ritual texts and materials of a number of others. My experience in watching these interact and illuminate one another suggests to me that other magicians interested in traditional esoteric systems, or in the often-vexing question of the management of magical groups, may find some of this material useful.

A few definitions will help to clarify matters. A lodge, in the present context, is a group of people who come together to prepare and perform initiations. An initiation is a formal process for bringing about specific long-term changes in human consciousness. Every lodge, magical or not, has at least one initiation to offer, and most have more than one. People outside the surviving lodges tend to think of these initiations as nothing more than an overelaborate process of being admitted to lodge membership, a kind of formalized hazing new members go through before getting access to what's really going on. In fact, the reverse is true: the initiation, centrally, is what's going on, and every other element of lodge organization and procedure is there primarily to support it.

This is true even in those fraternal orders which haven't completely decayed into social clubs or insurance companies. It is far more true, and far more critical, in a magical lodge worth the name. Magical initiation is to the new initiate what consecration is to a talisman: something inert and unformed receives energy, shape, direction. The same transformation can also be brought about by individual work—self-initiation is certainly a valid concept, and a valid path—but a ritual initiation combined with appropriate individual practice can allow enormous gains to be made in a relatively short time.

The methods of initiation differ. So, of course, do the models used to understand the process. One useful way of thinking about initiation posits two realms or worlds: one is the realm of matter, perceived by the ordinary senses; the other we may as well call the realm of meaning, perceived by that complex set of processes we usually call "the mind." (Some traditions see one or the other of these as primary, with the remaining one derived or even imaginary; for our present purposes, though, the distinction is a moot point.)

Ordinarily, these two realms exist cheek by jowl in our awareness, with a sort of uneasy mapping of one onto the other serving as the one link between them. Under certain circumstances, though, the gap between them can be bridged or even annihilated for a time: matter and meaning fuse, so that physical objects take on cognitive depth and catalyze transformations at all levels of consciousness.

Extreme physical or psychological states can do this; so can the effects of some drugs; and so can the technical devices of ceremonial magic. Some combination of these methods comes into most initiatory systems worldwide; in the Western esoteric tradition, by contrast, the first two rarely appear. If this needs any justification, it's that ceremonial magic can get the same results with less risk of long-term damage to physical or mental health.

This way of looking at the initiatory process is useful here because it highlights a critical feature of the traditional lodge system. Like Janus, the two-faced god of doorways and beginnings, a lodge looks two ways at the same time. As the support system for this coalescence of the realms, it must be able to organize space, time, personnel, and the other requirements of initiation in terms of matter and meaning alike.

On the side of matter, appropriate space and time need to be arranged for the initiatory work; people need to be selected, trained in ritual practice and the details of the initiation, and rotated from one role to another to prevent burnout and provide cross-training; and whatever physical properties, costumes, and consumables the ritual happens to require have to be provided and kept on hand. Arranging for these things generally involves a certain amount of money and labor, and ways to organize these and to resolve disputes concerning them need to be arranged as well.

All these things, in turn, have their precise correlates in the realm of meaning. The space used in the ritual is organized according to a symbolic map, the time structured in a ceremonial manner; the people are not merely trained in the ritual but also brought inside the initiation's system of meaning, not least by being initiated themselves; and the details of properties and internal organization shaped to fit the symbolism of the system.

The Janus quality of the elements of the lodge system has the potential for a great deal of awkwardness, of course; arrangements which make perfect sense in the context of one realm can fail utterly to work in that of the other. As an organic structure which has evolved through something like four centuries of trial and error, though, the lodge system has had the chance to work through most of the possibilities for mischief. Most of the details of what I will be calling the "standard kit" of lodge work have been selected because they face matter and meaning with equal effectiveness.

The remaining parts of this article will cover some of the issues and more of the details involved in working magic in the context of a traditional lodge. All of these issues, though—and the great majority of the details, even the strangest, of any lodge system—can be understood well enough if the central duality of the lodge as a magical technology is kept in mind.

Patterns in space and time

The traditional lodge system includes some fairly specific ways of organizing space and time as part of its "standard kit" of techniques. Some of the elements of these ways will seem needlessly ornate or formal to the modern magician; others will seem thoroughly boring. In practice, though, the system works well, and as often as not it is the apparently dull details which make for effective functioning.

Space

The process of initiation, as the first part of this article explained, is the primary purpose of the lodge system and the principal work of any functioning traditional lodge. While initiatory work can be done in any of a vast number of ways, the traditional initiations of Western magic (and, for that matter, of Western fraternal orders) tend to follow the same overall scheme and to use the same basic set of techniques. In outline, the candidate for initiation is placed in a receptive state by various technical methods, brought into a prepared space, moved through a set of specific experiences, and then given a set of symbolic and somatic triggers which allow the state of consciousness created by these experiences to be reawakened more or less at will.

This process places some fairly specific requirements on the space to be used. A lodge room needs to be large enough to allow the different stages of the initiation to be kept separate from one another, and for props, tableaus or symbolic images to be set up and removed easily. It also needs enough physical and sensory isolation from the outside world to keep the set experiences of the initiation from being interrupted.

At the same time, the initiatory work does not take place in a vacuum. The people, materials, and money needed for the process have to be collected, distributed and put to use, and any disputes resolved without rupturing the unity of the lodge. Spatial organization has more to say to these matters than may be apparent at first glance. Seating arrangements can help or hinder group discussion and decision-making processes, clarify or muddy roles and responsibilities within the lodge. Since the same room is normally used for a lodge's business meetings and its initiations, these factors come together with the needs of the initiation in the design of the lodge space.

The interplay between these two concerns has produced a standard lodge architecture that can be found in practically every lodge-based organization in the Western world. The basic form is an open rectangular space with a door on one of the short sides and seats around the perimeter. An anteroom outside the door allows a guard to control access and prevent interruptions. Inside, the primary lodge officers sit on the short sides, while the bulk of the members sit on the long sides. The center of the space may contain objects of symbolic importance, or it may be left empty; in either case, it will be used for the most important symbolic actions. The basic design is that of Diagram 1.

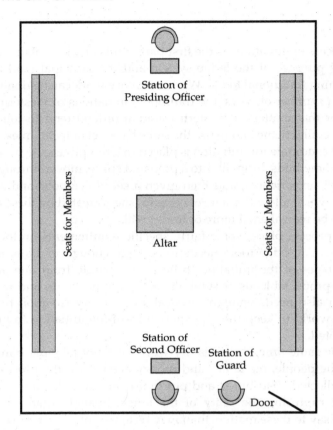

These are the material aspects of the use of space in a lodge. What of the other side of the equation, the realm of meaning? Most often, this comes out of the core symbolism of the specific lodge. A lodge working on Qabalistic lines will most likely map the Tree of Life onto the lodge room in some manner—the Golden Dawn is probably the best-known example of this; lodges of other traditions will use other mappings. In most systems, these maps determine the placement of the stations and movements of the initiatory process.

A few elements of this sort of mapping are common, enough to have a place in the "standard kit" of lodge technique. The most important of these is symbolic polarity—the identification of the parts and officers of a lodge with a set of symbolic opposites such as light and darkness, fire and water, or the like. Most often the two short ends of the lodge room, and the lodge officers who sit there, form the major polarity in the lodge. A second may be set up between officers who sit on the two long sides; alternatively, the first polarity may be resolved by a third officer sitting on one of the long sides or elsewhere; or both of these can be done in the same lodge.

A related "standard kit" ingredient has to do with the line connecting the chief officer's station with the central space of the lodge. This serves as the primary path for what we may as well call "energy"—dramatic, psychological, or magical, depending on your choice of interpretive filter. In most lodge systems this line is not crossed except at specific points in ceremonial work, and movement along it happens only at the critical moments in the initiatory process.

Time

The same needs that define the lodge's organization of space also shape its relationship to time. To carry out its work, a lodge must be able to define periods of time in which ritual consciousness is constructed, and it needs to have methods in place for moving smoothly from one level of ritual consciousness—"grade" or "degree" in lodge jargon—to another as well as from ordinary consciousness to any of these and back.

The usual method in these transitions is a simple ritual process given strength through regular practice. The ceremony used to open a lodge—to move from ordinary to ritual time—generally has four elements. First, the doors are closed, and those present show their right to be there; second, the lodge officers recite their duties; third, the powers governing the lodge symbolism are invoked; finally, the lodge is formally declared to be open. Each of these elements can be simple or complex, but all make use of familiar tactics for shaping consciousness.

Perhaps the most interesting, because the least obvious, is the central technique of the first element. Lodge members demonstrate their right to be present with one or more of the symbolic and somatic triggers— words, grips, gestures—received in initiation, and in this way evoke the emotional reactions to their first experience of the lodge.

A shorter ceremony, usually of two elements, closes a lodge. Banishings of the sort familiar to most magicians nowadays are all but unknown in lodge technique; instead, a second invocation designed to channel the energies of the ritual out into ordinary time is used. After this, the lodge is simply declared closed. A similar two-element ceremony moves the lodge from one grade to another; here a triggering symbol is used to link the lodge members with the desired grade's state of consciousness, and the lodge is then declared to be open in the new grade.

It's worth noting that fraternal lodges conduct their practical business while the lodge is ritually opened. Few magical lodges do the same. To some extent, this is sensible, given the different levels of energy involved: fraternal invocations normally approximate to ordinary prayers, while those of a magical lodge should be full-force magical rituals. There's something to be said, though, for carrying out lodge business in an open lodge, where (at least potentially) the unifying force of the lodge's energies can help counteract the usual problems of factionalism and ego inflation. The use of a low grade for business meetings, or the development of an "outer grade" along more or less fraternal lines, might be one way to explore these possibilities.

Patterns in organization

During the time when the lodge system was central to magic in the Western world, a great deal of nonsense and unneeded mystification about lodges and lodge methods went into circulation both in the magical community and outside it, both from romancers of the Dion Fortune variety and from Illuminati-hunting paranoids of the sort still published by John Birch Society presses. The resulting fog, combined with the habit of oaths of secrecy, has kept the whole subject of the lodge system far more obscure than it needs to be.

The lodge, in fact, can best be seen as a fairly simple technology of social organization, adapted for the purpose of bringing about specific changes in consciousness in its members. The differences between a lodge and other kinds of social structures come out of this. In the lodge system, as it exists in the Western world, these changes in consciousness are structured through formal ritual processes called initiations, which are themselves simply uses of another technology, one of personal transformation.

Both these technologies have a standard form in the Western world. Despite the usual claims of vast age circulated by magical and fraternal orders alike, these forms seem to have been developed in the latter part of the Renaissance, largely out of the remains of the old medieval guild system. Both went through a second period of development in the nineteenth century, during the golden age of fraternal orders in England and America.

From the perspective of the present, it's hard to imagine just how important these systems were in the Western world as recently as a hundred years ago. In 1897, it's estimated that forty percent of all adult Americans, of both genders and all ethnic backgrounds, belonged to at least one fraternal lodge. The rituals of these lodges were and are, in point of fact, the traditional initiation rituals of our culture, and the lodges themselves—democratically run, on the whole, and controlled by the local membership—also served as the foundation of a whole system, now all but forgotten, of decentralized social organization and mutual help.

With needs and (often) members in common, the lodge systems operating throughout these periods tended to share a great deal of technical material, so that even fine details of practice are identical in many different systems: for example, three knocks with a gavel or the equivalent will bring the members to their feet in nearly any lodge in North America. More important than these similarities of detail, though, are basic similarities of form and function, which are reflected in the lodge system in common structures of organization.

Functions and officers

A lodge, as an organization intended to carry out the work of initiation, has to be able to provide me with various items needed for that work and to organize the people involved in the process. Neither of these requirements is a particularly large burden—most initiations, magical or fraternal, can be performed competently given half a dozen trained people and a few hundred dollars' worth of costumes and props—but both need to be met regularly and reliably if the lodge is to function well.

The way in which these requirements are met is as much a part of the "standard kit" of lodge technique as the shape of the lodge room or the standard processes of initiation. Typically, each major task will have a specific officer to oversee it. Money is handled by a treasurer, necessary paperwork by a secretary; a chief officer presides over meetings of the lodge, and a second officer assists the chief and fills in when he or she is absent. There is usually an officer responsible for props and officers' regalia, and there may be another who serves as director for the rituals of initiation; still other officers will have charge of other aspects of the lodge's practical or ceremonial work. The principle behind all these offices is simple: responsibility is divided, so that no one person has too much to do, but it is also defined, so there's never any doubt about who is supposed to do what. There is always somewhere for the buck to stop.

This system of formal offices with set responsibilities has another advantage, one which goes against the grain of some of the stronger trends of our present culture. In a lodge setting, leadership is a function of office, not of personality; the chief officer of a lodge is not necessarily the most charismatic person in the lodge, or for that matter the worst bully, but he or she still presides over lodge meetings and has the final say in certain matters. Similarly, the duties and powers of each office are defined by lodge bylaws, not simply by interpersonal jockeying and buck-passing. This does not eliminate the political problems which so often occur in less organized groups—politics are inevitable whenever two human beings come within shouting distance—but it tends to keep politics from interfering with the work of the lodge.

This stress on offices rather than personalities is reinforced by a number of other parts of standard lodge practice. The different officers will have specific places to sit, defined in the physical and symbolic architecture of the lodge room; they will also wear symbolic regalia of office, which are formally conferred on them when they take office and just as formally passed on to their successors at the end of their terms. The point made by both these practices is that it is the position rather than the person which holds whatever authority is involved.

Decision-making in a lodge

Not all responsibilities in a lodge setting are routine enough that they can be assigned to a single officer. In fraternal lodges, in particular, a great deal of stress has been placed on bringing the whole lodge in on the more important decisions. The most obvious of these is the assignment of members to the different offices, but most decisions which involve lodge money also go to the membership as well, and so does the question of whether a given person will be admitted into the lodge.

These decisions, in fraternal lodges, are almost universally made by a vote of lodge members. This is one of the great strengths of the traditional lodge system; it helps prevent abuses of power and allows the voices of all lodge members to be heard. Unfortunately, it's a strength which has not usually been carried over into the magical community, where lodges have more often been oligarchies run by a clique of senior members. This habit has one excuse, which is that it can keep teachings from being watered down by a majority which does not understand them; still, there's a long history of abuse and exploitation on the part of lodges which are run this way. A possible compromise might be to place authority over rituals and instruction in the hands of a circle of senior members but keep day-to-day control over lodge business on a democratic basis. Control of money, above all, needs to be in the hands of the membership of each lodge; the temptation to dip into the lodge cookie jar has been too great for far too many "Secret Chiefs."

Decisions in the lodge are generally made by majority vote, except in certain specific cases. This has some problems—it can lead to the tyranny of the majority over a minority—but (unlike consensus-based systems) it has the advantage of ensuring that some decision does get made. Votes on special matters, such as bylaws or the expulsion of a member, may require a two-thirds vote. Voting on candidates for membership, though, is done on a far more exacting basis. In most lodges, a very small number of votes against admission—two or three—is enough to exclude a candidate. (The vote is usually taken with white and black balls, hence the term "blackballed.") This may seem unreasonable, but it has a solid basis in practical experience.

One of the most common factors in the breakup of lodges is personal quarrels between members. If more than one or two lodge members dislike a candidate enough to vote against admission, the risk of that dislike becoming a problem within the lodge is a real one. A lodge, again, is a specific group of people who work together for the purpose of offering a specific initiation. It is not, and does not need to be, open to everyone.

Patterns of initiation

"Initiation" is another concept which has been piled with an obscurity it doesn't require. In magical circles, until quite recently, people tended to speak of it in the same tone of hushed melodrama given to solemn gibberish about Atlantis and the Secret Masters. In the fraternal orders, on the other hand, rites of initiation have too often been treated as though they were nothing more than a sort of formalized hazing. In both settings, too much mystification and not enough thought have kept the process of initiation from being understood with any kind of clarity at all.

The sad thing is that this clarity can be managed quite easily without violating the obligation of secrecy which, for reasons we'll examine in a moment, is standard in nearly all lodge systems. The material I'll be covering here does not include any of the things which are considered secret, either by the order in which I have been initiated or by any other; revelations of lodge "secrets" have been made before, with no noticeable benefit to anyone in most cases. Rather, what I've given is the framework in which these secrets are placed—a framework which, in the lodge system, is what gives the secrets their importance and effect.

Methods of initiation

As mentioned earlier in this essay, the process of initiation works by bringing about a fusion between the realms of matter and meaning in the consciousness of the initiate. There are any number of methods for doing this. In the lodge systems of the Western world, it's typically done by means of a set of fairly simple psychological methods.

These psychological methods take many forms, but they all rely on the induction of a certain kind of receptive state in the person receiving the initiation. That state is not particularly hard to achieve; everyone who's lost a couple of hours while staring at the TV has experienced a shallow form of it, whence comes the effectiveness of TV advertising. In a lodge setting, the specific methods used to bring about this state are sensory deprivation, disorientation, sonorous and hypnotic language, and the deliberate use of mild and carefully controlled shock and fear.

One other means of bringing about this state deserves a little more comment, if only because it has been thoroughly misunderstood in modern times. Secrecy has a range of purposes in a fraternal or magical setting, but one of its most important uses is as a means of transforming consciousness in ritual. The specific things which are kept secret by orders using the lodge system are rarely of any importance by themselves, but the fact that these things are secret—and the fact that those outside the orders know that there are secrets inside them—shapes the way in which candidates for initiation approach the experiences of the ceremony. The idea that secrets will be revealed in an initiation creates a sense of expectancy, and can also give rise to a certain kind of fear; both of these are useful in the work of initiation.

The production of this receptive state forms the first phase of the initiatory process. Once it has been reached, the process of lodge initiation moves to a second phase, in which a set of carefully chosen images or events are experienced by the initiate, and then explained. These experiences and their explanations are heightened by the receptive state, and are intended to offer a new pattern for some portion of the initiate's mental map of the world; the pattern may also be encoded, more subtly, in the underlying structure of the ritual itself. If the initiate accepts this new pattern—which does not always happen—the initiation has "taken."

At this point, the process enters its third phase. The new initiate is given a set of conceptual, verbal and somatic triggers for the new pattern. Just as a memento from an emotionally charged event in the past can awaken not merely memories but states of emotion and consciousness, these triggers reinforce the new pattern every time they are used. They serve, in an important sense, as anchors fur the initiation.

The three-phase process of initiation can be handled in various ways, and has been handled with various levels of effectiveness in the initiations used by different magical and fraternal orders. Like any other art, the art of initiation has its failures as well as its masterpieces. Making the situation more complex is the fact that most orders of both kinds use a series of initiations—the usual terms are "Grades" or "Degrees"—to carry out an extended program of transformation, each change building on the ones already made. In the fraternal orders, the goal of this program is typically nothing more profound (or more sinister) than basic personal maturity. In magical orders, by contrast, the possibilities for change are far greater.

An initiation in outline

It's possible, though, to sketch an example of the technology of initiation at work, in order to show how the techniques described above work out in practice.

The initiation begins with the ritual opening of the lodge space, following the pattern covered earlier in this essay. Props and other materials needed for the initiation are already in place. The candidate for initiation is outside the lodge room in an antechamber, separated* from the outside world but unable to see or hear what is going on inside the lodge.

At the conclusion of the opening, one or more lodge officers leave the lodge room for the antechamber. Their job is to prepare the candidate;

this typically involves blindfolding, the most common means of sensory deprivation, and may involve binding the arms or hands as well. In some rituals, the candidate may be given a preliminary oath of secrecy at this point. Meanwhile, inside the lodge room, the lodge officers take their places and the lights are turned down.

The candidate is then brought into the lodge room and moved through unfamiliar space. Darkness and silence, broken only by the specific sights and sounds of the ritual, intensify the experience. Unable to get his or her bearings, the candidate quickly becomes disoriented. The lodge officers recite the sonorous words of the ritual; the candidate may be threatened or challenged, startled or frightened, although this element is best kept under tight control; simple surprise and uncertainty induce the required state more effectively than the more extreme levels of fear and shock. At intervals, the blindfold may be raised to show some brightly illuminated scene or symbol, and then lowered again. At some time during this part of the ritual—different initiations place it at different points—the candidate is given the principal oath or obligation of secrecy and fellowship, and the core transformative experiences of the initiation are enacted.

At this stage, the so-called "secrets of the degree" are given to the candidate. These typically take the form of a word, a grip, and a gesture. Evolved from security devices meant to preserve secrecy, and still usually presented as such, these are in many ways the most interesting part of the entire technology. They serve as the triggering elements we've already discussed; first presented in the heightened state of the initiation, and only repeated by the candidate in an open lodge, they serve to recall and thus stabilize the new pattern of consciousness created by the initiation.

The candidate is now an initiate and is welcomed by the members of the lodge and seated among them. He or she may be lectured, sometimes at some length, about the meaning of the symbols and scenes shown in the initiation. Finally, the lodge is ritually closed, and by this process the new initiate and the other lodge members return to a more ordinary state of consciousness.

The results of the system are variable, as with any system of transformation, and depend on (among other things) the skill of the initiating officers and the mental state of the candidate. Still, it's possible to get remarkable results by means of this system, when the rituals are performed well and presented to those ready to receive them.

Ars Memorativa: an introduction to the Hermetic Art of Memory

In 1995, I helped found a magazine on occult subjects titled Caduceus: The Hermetic Quarterly. *While it lasted only three years before disputes among the founders shut it down, it featured some first-rate articles on occultism in its time. This was my first piece for* Caduceus; *Part One appeared in the Spring 1995 issue, Part Two in the Summer issue of the same year. It was among other things the first published essay in which I began to develop my critique of modern industrial society as a prosthetic culture, in which human capacities are amputated and then replaced by machines.*

Part One: The Uses of Memory

In the current occult revival, the Art of Memory is perhaps the most thoroughly neglected of all the technical methods of Renaissance esotericism. While the researches of the late Dame Frances Yates[1] and, more recently, a revival of interest in the master mnemonist Giordano Bruno[2] have made the Art something of a known quantity in academic circles, the same is not true in the wider community; to mention the Art of Memory in most occult circles nowadays, to say nothing of the general public, is to invite blank looks.

27

In its day, though, the mnemonic methods of the Art held a special place among the contents of the practicing magician's mental toolkit. The Neoplatonic philosophy which underlay the whole structure of Renaissance magic gave memory, and thus techniques of mnemonics, a crucial place in the work of inner transformation. In turn, this interpretation of memory gave rise to a new understanding of the Art, turning what had once been a purely practical way of storing useful information into a meditative discipline calling on all the powers of the will and the imagination.

This article seeks to reintroduce the Art of Memory to the modern Western esoteric tradition as a practical technique. This first part, "The Uses of Memory," will give an overview of the nature and development of the Art's methods, and explore some of the reasons why the Art has value for the modern esotericist. The second part, "The Garden of Memory," will present a basic Hermetic memory system, designed along traditional lines and making use of Renaissance magical symbolism, as a basis for experimentation and practical use.

The method and its development[3]

It was once almost mandatory to begin a treatise on the Art of Memory with the classical legend of its invention. This habit has something to rec-ommend it, for the story of Simonides is more than a colorful anecdote; it also offers a good introduction to the basics of the technique.

The poet Simonides of Ceos, as the tale has it, was hired to recite an ode at a nobleman's banquet. In the fashion of the time, the poet began with a few lines in praise of divinities—in this case, Castor and Pollux—before going on to the serious business of talking about his host. The host, however, objected to this diversion of the flattery, deducted half of Simonides' fee, and told the poet he could seek the rest from the gods he had praised. Shortly thereafter, a message was brought to the poet that two young men had come to the door of the house and wished to speak to him. When Simonides went to see them, there was no one there, but in his absence the banquet hall collapsed behind him, killing the impious nobleman and all the dinner guests as well. Castor and Pollux, traditionally imaged as two young men, had indeed paid their half of the fee.

Tales of this sort were commonplace in Greek literature, but this one has an unexpected moral. When the rubble was cleared away, the victims were found to be so mangled that their own families could not identify them. Simonides, however, called to memory an image of the banqueting hall as he had last seen it, and from this was able to recall the order of the guests at the table. Pondering this, according to the legend, he proceeded to invent the first classical Art of Memory. The story is certainly apocryphal, but the key elements of the technique it describes—the use of mental images placed in ordered, often architectural settings—remained central to the whole tradition of the Art of Memory throughout its history, and provided the framework on which the Hermetic adaptation of the Art was built.

In Roman schools of rhetoric, this approach to memory was refined into a precise and practical system. Students were taught to memorize the insides of large buildings according to certain rules, dividing the space into specific *loci* or "places" and marking every fifth and tenth *locus* with special signs. Facts to be remembered were converted into striking visual images and placed, one after another, in these *loci*; when needed, the rhetorician needed only to stroll in his imagination through the same building, noticing the images in order and recalling their meanings. At a more advanced level, images could be created for individual words, or sentences, so that large passages of text could be stored in the memory in the same way. Roman rhetoricians using these methods reached dizzying levels of mnemonic skill; one famous practitioner of the Art was recorded to have sat through a day-long auction and, at its end, repeated from memory the item, purchaser, and price for every sale of the day.

With the disintegration of the Roman world, these same techniques became part of the classical heritage of Christianity. The Art of Memory took on a moral cast as memory itself was defined as a part of the virtue of prudence, and in this guise the Art came to be cultivated by the Dominican Order. It was from this source that the ex-Dominican Giordano Bruno (1548–1600), probably the Art's greatest exponent, drew the basis of his own techniques.[4]

Medieval methods of the Art differed very little from those of the classical world, but certain changes in the late Middle Ages helped lay the foundations for the Hermetic Art of Memory of the Renaissance. One of the most important of these was a change in the frameworks used for memory *loci*. Along with the architectural settings most often used in the classical tradition, medieval mnemonists also came to make use of the whole Ptolemaic cosmos of nested spheres as a setting for memory images. Each sphere from God at the periphery through the angelic, celestial and elemental levels down to Hell at the center thus held one or more loci for memory images.

Between this system and that of the Renaissance Hermeticists, there is only one significant difference, and that is a matter of interpretation, not of technique. Steeped in Neoplatonic thought, the Hermetic magicians of the Renaissance saw the universe as an image of the divine Ideas, and the individual human being as an image of the universe; they also knew Plato's claim that all "learning" is simply the recollection of things known before birth into the realm of matter. Taken together, these ideas raised the Art of Memory to a new dignity. If the human memory could be reorganized in the image of the universe, in this view, it became a reflection of the entire realm of Ideas in their fullness, and thus the key to universal knowledge. This concept was the driving force behind the complex systems of memory created by several Renaissance Hermeticists, and above all those of Giordano Bruno.

Bruno's mnemonic systems form, to a great extent, the high-water mark of the Hermetic Art of Memory. His methods were dizzyingly complex, and involve a combination of images, ideas, and alphabets which require a great deal of mnemonic skill to learn in the first place! Hermetic philosophy and the traditional images of astrological magic constantly appear in his work, linking the framework of his Art to the wider framework of the magical cosmos. The difficulty of Bruno's technique, though, has been magnified unnecessarily by authors whose lack of personal experience with the Art has led them to mistake fairly straightforward mnemonic methods for philosophical obscurities.

A central example of this is the confusion caused by Bruno's practice of linking images to combinations of two letters. Yates' interpretation of Brunonian memory rested largely on an identification of this with the letter combinations of Lullism, the half-Cabalistic philosophical system of Ramon Lull (1235–1316).[5] While Lullist influences certainly played a part in Bruno's system, interpreting that system solely in Lullist terms misses the practical use of the combinations: they enable the same set of images to be used to remember ideas, words, or both at the same time.

An example might help clarify this point. In the system of Bruno's *De Umbris Idearum* (1582), the traditional image of the first decan of Gemini, a servant holding a staff, could stand for the letter combination *be*; that of Suah, the legendary inventor of chiromancy or palmistry, for *ne*.

The decan-symbols are part of a set of images prior to the inventors, establishing the order of the syllables. Put in one *locus*, the whole would spell the word *bene*, "good."[6]

The method has a great deal more subtlety than this one example shows. Bruno's alphabet included thirty letters, the Latin alphabet plus those Greek and Hebrew letters which have no Latin equivalents; his system thus allowed texts written in any of these alphabets to be memorized. He combined these with five vowels and provided additional images for single letters to allow for more complex combinations. Besides the astrological images and inventors, there are also lists of objects and adjectives corresponding to this set of letter combinations, and all these can be combined in a single memory-image to represent words of several syllables. At the same time, many of the images stand for ideas as well as sounds; thus, the figure of Suah mentioned above can also represent the art of palmistry if that subject needed to be remembered.

Bruno's influence can be traced in nearly every subsequent Hermetic memory treatise, but his own methods seem to have proved too demanding for most magi. Masonic records suggest that his mnemonics, passed on by his student Alexander Dicson, may have been taught in Scots Masonic lodges in the sixteenth century;[7] more common, though, were methods like the one diagrammed by the Hermetic encyclopedist Robert Fludd in his *History of the Macrocosm and Microcosm*. This was a fairly straightforward adaptation of the late medieval method, using the spheres of the heavens as *loci*, although Fludd nonetheless classified it along with prophecy, geomancy, and astrology as a "microcosmic art" of human self-knowledge.[8] Both this approach to the Art and this classification of it remained standard in esoteric circles until the triumph of Cartesian mechanism in the late seventeenth century sent the Hermetic tradition underground and the Art of Memory into oblivion.

The method and its value

This profusion of techniques begs two questions, which have to be answered if the Art of Memory is to be restored to a place in the Western esoteric tradition. First of all, are the methods of the Art actually superior to rote memorization as a way of storing information in the human memory? Put more plainly, does the Art of Memory *work*?

It's fair to point out that this has been a subject of dispute since ancient times. Still, then as now, those who dispute the Art's effectiveness are generally those who have never tried it. In point of fact, the Art does work; it allows information to be memorized and recalled more reliably, and in far greater quantity, than rote-methods do. There are good reasons, founded in the nature of memory, why this should be so. The human mind recalls images more easily than ideas, and images charged with emotion more easily still; one's most intense memories, for example, are rarely abstract ideas. It uses chains of association, rather than logical order, to connect one memory with another; simple mnemonic tricks like the loop of string tied around a finger rely on this. It habitually follows rhythms and repetitive formulae; it's for this reason that poetry is often far easier to remember than prose. The Art of Memory uses all three of these factors systematically. It constructs vivid, arresting images as anchors for chains of association, and places these in the ordered and repetitive context of an imagined building or symbolic structure in which each image and each locus leads on automatically to the next. The result, given training and practice, is a memory which works in harmony with its own innate strengths to make the most of its potential.

The fact that something can be done, however, does not by itself prove that it should be done. In a time when digital data storage bids fair to render print media obsolete, in particular, questions of how best to memorize information might well seem as relevant as the choice between different ways of making clay tablets for writing. Certainly, some methods of doing this once-vital chore are better than others; so what? This way of thinking leads to the second question a revival of the Art of Memory must face: what is the value of this sort of technique?

This question is particularly forceful in our present culture because that culture, and its technology, have consistently tended to neglect innate human capacities and replace them where possible with mechanical equivalents. It would not be going too far to see the whole body of modern Western technology as a system of prosthetics. In this system, print and digital media serve as a prosthetic memory, doing much of the work once done in older societies by the trained minds of mnemonists. It needs to be recognized, too, that these media can handle volumes of information which dwarf the capacity of the human mind; no conceivable Art of Memory can hold as much information as a medium-sized public library.

The practical value of these ways of storing knowledge, like that of much of our prosthetic technology, is real. At the same time, there is another side to the matter, a side especially relevant to the Hermetic tradition. Any technique has effects on those who use it, and those effects need not be positive ones. Reliance on prosthetics tends to weaken natural abilities; one who uses a car to travel anywhere more than two blocks away will come to find even modest walks difficult. The same is equally true of the capacities of the mind. In Islamic countries, for example, it's not at all uncommon to find people who have memorized the entire Quran for devotional purposes. Leave aside, for the moment, questions of value; how many people in the modern West would be *capable* of doing the equivalent?

One goal of the Hermetic tradition, by contrast, is to maximize human capacities, as tools for the inner transformations sought by the Hermeticist Many of the elementary practices of that tradition— and the same is true of esoteric systems worldwide—might best be seen as a kind of mental calisthenics, intended to stretch minds grown stiff from disuse. This quest to expand the powers of the self stands in opposition to the prosthetic culture of the modern West, which has consistently tended to transfer power from the self to the exterior world. The difference between these two viewpoints has a wide range of implications—philosophical, religious, and (not the least) political— but the place of the Art of Memory can be found among them.

From what might be called the prosthetic standpoint, the Art is obsolete because it is less efficient than external data-storage methods such as books, and distasteful because it requires the slow development of inner abilities rather than the purchase of a piece of machinery. From a Hermetic standpoint, on the other hand, the Art is valuable in the first place as a means of developing one of the capacities of the self, the memory, and in the second place because it uses other capacities— attention, imagination, mental imagery—which have a large role in other aspects of Hermetic practice.

Like other methods of self-development, the Art of Memory also brings about changes in the nature of the capacity it shapes, not merely in that capacity's efficiency or volume; its effects are qualitative as well as quantitative—another issue not well addressed by the prosthetic approach. Ordinarily, memory tends to be more or less opaque to consciousness. A misplaced memory vanishes from sight, and any amount of random fishing around may be needed before an associative chain leading to it can be brought up from the depths. In a memory trained by the methods of the Art, by contrast, the chains of association are always in place, and anything memorized by the Art can thus be found as soon as needed. Equally, it's much easier for the mnemonist to determine what exactly he or she does and does not know, to make connections between different points of knowledge, or to generalize from a set of specific memories; what is stored through the Art of Memory can be reviewed at will.

Despite our culture's distaste for memorization, and for the development of the mind generally, the Art of Memory thus has some claim to practical value, even beyond its uses as a method of esoteric training. In the second part of this article, "The Garden of Memory," some of these potentials will be explored through the exposition of an introductory memory system based on the traditional principles of the Art.

Notes to Part One

1. Yates, F.A., *The Art of Memory* (University of Chicago Press, 1966) remains the standard English-language work on the tradition.
2. Bruno, G., *On the Composition of Images. Signs and Ideas* (Willis, Locker & Owens, 1991), and Culianu, I., *Eros and Magic in the Renaissance* (University of Chicago Press, 1987) are examples.
3. The brief history of the Art given here is drawn from Yates, op. cit.
4. For Bruno, see Yates, op. cit., Ch. 9, 11, 13–14, as well as Yates, F.A., *Giordano Bruno and the Hermetic Tradition* (University of Chicago Press, 1964).
5. See Yates, *The Art of Memory*, Ch. 8.
6. *Ibid.*, pp. 208–222.
7. Stevenson, D., *The Origins of Freemasonry: Scotland's Century* (Cambridge University Press, 1988, p. 95).
8. See Yates, *The Art of Memory*, Ch. 15.

Bibliography

Bruno, G., *On the Composition of Images. Signs and Ideas* (Willis, Locker & Owens, 1991).

Culianu, I., *Eros and Magic in the Renaissance* (University of Chicago Press, 1987).

Stevenson, D., *The Origins of Freemasonry: Scotland's Century* (Cambridge University Press, 1988, p. 95).

Yates, F.A., *Giordano Bruno and the Hermetic Tradition* (University of Chicago Press, 1964).

Yates, F.A., *The Art of Memory* (University of Chicago Press, 1966).

Part Two: The Garden of Memory

During the Renaissance, the age in which it reached its highest pitch of development, the Hermetic Art of Memory took on a wide array of different forms. The core principles of the Art, developed in ancient times through practical experience of the way human memory works best, are common to the whole range of Renaissance memory treatises; the structures built on this foundation, though, differ enormously. As we'll see, even some basic points of theory and practice were subjects of constant dispute, and it would be impossible as well as unprofitable to present a single memory system, however generic, as somehow "representative" of the entire field of Hermetic mnemonics.

That is not my purpose here. As the first part of this essay pointed out, the Art of Memory has potential value as a practical technique even in today's world of information overload and digital data storage. The memory system which will be presented here is designed to be used, not merely studied; the techniques contained in it, while almost entirely derived from Renaissance sources, are included for no other reason than the simple fact that they work.

Traditional writings on mnemonics generally divide the principles of the Art into two categories. The first consists of rules for places—that is, the design or selection of the visualized settings in which mnemonic images are located; the second consists of rules for images—that is, the building up of the imagined forms used to encode and store specific memories. This division is sensible enough and will be followed in this essay, with the addition of a third category: rules for practice, the principles which enable the Art to be effectively learned and put to use.

Rules for places

One debate which went on through much of the history of the Art of Memory was a quarrel over whether the mnemonist should visualize real places or imaginary ones as the setting for the mnemonic images of the Art. If the half-legendary classical accounts of the Art's early phases can be trusted, the first places used in this way were real ones; certainly, the rhetors of ancient Rome, who developed the Art to a high pitch of efficacy, used the physical architecture around them as the framework for their mnemonic systems. Among the Hermetic writers on the Art, Robert Fludd insisted that real buildings should always be used for memory work, claiming that the use of wholly imaginary structures leads to vagueness and thus a less effective system.[1] On the other hand, many ancient and Renaissance writers on memory, Giordano Bruno among them, gave the opposite advice. The whole question may, in the end, be a matter of personal needs and temperament.

Be that as it may, the system given here uses a resolutely imaginary set of places, based on the numerical symbolism of Renaissance occultism. Borrowing an image much used by the Hermeticists of the Renaissance, I present the key to a garden: Hortus Memoriae, the Garden of Memory.

The Garden of Memory is laid out in a series of concentric circular paths separated by hedges; the first four of these circles are mapped in Diagram 1. Each circle corresponds to a number and has the same number of small gazebos set in it. These gazebos—an example, the one in the innermost circle, is shown in Diagram 2—bear symbols which are derived from the Pythagorean number-lore of the Renaissance and later magical traditions, and serve as the places in this memory garden.[2] Like all memory places, these should be imagined as brightly lit and conveniently large; in particular, each gazebo is visualized as large enough to hold an ordinary human being, although it need not be much larger.

The first four circles of the garden are built up in the imagination as follows:

The first circle

This circle corresponds to the Monad, the number One; its color is white, and its geometrical figure is the circle. A row of white flowers grows at the border of the surrounding hedge. The gazebo is white, with gold trim, and is topped with a golden circle bearing the number 1. Painted on the dome is the image of a single open eye, while the sides bear the image of the Phoenix in flames.

The second circle

The next circle corresponds to the Dyad, the number Two and to the concept of polarity; its color is gray, its primary symbols are the Sun and Moon, and its geometrical figure is the vesica piscis, formed from the common area of two overlapping circles. The flowers bordering the hedges in this circle are silver-gray; in keeping with the rule of puns, which we'll cover a little later, these might be tulips. Both of the two gazebos in this circle are gray. One, topped with the number 2 in a white vesica, has white and gold trim, and bears the image of the Sun on the dome and that of Adam, his hand on his heart, on the side. The other, topped with the number 3 in a black vesica, has black and silver trim, and bears the image of the Moon on the dome and that of Eve, her hand touching her head, on the side.

The third circle

This circle corresponds to the Triad, the number Three; its color is black, its primary symbols are the three alchemical principles of Sulfur Mercury and Salt, and its geometrical figure is the triangle. The flowers bordering the hedges are black, as are the three gazebos. The first of the gazebos has red trim, and is topped with the number 4 in a red triangle; it bears, on the dome, the image of a red man touching his head with both hands, and on the sides the images of various animals. The second gazebo has white trim, and is topped by the number 5 in a white triangle; it bears, on the dome, the image of a white hermaphrodite touching its breasts with both hands, and on the sides the images of various plants. The third gazebo is unrelieved black, and is topped with the number 6 in a black triangle; it bears, on the dome, the image of a black woman touching her belly with both hands, and on the sides the images of various minerals.

The fourth circle

This circle corresponds to the Tetrad, the number Four. Its color is blue, its primary symbols are the four elements, and its geometrical figure is the Square. The flowers bordering the hedges are blue and four-petaled, and the four gazebos are blue. The first of these has red trim and is topped with the number 7 in a red square; it bears the image of flames on the dome and that of a roaring lion on the sides. The second has yellow trim and is topped with the number 8 in a yellow square; it bears the images of the four winds blowing on the dome, and that of a man pouring water from a vase on the sides. The third is unrelieved blue and is topped with the number 9 in a blue square; it bears the image of waves on the dome and those of a scorpion, a serpent and an eagle on the sides. The fourth has green trim and is topped with the number 10 in a green square; it bears, on the dome, the image of the Earth, and that of an ox drawing a plow on the sides.

To begin with, these four circles and ten memory places will be enough, providing enough room to be useful in practice, while still small enough that the system can be learned and put to work in a fairly short time. Additional circles can be added as familiarity makes work with the system go more easily. It's possible, within the limits of the traditional number symbolism used here, to go out to a total of eleven circles containing sixty-seven memory places.[3] It's equally possible to go on to develop different kinds of memory structures in which images may be placed. So long as the places are distinct and organized in some easily memorable sequence, almost anything will serve.

The Garden of Memory as described here will itself need to be committed to memory if it's to be used in practice. The best way to do this is simply to visualize oneself walking through the garden, stopping at the gazebos to examine them and then passing on. Imagine the scent of the flowers, the warmth of the sun; as with all forms of visualization work, the key to success is to be found in concrete imagery of all five senses. It's a good idea to begin always in the same place—the first circle is best, for practical as well as philosophical reasons—and, during the learning process, the student should go through the entire garden each time, passing each of the gazebos in numerical order. Both of these habits will help the imagery of the garden take root in the soil of memory.

Rules for images

The garden imagery described above makes up half the structure of this memory system—the stable half, one might say, remaining unchanged so long as the system itself is kept in use. The other, changing half consists of the images which are used to store memories within the garden. These depend much more on the personal equation than the framing imagery of the garden; what remains in one memory can evaporate quickly from another, and a certain amount of experimentation may be needed to find an approach to memory images which works best for any given student.

In the classical Art of Memory, the one constant rule for these images was that they be striking—hilarious, attractive, hideous, tragic, or simply bizarre, it made (and makes) no difference, so long as each image caught in the mind and stirred up some response beyond simple recognition. This is one useful approach. For the beginning practitioner, however, thinking of a suitably striking image for each piece of information which is to be recorded can be a difficult matter. It's often more useful, therefore, to use familiarity and order rather than sheer strangeness in an introductory memory system, and the method given here will do precisely this.

It's necessary for this method, first of all, to come up with a list of people whose names begin with each letter of the alphabet except K and X (which very rarely begin words in English). These may be people known to the student, media figures, characters from a favorite book— my own system draws extensively from J.R.R. Tolkien's Ring trilogy, so that Aragorn, Boromir, Cirdan the Shipwright, and so on tend to populate my memory palaces. It can be useful to have more than one figure for letters which often come at the beginning of words (for instance, Saruman as well as Sam Gamgee for S), or figures for certain common two-letter combinations (for example, Theoden for Th, where T is Treebeard), but these are developments which can be added later on. The important point is that the list needs to be learned well enough that any letter calls its proper image to mind at once, without hesitation, and that the images are clear and instantly recognizable.

Once this is managed, the student will need to come up with a second set of images for the numbers from 0 to 9. There is a long and ornate tradition of such images, mostly based on the simple physical similarity between number and image—a javelin or pole for 1, a pair of eyeglasses or of buttocks for 8, and so on. Any set of images can be used though, so long as they are simple and distinct. These should also be learned by heart, so that they can be called to mind without effort or hesitation. One useful test is to visualize a line of marching men, carrying the images which correspond to one's telephone number; when this can be done quickly, without mental fumbling, the images are ready for use.

That use involves two different ways of putting the same imagery to work. One of the hoariest of commonplaces in the whole tradition of the Art of Memory divides mnemonics into "memory for things" and "memory for words." In the system given here, however, the line is drawn in a slightly different place; memory for concrete things—for example, items in a grocery list—requires a slightly different approach than memory for abstract things, whether these be concepts or pieces of text. Concrete things are, on the whole, easier, but both can be done using the same set of images already selected.

We'll examine memory for concrete things first. If a grocery list needs to be committed to memory—this, as we'll see, is an excellent way to practice the Art—the items on the list can be put in any convenient order. Supposing that two sacks of flour are at the head of the list, the figure corresponding to the letter F is placed in the first gazebo, holding the symbol for two in one hand and a sack of flour in the other, and carrying or wearing at least one other thing which suggests flour: for example, a chaplet of plaited wheat on the figure's head. The garments and accessories of the figure can also be used to record details: for instance, if the flour wanted is whole-grain, the figure might wear brown clothing. This same process is done for each item on the list, and the resulting images are visualized, one after another, in the gazebos of the Garden of Memory. When the Garden is next visited in the imagination—in the store, in this case—the same images will be in place, ready to communicate their meaning.

This may seem like an extraordinarily complicated way to go about remembering one's groceries, but the complexity of the description is deceptive. Once the Art has been practiced, even for a fairly short time, the creation and placement of the images literally takes less time than writing down a shopping list, and their recall is an even faster process. It quickly becomes possible, too, to go to the places in the Garden out of their numerical order and still recall the images in full detail. The result is a fast and flexible way of storing information—and one which is unlikely to be accidentally left out in the car!

Memory for abstract things, as mentioned earlier, uses these same elements of practice in a slightly different way. A word or a concept often can't be pictured in the imagination the way a sack of flour can, and the range of abstractions which might need to be remembered, and discriminated, accurately is vastly greater than the possible range of items on a grocery list (how many things are there in a grocery store that are pale brown and start with the letter F?). For this reason, it's often necessary to compress more detail into the memory-image of an abstraction.

In this context, one of the most traditional tools, as well as one of the most effective ones, is a principle we'll call the rule of puns. Much of the memory literature throughout the history of the Art can be seen as an extended exercise in visual and verbal punning, as when a pair of buttocks appears in place of the number 8, or when a man named Domitian is used as an image for the Latin words *domum itionem*.

An abstraction can usually be memorized most easily and effectively by making a concrete pun on it and remembering the pun, and it seems to be regrettably true that the worse the pun, the better the results in mnemonic terms.

For instance, if—to choose an example wholly at random—one needed to memorize the fact that streptococcus bacteria cause scarlet fever, rheumatic fever, and streptococcal sore throat, the first task would be the invention of an image for the word "streptococcus." One approach might be to turn this word into "strapped to carcass," and visualize the figure who represents the letter S with a carcass strapped to his or her back by large, highly visible straps. For scarlet fever—perhaps "Scarlett fever"—a videotape labeled "Gone With The Wind" with a large thermometer sticking out of it and an ice pack on top would serve, while rheumatic fever—perhaps "room attic fever"—could be symbolized by a small model of a house, similarly burdened, with the thermometer sticking out of the window of an attic room; both of these would be held by the original figure, whose throat might be red and inflamed to indicate the sore throat. Again, this takes much longer to explain, or even to describe, than it does to carry out in practice.

The same approach can be used to memorize a linked, series of words, phrases or ideas, placing a figure for each in one of the gazebos of the Garden of Memory (or the places of some more extensive system). Different linked series can be kept separate in the memory by marking each figure in a given sequence with the same symbol—for example, if the streptococcus image described above is one of a set of medical items, it and all the other figures in the set might wear stethoscopes. Still, these are more advanced techniques and can be explored once the basic method is mastered.

Rules for practice

Like any other method of Hermetic work, the Art of Memory requires exactly that—work—if its potentials are to be opened up. Although fairly easy to learn and use, it's not an effort-free method, and its rewards are exactly measured by the amount of time and practice put into it. Each student will need to make his or her own judgment here; still, the old manuals of the Art concur that daily practice, if only a few minutes each day, is essential if any real skill is to be developed.

The work that needs to be done falls into two parts. The first part is preparatory, and consists of learning the places and images necessary to put the system to use; this can be done as outlined in the sections above. Learning one's way around the Garden of Memory and memorizing the basic alphabetical and numerical images can usually be done in a few hours of actual work, or perhaps a week of spare moments.

The second part is practical and consists of actually using the system to record and remember information. This has to be done relentlessly, on a daily basis, if the method is to become effective enough to be worth doing at all. Its best by far to work with useful, everyday matters like shopping lists, meeting agendas, daily schedules, and so on. Unlike the irrelevant material sometimes chosen for memory work, these can't simply be ignored, and every time one memorizes or retrieves such a list the habits of thought vital to the Art are reinforced.

One of these habits—the habit of success—is particularly important to cultivate here. In a society which tends to denigrate human abilities in favor of technological ones, one often has to convince oneself that a mere human being, unaided by machines, can do anything worthwhile! As with any new skill, therefore, simple tasks should be tried and mastered before complex ones, and the more advanced levels of the Art mastered one stage at a time.

Notes to Part Two

1. See Yates, F.A., *Theatre of the World* (University of Chicago Press, 1969, pp. 147–149 and 207–209).
2. The symbolism used here is taken from a number of sources, particularly McLean, A., ed., *The Magical Calendar* (Magnum Opus, 1979) and Agrippa, H.C., *Three Books of Occult Philosophy* (Tyson, D., rev. and ed., Llewellyn, 1993, pp. 241–298). I have, however, borrowed from the standard Golden Dawn color scales for the colors of the circles.
3. The numbers of the additional circles are 5–10 and 12; the appropriate symbolism may be found in McLean and Agrippa, and the colors in any book on the Golden Dawn's version of the Cabala. The Pythagorean numerology of the Renaissance defined the number 11 as "the number of sin and punishment, having no merit" (see McLean, p. 69) and so gave it no significant imagery. Those who wish to include an eleventh circle might, however, borrow the eleven curses of Mount Ebal and the associated Qlippoth or daemonic primal powers from Cabalistic sources.

Bibliography

Agrippa, H.C., *Three Books of Occult Philosophy* (Tyson, D., rev. and ed., Llewellyn, 1993, pp. 241–298).

McLean, A., ed., *The Magical Calendar* (Magnum Opus, 1979).

Yates, F.A., *Theatre of the World* (University of Chicago Press, 1969, pp. 147–149 and 207–209).

The Hall of Thmaa: sources of the
Golden Dawn lodge system

My experiences in the Independent Order of Odd Fellows led me to a variety
of insights into the way the lodge system had shaped the traditions and history
of the Hermetic Order of the Golden Dawn. When the opportunity arose to
submit an essay to The Golden Dawn Journal, *an annual published at that*
time by Llewellyn Publications, I chose that as the theme. My essay started out
as an adaptation of "The Magical Lodge"—and attentive readers will notice
certain passages that made it unchanged into the final essay—but went veer-
ing off in its own directions. One source I didn't cite at the time was the Portal
Grade essay I had written in the course of my Golden Dawn studies; a revised
version of this appeared in a later issue of the same journal and is included in
this volume under the title "Osiris and Christ."

In the flurry of attention given in recent years to the magical system
of the Hermetic Order of the Golden Dawn, certain elements of that
system have received a great deal of notice, while others have not.
Golden Dawn approaches to ritual magic, Tarot symbolism and the
Cabala, among other topics, have become all but standard in magical
circles throughout the English-speaking world. At the same time, other
elements have remained in obscurity.

One of these neglected elements, paradoxically, was the cornerstone of the entire system in its original context. The Golden Dawn, it's worth remembering, was not a "tradition" in the vague modern sense of that word; it was an organization of a particular type. All the other elements of the Golden Dawn system were first brought in to serve specific roles within the Order's organizational structure and reshaped—sometimes drastically—to fit that structure's needs.

As an organization, the Golden Dawn derived its structure from what this essay will call the traditional lodge system. Historians of this system, most of them Freemasons, have tended to see their subject as a Masonic affair first and foremost. This is an oversimplification, however. Freemasonry was, and is, only one of a remarkable diversity of organizations which have made use of the lodge system and contributed to its growth. For a period of more than a century—a period which included the entire lifespan of the original Golden Dawn, from its formation in 1887 to its disintegration in 1900–1903—the traditional lodge system served as a kind of organizational template, on which an astonishing array of societies, clubs, sects, fraternal orders, and business enterprises were based.

So, in its turn, was the Golden Dawn. Still, the development of the Order's system was as much a work of alchemy as anything taught in its knowledge lectures; the prima maferia of its sources underwent a transmutation of astonishing scope on its way to becoming the Philosopher's Stone of the completed system. The founders of the Golden Dawn borrowed the framework of their Order's structure from the traditional lodge system but transformed that system from a means of organization into a tool of magic.

Sources of the lodge system

The origins of the traditional lodge system are largely a matter for conjecture, despite the efforts of several generations of Masonic historians.[1] Equally uncertain, and more controversial, is the question of the role that occultism and magical secret societies played in those origins. Most of the early lodge organizations, magical or not, were secret to one degree or another, and left behind only the most fragmentary of traces. Before approximately 1700, any attempt at a coherent history is a matter of groping one's way in the mist.

It's fairly clear, though, that in England during the seventeenth century a number of organizations emerged which followed something not too far from the later lodge system. The most visible of these organizations, in hindsight, was Freemasonry; at the time, though, it was one of many social and charitable societies, and not particularly distinguishable among them. That period in English history has been called "an age of clubs." From these clubs, the earliest handful of fraternal orders emerged, among them the Freemasons, the Odd Fellows, and the Ancient Order of Druids—organizations marked by regular lodge meetings with ceremonial openings and closings; by initiation ceremonies for new members; and by the use of grips, passwords, and secret signs for recognition.[2]

From the perspective of the modern magician, these may seem like sure signs of an esoteric tradition. In fact, they were common to a wide range of private social groups in that period. At the same time in history, though, the great resurgence in the Western magical tradition which began in the Renaissance (and may have sparked it in the first place)[3] gave rise to a multitude of secret societies which were devoted to magic, alchemy, and "heretical" religious beliefs. Most of these organizations were shadowy presences, attested by a few references in once-private documents or by Inquisition papers. The fiery Hermetic magus Giordano Bruno seems to have established circles of students at various places in Europe.[4] John Dee, creator or recipient of the Enochian system, may have done the same.[5] And the furor over the Rosicrucian manifestoes in the same century argues that, whatever might have been behind those mysterious documents, the idea of a secret society possessing magical secrets was familiar enough at the time to be believable to many people.[6]

Some of the papers of one such secret magical group have survived. This group, the Society of Hermetick Adepti, was founded in England sometime toward the middle of the seventeenth century. According to its constitution, it had three degrees of membership—Probationer, Son, and Father—with a prescribed curriculum of study and formal ceremonies of initiation. Members took an obligation of secrecy; the true name of the group itself was one of the matters to be kept secret. The Fathers met at the Spring Equinox each year in a secret conclave.[7] The similarities between this group and later magical groups, the Golden Dawn among them, are obvious.

Both of these currents, fraternal order and magical society, drew on the commonplace ideas of their time, and it's impossible to tell whether similarities between them come from this source or a closer connection. The spread of Freemasonry outside England in the eighteenth century, though, made the whole question a moot point. In the Europe of the time, ruled as it was by absolute monarchs and an oppressive Church, the relative freedom and religious toleration of English society made the very English institution of Freemasonry irresistibly appealing to liberals and radicals of all stripes. Among these were magicians, alchemists, and students of ancient lore, who saw in Masonic initiations an echo of the mystery cults of the classical world and a potent tool for magical work. In continental Europe and, to a lesser extent, in England as well, fraternal and magical traditions became the warp and weft of a single fabric. Even plain fraternal orders with purely social goals began to use names, symbols, and initiatory techniques of surprising depth. It is from this period that the expansion of Masonic grades—from the three original grades to the astonishing total of ninety-nine in the nineteenth-century Rite of Memphis and Mizraim can be traced. From this period, too, descend the core elements of the traditional lodge system used by the Golden Dawn.

Elements of the lodge system

The diversity of eighteenth and nineteenth century fraternal and magical orders, real though it is, is founded on a set of common ideas and structures amounting to a kind of "standard kit."[8] The elements of this kit may be combined in different ways or used in different proportions, but they themselves vary only slightly from order to order. Thus (to name a very minor example) three knocks with a gavel will bring the members of nearly any fraternal lodge in existence to their feet, and one knock will seat them.

The fundamentals of this "kit" may become a little more clear if some definitions are provided. A lodge, in the present context, is a group of people who come together to prepare and perform initiations. An initiation can be seen as a formal process for bringing about specific long-term changes in human consciousness. Every lodge, magical or not, has at least one initiation to offer, and most have more than one. People outside the surviving lodges tend to think of these initiations as nothing more than an overelaborate process of being admitted to lodge membership—a kind of formalized hazing that new members go through before getting access to what's really going on. In fact, the reverse is true. The initiation, centrally, is what's going on, and every other element of lodge organization and procedure is there primarily to support it.

This was true of all orders in the heyday of the lodge system and is still true in those fraternal orders which haven't completely decayed into social clubs or insurance companies. Initiation is to the new initiate what consecration is to a talisman: something inert and unformed receives energy, shape, and direction. (The same transformation can also be brought about by individual work; self-initiation remains a valid concept and a valid path.)

The methods of initiation differ. So, of course, do the models used to understand the process. One useful way of thinking about initiation, a way deriving from the Neoplatonic background of the Renaissance magical societies, posits two realms or worlds. One is the realm of matter, perceived by the ordinary senses. The other we may as well call the realm of meaning, perceived by that complex set of processes we usually call "the mind." (Some traditions see one or the other of these as primary, with the remaining one derived or even imaginary. For our present purposes, though, the distinction is a moot point.)

Ordinarily, these two realms exist cheek by jowl in our awareness, with a sort of uneasy mapping of one onto the other serving as the one link between them. Under certain circumstances, though, the gap between them can be bridged or even annihilated for a time: matter and meaning fuse, so that physical objects take on cognitive depth and catalyze transformations at all levels of consciousness. Extreme physical or psychological states can do this, so can the effects of some drugs, and so can the technical devices of ceremonial magic. Some combination of these methods comes into most initiatory systems worldwide; in the traditional lodge system, by contrast—even in its magical forms—the first two rarely appear. If this needs any justification, it's that ceremonial magic can get the same results with less risk of long-term damage to physical or mental health.

This way of looking at the initiatory process is useful here because it highlights a critical feature of the traditional lodge system. Like Janus, the two-faced god of doorways and beginnings, a lodge looks two ways at the same time. As the support system for this coalescence of the realms, it must be able to organize space, time, personnel, and the other requirements of initiation in terms of matter and meaning alike.

Patterns in space and time

In the traditional lodge system, the organization of space and time follows a set of patterns that will be familiar at once to the student of Golden Dawn ceremonies. Some of these patterns will seem needlessly ornate or formal to the modern magician—others will seem thoroughly boring. In practice, though, the system works well, and as often as not it is the apparently dull details which make for effective functioning.

The lodge system's use of space and time derives from the dual function of the lodge, as described a little earlier. This duality places some fairly specific requirements on the space to be used. A lodge room is typically used both for initiation ceremonies and for meetings of the members. As an initiatory space, it needs to be large enough to allow for easy movement, and for props, tableaus, or symbolic images to be set up and removed easily. It also needs enough physical and sensory isolation from the outside world to keep the experience of the initiation from being disturbed by unwanted noise or intrusion. As a meeting space, it needs to permit all of the members to see and speak to one another, while at the same time (since members typically rotate between different functions in a lodge setting) it can be used to help clarify the different responsibilities of lodge officers and members.

The interplay between these two concerns has produced a standard lodge architecture that can be found in practically every lodge-based organization in the Western world. The basic form is an open rectangular space with a door on one of the short sides and seats around the perimeter. An anteroom outside the door allows a guard to control access and prevent interruptions. Inside, the primary lodge officers sit on the short sides, while the bulk of the members sit on the long sides. The center of the space may contain objects of symbolic importance, or it may be left empty. In either case, it will be used for the most important symbolic actions. The basic design is shown in Diagram 1.

These are the material aspects of the use of space in a lodge. What of the other side of the equation, the realm of meaning? Most often, this comes out of the core symbolism of the specific lodge. Such symbolism is a critical element of the lodge system, but it is not a part of the "standard kit"—each order, magical or not, has one of its own, simple or complex. The use of the lower half of the Tree of Life as a map of the Neophyte Grade Temple in the Golden Dawn is a good example.

In most systems, these maps determine the placement of the stations and movements of the initiatory process, as well as the location of the officers in ordinary meetings.

A few elements of this sort of mapping are common enough, though, that they very nearly have a place in the "standard kit" of lodge technique. The most important of these is symbolic polarity—the identification of the parts and officers of a lodge with a set of symbolic opposites such as light and darkness, fire and water, or the like. Most often the two short ends of the lodge room, and the lodge officers who sit there, form the major polarity in the lodge. A second may be set up between officers who sit on the two long sides. Alternatively, the first polarity may be resolved by a third officer sitting on one of the long sides or elsewhere (like the Hegemon in the Golden Dawn's Neophyte Grade.) Or both of these can be done in the same lodge. (Again, the Golden Dawn's 0=0 lodge is an example.)

A related "standard kit" ingredient has to do with the line connecting the chief officer's station with the central space of the lodge. This serves as the primary path for what we may as well call "energy"—dramatic, psychological, or magical, depending on your choice of interpretive filter. In most lodge systems this line is not crossed except at specific points in ceremonial work, and movement along it happens only at the critical moments in the initiatory process.

The same needs that define the lodge's organization of space also shape its relationship to time. To carry out its work, a lodge must be able to define periods of time in which ritual consciousness is constructed, and if it offers more than one initiation it needs to have methods in place for moving smoothly from one level of ritual consciousness ("grade" or "degree" in lodge jargon) to another as well as from ordinary consciousness to any of these and back.

The usual method in these transitions is a simple ritual process given strength through regular practice. The ceremony used to open a lodge—to move from ordinary to ritual time—generally has four elements. First, the doors are closed, and those present show their right to be there; second, the lodge officers recite their duties; third, the powers governing the lodge symbolism are invoked; finally, the lodge is formally declared to be open. Each of these elements can be as simple or complex as the tastes of the founders may dictate.

A shorter ceremony, usually of two elements, closes a lodge. Banishings of the sort familiar to most magicians nowadays are all but unknown in lodge technique; instead, a second invocation designed to channel the energies of the ritual out into ordinary time is used. After this, the lodge is simply declared closed. A similar two-element cere-mony moves the lodge from one grade to another. Here members dem-onstrate their right to be present in the new grade, and the lodge is then declared to be open in that grade.

Organization and officers

The carrying out of regular initiatory ceremonies requires a certain amount of organization of people, materials, and money. In the tradi-tional lodge system, this is handled according to a system which most Americans will recognize at once. A set of officers, each with speci-fied duties, is elected by the lodge membership for fixed terms by a secret ballot. Once elected, officers have powers and responsibilities set for them by the laws of their order. If they fail to carry out their duties, they may be removed by a vote of the lodge. In all matters, particularly those involving money, the lodge has final say within the limits of the laws. (It may come as no surprise that all but two of the signers of the Declaration of Independence were Freemasons.)

The titles of officers in different orders vary wildly. The functions of the offices, however, do not—these belong to the "standard kit." Whether a lodge is governed by a Worshipful Master, a Noble Grand, a Supreme Oracle, or a Chancellor Commander[9] (or, for that matter, a Greatly Honored Hierophant), that officer will sit at the end of the lodge room furthest from the door, preside over lodge meetings, and begin the opening ceremony with a single knock with a gavel or the equiva-lent. Similarly, whatever the name of the officer corresponding to the Golden Dawn Kerux, he or she will probably be instructed by the pre-siding officer to proclaim the lodge formally open or closed.

The usual set of lodge officers, then, includes a presiding officer (in the Golden Dawn, the Hierophant), a second officer who has primary charge of the door (the G.D. Hiereus), one or more business officers with secretarial and financial duties (the G.D. Cancellarius or, more broadly speaking, the Three Chiefs), an officer who makes announcements and leads movements in the lodge (the G.D. Kerux), and a guard between the inner and outer doors (the G.D. Sentinel). Additional officers (there are often several) are provided for as required by the initiation rites. (The G.D. Hegemon, Stolistes, and Dadouchos fall into this category.)

The presiding officer of the previous term (the G.D. Past Hierophant) often has a special place to sit and a role in the ritual. There is a certain amount of variation in where these officers sit, although the positions of the presiding and second officers are all but universal. The locations in Diagram 1 will serve as a general guide. As with the lodge space, the lodge officers will be linked to the governing symbolism of the lodge. The existence of such a link is an important part of the "standard kit"; however, the specifics are not, and will vary from order to order.

The methods of initiation

The process of initiation, then, is the primary purpose of the lodge system and the principal work of any functioning group using the traditional lodge system. While initiatory work can be done in any of a vast number of ways, the traditional initiations of the Western world tend to follow the same overall scheme and to use the same basic set of techniques. (It may be worth stressing here that these ceremonies are, in point of fact, the traditional initiation rituals of our own culture, and once served the same functions as the vision quests and rites of passage itch many Westerners are currently borrowing, if that is the word, from other cultures. It's been remarked that if the existing fraternal orders were to be imported today from some distant continent, they could charge initiation fees in four figures and still be swamped with applications. This is a sad comment on our culture's inability to recognize its own resources).

In bare outline, the candidate for initiation is placed in a receptive state by various simple non-invasive methods sensory restrictions such as hoodwinks, combined with movement into an unfamiliar space, play an important role here, as do deliberate and carefully controlled shocks. These last must not be overdone. Surprise and mild fear heighten the initiatory experience, but extreme fear can easily destroy it. The cold touch of the Hiereus' sword on the candidate's neck in the 0=0 ceremony, and the rejection of the candidate for spiritual pride in the first part of the 5=6, are good examples the technique in use.

While in the receptive state, the candidate is moved through a prepared space, in which he or she encounters a set of specific experiences designed to elicit particular emotional and mental reactions. These experiences are structured according to a particular symbolism; the nature of this symbolism varies from order to order and, in many cases, from degree to degree, but the "standard kit" requires that some such structure be part of the rite, to serve as a template upon which the experiences of the initiation are organized. The candidate is then given a set of symbolic and somatic triggers (the words, signs, grip, and so forth of the degree), which allow the state of consciousness created by these experiences to be reawakened more or less at will. The ceremony is brought to an end with the formal closing of the lodge and the transition out of ritual consciousness.

The triggers referred to above are, in some sense, the most interesting as well as the most important of the technical methods of the traditional lodge system. The various "secrets of the degrees," as they are often called, have generally been treated as though they were simply security devices. In fact, they are central to the whole lodge system. When a lodge is formally opened in a given degree, all the members typically give the password, grip, and sign of that degree in the course of the opening ceremony. Just as a memento from some emotionally charged event in the past can awaken not only memories but states of emotion and awareness, these triggering devices serve to reawaken in the initiate the effects of the initiatory process. With practice and participation in the work of the lodge, the triggers become, in effect, "switches" by which specific states can be established and used in a lodge context.

The details of initiation vary enormously from order to order and from degree to degree. This is not simply a matter of variations in symbolism. Initiations have different purposes, not just different imagery. Given a grasp of the techniques of initiation, it would be possible to construct an initiatory ritual to foster any conceivable change, positive or negative, in those who undergo it. (This may well be one of the reasons for the intensity of the traditional secrecy surrounding such rites.) In most fraternal orders, the degree rituals aim principally at fostering one aspect or another of simple personal maturity, a commodity uncommon enough that the orders' work is well worth doing. In magical orders, of course, the possibilities for transformation are much greater.

The Golden Dawn lodge system

By the time the Golden Dawn was founded in 1887, the full set of techniques described above had been in common use in fraternal and magical circles alike for more than a century. The fraternal orders themselves were at or near the peak of their power and influence throughout the

English-speaking countries. At the same time, the magical arts were undergoing a renaissance on a scale not seen since the 1600s, and a great deal of forgotten material was being unearthed from old manuscripts and a handful of living traditions. The time was ripe for a synthesis.

A central figure in the emergence of that synthesis was the redoubtable Dr. William Wynn Westcott.[10] Cabalist, magician, Freemason, and Rosicrucian, he stood at the interface between magical and fraternal traditions. His connections extended to esoteric groups all over Europe. He was an active member of Quatuor Coronati Lodge, the English association for Masonic historical research, and joined and (from 1892 on) headed the Societas Rosicruciana in Anglia (SRIA), a Masonic auxiliary order deeply involved in esoteric studies. It was around Westcott that the "Hermetic Students," an informal group including many future Golden Dawn Adepti, gathered in the early 1880s; and it was from Westcott that the famous Cipher Manuscripts, the core of the Golden Dawn system, and the much-debated Anna Sprengel correspondence issued.

With the aid of Samuel Mathers, also a Mason, an SRIA member, and a brilliant if unstable magician, the rituals from the Cipher Manuscripts were revised, expanded, and made into the framework of the First Order of the complete Golden Dawn system. This First Order, it's worth noting, did not teach practical magic—it offered initiations and provided instruction in what that age called "occult philosophy": the basics of Cabala, Tarot, astrology, and magical symbolism. In this, it was line with many of the other magical orders at work in the same period, and not greatly different from the better grade of fraternal orders.

It was with the coming of the Second Order in 1891, founded in rituals and writings of Mathers' creation, that the Golden Dawn became something more than this. The Second Order (to give it its full name, the *Ordo Rosae Rubeae et Aureae Crucis*, "Order of the Red Rose and Golden Cross") moved from occult philosophy to occult practice. Members were expected to study and master the extensive body of magical lore which today passes as the "Golden Dawn system," along with certain other disciplines (for instance, horary astrology), which have largely vanished from the curriculum of most Golden Dawn groups.

This shift did not, however, involve a turning away from the elements of the traditional lodge system described above. On the contrary, lodge technique and lodge symbolism was at the core of the Second Order's curriculum; at the same time, these were transformed and expanded in ways no previous magical order seems to have done. This process of transformation is critical to an understanding of the Golden Dawn's lodge technique.

Central to the Second Order teachings were the so-called "Z Manuscripts," a set of papers analyzing the Neophyte Ritual of the First Order.[11] These had to be mastered before the first sub-Grade of the Second Order could be achieved. Their content, in terms of the traditional lodge system explored above, can only be described as revolutionary.

In the discussion of the traditional lodge system, earlier in this essay, it was suggested that a lodge should be seen as a Janus-faced entity looking toward the two realms of matter and meaning. In the Z Manuscripts, both these realms are dealt with. Thus, each part of the lodge structure and the ritual of the 0=0 initiation has a practical meaning in terms of the mechanics of lodge functioning, and a symbolic meaning in terms of the structure of lodge interpretation. But it also has a third meaning—a magical meaning in terms of the application of lodge practice to the disciplines of the magical arts. The two faces have become three: Janus, to extend the metaphor, was replaced by Hecate, the goddess of crossroads and of sorcery.

A specific example may help to clarify the way this worked in practice. The following passage is from Manuscript Z-3, "The Symbolism of the Admission of the Candidate"—the numbers at the head of the paragraphs relate them to (1) practical, (2) symbolic, and (3) magical levels of meaning.

The Password

1. *Merely to guard the Secrets of the Order against any Members resigned or not working; hence changed each Equinox.*
2. *It is an affirmation of the different spiritual as well as the different physical constitutions of the candidates—that all natures cannot be the same without evil and injury resulting thereby—but that each nature should be brought to its own Kether—the best of its kind. This too, may be done in all things. It is the basis of alchemy.*
3. *It should be pronounced as if attracting the Solar Force—the Light of Nature, during the six months following the Equinox at which it is issued, as a link with the Solar Force, between that and the Order. This password, therefore, may also be used in a magical ceremony as attracting the support of the Light of Nature acting on natural forces.*[12]

The first interpretation given here is a straightforward matter of fraternal practice, a means of telling those who belong to a given lodge from those who do not. The second one is an interpretation on a symbolic level, a little subtler than the sort commonly found in other fraternal or magical orders, but not different from them in kind. The third one is, so far as I know, unique to the Golden Dawn and some of its descendants—an application of the method to magical practice. An initiate of the Golden Dawn who wished to carry out a working to shape the forces of nature might use the password in this sense, as a way to bring the state of consciousness awakened by the Equinox ceremony into focus in the ritual he or she was working. Thus, the collective work of the initiations and other group rituals of the Order became the foundation for the individual magical work of its members.

The same principle, used in a much broader manner, gives shape to the Neophyte Formula rituals presented in Manuscript Z-2. These are in many ways the crown jewels of the Golden Dawn system, complex and effective rites for carrying out many of the major operations of practical magic. Each of them derives its structure, its symbolism, and its focus from the Neophyte initiation ritual; the Golden Dawn magician working one of them makes use not only of his or her own abilities but of the reactions of consciousness established by his or her own initiation, and strengthened by all the other 0=0 ceremonies in which he or she has taken part. In turn, the practice of the Z-2 rituals helps prepare the magician for participation in the initiatory work itself. Where older magical lodge systems had treated personal practice and lodge work as two distinct subjects, the Golden Dawn fused the two into a single structure that strengthened both. The Order's own rather florid terminology described the lodge in which the Neophyte Ritual was performed as the "Hall of Thmaa" or the "Hall of the Dual Manifestation of Truth." But the manifestation of the lodge system's potentials which emerged from the Order's workings was not dual but triple.

The symbolism of initiation

The same fusion of fraternal and magical elements occurred at a deeper level of the Golden Dawn's magical system as well. As mentioned earlier, different groups using the traditional lodge system have made use of an enormous range of different systems of symbolism in their work. During the heyday of the fraternal orders in the late nineteenth century, lodges were organized around almost any symbolism one can imagine. For example, the publication of Lew Wallace's best-selling novel *Ben-Hur* in 1880 was followed by the birth of a fraternal order, the Tribe of Ben-Hur, which used the events of the novel as the basis for its scheme of degrees; candidates even took part in a mock chariot race during one ceremony.

The promoters who floated the Tribe of Ben-Hur had their eyes on nothing more profound than a share of the substantial fraternal life-insurance market. The founders of the Golden Dawn had deeper issues in mind, and whatever the origin of the Cipher Manuscripts they used as a foundation, the rituals they developed show it. Unlike most fraternal initiations, and many magical ones, the Golden Dawn grades below Adeptus Minor were not structured around a single myth or legendary story; rather, they consist of a complex layering of images and ideas built on a framework which the Order's papers themselves rarely discuss.

The complexity of the Order's grade rituals has caused a good deal of confusion and misunderstanding among some scholars, who have tended to regard the rites as simply a hodgepodge of material thrown together for theatrical effect. Such an approach severely understates both the level of structure within the grade rituals and the sophistication of the Golden Dawn's founders. It also fails to grasp the nature of an intellectual revolution which, during the years of the Golden Dawn's emergence, was shaking the foundations of Western society and played a significant part in giving the Order's rituals and practices their shape.

This revolution was the rise of the first real comparative approaches to the study of religion and myth. The work of the anthropologist Sir James Frazer, whose monumental *The Golden Bough* was first published in 1890, showed that many elements of Christian belief could be found in the religions of ancient cultures and so-called "primitive" peoples worldwide. This book served as capstone to a movement among scholars which had been busy undermining the core notions of Western ethnocentrism since the beginning of the nineteenth century. To these researchers, all of the world's religions—Christianity, for the first time in modern history, included—could be studied together, as individual expressions of a common basic approach to the world. Groups such as the Theosophical Society (founded in 1875) built on this foundation, suggesting that all faiths and mystical traditions were in fact fragments of a single, coherent system of spiritual science dating from the forgotten past.

In the context of the time, then, the profusion of sources and traditions which went into the Golden Dawn's rituals should not be seen as a kind of Fibber McGee's closet of old lore; rather, it was a careful attempt to combine what the Order's founders believed were equivalent elements from different but coordinate systems. Nor were these elements simply piled together around the basic lodge initiation pattern, or (as was done in other groups) encrusted on some mythic or legendary story. Instead, they were used to fill out the framework of an explicitly magical pattern of inner transformation.

The outline of this pattern can be traced, not coincidentally, in the work by Sir James Frazer mentioned above. The central thesis of *The Golden Bough* is that a single core myth, the myth of the so-called Dying God, is at the heart of many of the world's religions, legends, and folk customs. The Dying God is, in some sense, the god of vegetation. He represents the seed buried in the ground, the green plant dying with the coming of Winter, and like the seed, he rises again from the earth in the resurrection of Spring. The Biblical legends of Jesus are among the many myths which follow elements of this pattern.

In nineteenth-century magical circles, however, this mythic pattern was read not as an allegory of vegetation so much as a map of the process of inner transformation. It was recognized, too, that there are two different Dying God formulae, not just one—a greater and a lesser—both of which appear together in many mythologies. In the lesser formula, the Dying God descends into the Earth, and there is decapitated or dismembered. A sword and a shield or platter often appear in this formula's myths. In the greater formula, on the other hand, the Dying God is raised up above the earth to die (by hanging, crucifixion, or some similar method), and a spear and cup often appear in the myths. To the lesser formula belong the deaths of Orpheus and Dionysus, of Bran the Blessed, and of the many Primal Beings—Prajapati, Ymir, Tiamat—whose dismemberment provides the raw materials for the creation of the universe. To the greater formula belong Odin's self-sacrifice on the world-tree, among many others. In terms of "vegetation myth," the first formula is that of the seed "dying" in its germination underground, reborn in the plant. The second is the plant dying at harvest above ground, reborn in the seed. In Christian mythology, these two formulae are represented by John the Baptist and Jesus. In the Golden Dawn, they were referred to as the Formula of Osiris and that of Christ.[13]

Crucial to an understanding of the magical use of these myths is Flying Roll X, one of a series of documents circulated among Golden Dawn Adepts.[14] This paper, a copy of a lecture given by Mathers in 1893, is titled "Concerning the Symbolism of Self-Sacrifice and Crucifixion contained in the 5=6 Grade." A dense and rather difficult essay, it analyzes the altar diagrams from the grade rituals, and goes on through the Adeptus Minor ceremony in detail, drawing on Cabalistic, magical, and Egyptian sources—even, at one point, the Norse Elder Edda—in Mathers' inimitably murky style. Its main point, though, is clear. The characters of myth, in this interpretation, are to be understood as the different parts of the soul, as analyzed in Cabalistic writings; the events of myth are read in turn as guides to the technical processes of inner awakening, by which the ordinary awareness unites itself to the Lower Genius, the normally hidden powers of human consciousness, and then to the Higher Genius, the "Augoeides" or self-luminous divine presence in humanity.

The first phase of this process, equivalent to the lesser Dying God formula, requires the conscious self (in Cabalistic language, the Ruach) to descend into its own hidden places, to come to self-knowledge, and to cast out the "Evil Persona" or false self-image. This is experienced by consciousness as a dismemberment, since that false image is literally the only "self" the unawakened mind has ever known. The second phase, equivalent to the greater formula, requires the transformed Ruach to ascend to the Neshamah, the transcendent and immortal portion of the self, and to merge with that higher aspect so that every level of the self including the physical body is transformed utterly. In Mathers' words:

> ... if you can once get the great force of the Highest to send its ray clean down through the Neshamah into the mind, and thence, into your physical body, the Nephesh would be so transformed as to render you almost like a God walking on this Earth.[15]

This pattern is central to the Golden Dawn's path of inner transformation. What is not often recognized is that it is also central to the Golden

Dawn Grade rituals themselves. The lesser formula, the Formula of Osiris, dominates the Neophyte Ritual—even the symbolic decapitation is present in the touch of the Hiereus' sword on the back of the candidate's neck at the end of the obligation. The Z Manuscripts themselves make it clear that this symbolism is intended:

> When the Candidate stands before the Altar before the Obligation ... rarely in his life has he been nearer death, seeing that he is, as it were, disintegrated into his component parts.[16]

The grades from Zelator through Philosophus continue the symbolism of the Osiris Formula. These Elemental Grades represent, in a sense, the scattering of the symbolic body of the initiate, or more technically the differentiation of the aspects of consciousness, so that the senses of Malkuth, the intuition of Yesod, the intellect of Hod, and the emotions of Netzach can be known and experienced clearly for the first time. These aspects, in turn, are gathered up again in the Portal Grade:

> The Candidate in the Portal by a single circumambulation for each, recalls his past Grades and, at the end of the first point regards their symbols upon the Altar as parts of his body, and contemplates them as coming together in one place—the unity of his person.[17]

These symbols then are cast into a brazier as the candidate's self-sacrifice on the Altar of Spirit. This forms the transition from the lesser to the greater formula of the Dying God, while the remainder of the Portal Ritual, and above all the Adeptus Minor Grade, carry out the symbolism of that formula. It is for this reason that the candidate in the 5=6 is symbolically crucified, enters into the Pastos, and comes forth from it bearing the emblems of the Chief Adept—who, here as elsewhere in the Order's ceremonies, is a representation of the candidate's own Higher Genius.

The Golden Dawn's development of rituals around this map of the process of inner transformation is remarkable enough. What is extraordinary is that, here again, those rituals were not simply symbolic expressions of the map, but were meant to be used as the foundations of practical work with it. The transformations of the Neophyte Ritual were repeated and reinforced in the Z-2 ceremonies, allowing the core aspects of the Osiris Formula to be put to use in individual prac- tice. The consecration and use of the elemental weapons extended the work of the Elemental Grades into the personal sphere, while Golden Dawn Adepts were urged to make use of the Vault structure itself for individual work.[18] Once again, the Order took a relatively ordinary matter of fraternal practice and reshaped it into a potent tool for magi- cal transformation.

The grades and the path

This same tendency to merge lodge technique from traditional sources with magical symbolism and practice pervaded the Golden Dawn's lodge system. Its results, however, were not always as constructive as the examples already given might suggest. Sometimes, the fusion of fra- ternal and magical elements produced unexpected problems. One good example of this is the symbolic organization of the Golden Dawn's grade system.

The organization of grades or degrees within groups using the tra- ditional lodge system tends to vary widely. Some systems are a hodge- podge of different initiations thrown together more or less at random, while others take a more orderly approach. These patterns of organiza- tion need not have anything in particular to do with the inner symbolism of the rituals. (There are orders whose initiatory systems seem chaotic at first glance, but which arrange disparate rituals into a symbolically valid sequence.) Instead, it can be a matter of classification and, often, of linking ritual symbolism to the overall symbols and teachings of the order. The Golden Dawn falls into the more orderly group. Its grade organization is based, like so many of the details of the Order's work- ing, on the Cabalistic Tree of Life, with one grade assigned to each of the ten Sephiroth of the Tree. This pattern overlays the deeper initiatory structure discussed earlier and, to a great extent, reinforces it. The for- mulae used in the Adeptus Minor Grade, for example, correspond well to Tiphareth, the 5=6 Grade's Sephirothic attribution.

It's worth noting that this system was developed out of a grade structure apparently used by German Rosicrucian lodges in the eighteenth century. First published in 1781, it lists nine grades instead of ten, but these grades may seem quite familiar to students of the Golden Dawn system (see Table 1).[19]

Table 1

Degree	Name	Symbol	Brotherhood name
1,9	Magi	Equilateral Triangle	Luxianus Renaldus de Perfectis
2,8	Magistri	Compass	Pedemontanus de Rebis
3,7	Adepti Exempti	Hitakel	Janus de Aure Campis
4,6	Maiores	Phrath	Sphaere Fontus de Sales
5,5	Minores	Pison	Hodus Camlionis
6,4	Philosophi	Gihon	Pharos Illuminans
7,3	Practici	Wetharetz	Monoceros de Astris
8,2	Theoretici	Maim	Poraius de Reiectis
9,1	Juniores	Aesch	Periclinus de Faustis

Despite the obvious borrowings from this system in the Golden Dawn's own grade structure, though, the underlying patterns of the two have little in common. While there are certainly Cabalistic references in the Rosicrucian system, the direct mapping of grades to Sephiroth that governs the Golden Dawn structure is absent. Thus, the Rosicrucian system seems to have provided the Golden Dawn's founders with a series of titles and symbols, and little more—the governing pattern was the Order's own creation.

The construction of the full Golden Dawn grade structure, then, represented the same sort of innovation in lodge systems as the other examples already explored: the transformation of an existing element of the traditional system to serve the needs of magical work. In place of an arbitrary sequence of levels and initiations, the Golden Dawn's founders set out to establish one which would mirror the Cabala's map of levels of being and of the stages of spiritual and magical growth. It was a logical result of the same process which produced so much of value in the Order's system.

It was also, in practical terms, a source of serious problems, and one which played a major role in the troubles which overtook the Order. The core of the problem, as Israel Regardie pointed out many years ago,[20] was that the assignment of the grades to the Sephiroth could have practical meaning only if the grade initiations actually conferred the powers and transformative experiences of the Sephiroth to which they were assigned—and this they could not always be relied upon to do.

The methods of initiation used in the traditional lodge system are capable of fostering changes in awareness, but they cannot force these. It sometimes happens that a candidate goes through an initiation ritual without any reaction deeper than puzzlement and boredom. In some cases, this is a function of individual differences; a given set of experiences and symbols cannot be counted on to have exactly the same effect on everyone who experiences it. In other cases, unfortunately, it is a function of incompetence or inattention on the part of the initiators. Israel Regardie has written with some feeling about his own initiation into the Adeptus Minor Grade, in which important parts of the ceremony were read out as though they were grocery lists.[21]

In addition, even when the initiation has been properly performed and had its intended effect, the reactions and triggers placed in the initiate's mind will lose effectiveness like any other stimulus unless they are strengthened and reinforced through repetition and regular practice. The word "initiation," it should be remembered, literally means "beginning," and even the most effective initiation is only the beginning of a process that must be carried out through further effort and time. This is true even in fraternal contexts. It is far more true in the case of a magical order.

This point was not lost on all the Golden Dawn's members, by any means, and several papers issued to Golden Dawn initiates stress the necessity for personal work. In practice, unfortunately, this principle too often received little more than lip service. Part of the problem stemmed from the fact that the grades of the Outer Order were normally taken within a matter of months, with no more required for passage from one to the next than the memorization of a few scraps of magical symbolism. This led far too many members to believe, and act, as though the mere process of undergoing a ritual initiation was enough to confer exalted levels of spiritual development. The result, unavoidably, was that the grades of the Order were treated as mere honorific titles, and the hard work of magical training and discipline was too often neglected or discarded. The later decline of the Order, in which requirements for advancement were progressively cut and manuscripts pulled from circulation, seems to have taken its shape largely from this factor.

The problems caused by the Golden Dawn grade structure were by no means impossible to solve. A stronger emphasis on personal practice and training, a better grasp of the limitations of the initiatory process, and a single "knowledge lecture" drawing a clear distinction between the grades as reflections of (and first steps toward) Sephirothic states of consciousness and those states themselves, might have done much. At the same time, the troubles that did arise are evidence that the Golden Dawn's core strategy of infusing the traditional lodge system with magical meaning was not without its potential pitfalls.

The government of the order

The risks inherent in the Order's strategy had a larger role, and a far more disastrous one, in the political and organizational troubles which shattered the Golden Dawn in the years 1900–1903. These troubles arose when the system of government which had been adopted by the Order proved unable to deal with a crisis among the top leadership. Previous accounts of the crisis have tended to stress the role of personalities in the Order's breakup. While these certainly had their part to play, much of what happened was a direct consequence of the way the Order's founders had adapted the governmental structures of the traditional lodge system to suit the needs of magical symbolism.

Hundreds of years of experience with human fallibility had led traditional orders to develop a flexible and carefully defined system of lodge governance, with the same sort of checks and balances American school children once studied in civics class. Typically, the officers in a lodge are elected for terms of six months to a year by the lodge membership, and they rotate through the offices so that no one person gains a stranglehold on any one position. Financial matters are assigned to one or more business officers, but lodge funds cannot be spent without a vote of the lodge itself. This same pattern repeats itself at the level of the "Grand Lodge," the regional or overall organization. Each lodge usually has a voting representative at the Grand Lodge level, and Grand Lodge officers are elected and serve under the same constraints. (In an Order with many organizational levels—some have as many as four, with local, county, state, and national lodges—each one relates to the next in the same fashion.)

Substantial elements of this system were built into the Golden Dawn's structure. For example, the regular rotation of Temple officers at six-month intervals was an important part of the function of the Equinox ceremony. On the other hand, the system of checks and balances which protect members and lodges from abuses on the part of the leadership was almost entirely absent. Temple officers were not elected but appointed by the Chiefs of the Order, who also held the power to change or suspend the Order's bylaws at will. The only recourse given to members who disagreed with an action of the Chiefs was the right to appeal to the Chiefs themselves![22] The entire system was designed as an autocracy, and once the control of that system passed into the hands of someone willing to abuse it—as happened when Samuel Mathers took sole control of the Order in 1897—the only way members had to resist such abuses was open revolt.

Another important influence, though, was the idea (then immensely popular in magical circles) that a body of "Secret Chiefs" or "Masters," unknown beings either human or once-human but in any case possessed of vast powers and the wisdom of the ages, were the true source of all magical knowledge and of all true initiation. This notion is often tied to Theosophical ideas about Mahatmas, but it actually goes much further back in Western magical thought. It appears in a range of eighteenth-century writings, and it had been used in several previous magically oriented orders, most notably the *Gold und Rosenkreuz* in Germany a century before.[23] It was a logical part of the magical tradition for the Golden Dawn to borrow—as well as a highly useful one.

Why did the Golden Dawn's original Chiefs—experienced Freemasons all—break with the traditional lodge structure in this way? Simple issues of personal power may well have played a role; the founders of the Order were human and had their share of human faults. However, there were at least two additional factors involved, factors which derived from the Order's magical concerns. One of these was the danger that the magical teachings of the Golden Dawn might be distorted in a more democratic system. The other was a central image of the magical symbolism of the time, which, in keeping with the Golden Dawn strategy already explored, was brought into this part of the traditional lodge system to adapt it to magical use.

It's hard to tell just how deeply committed the founders of the Golden Dawn themselves were to the idea of the Secret Chiefs. On the one hand, neither Westcott nor Mathers seem to have been averse to a certain amount of fraud, and the "Anna Sprengel letters," on which the Order based its claims, were almost certainly forgeries perpetrated by Westcott.[24] On the other hand, Golden Dawn papers contain detailed instructions on methods of communicating clairvoyantly with the Secret Chiefs,[25] and it seems somewhat unlikely that these instructions would have been issued by the Order's founders if those gentlemen did not expect messages to be received.

The risk of losing control of the Order's teachings was a real one, as the later history of the Golden Dawn and its successor groups proved. Westcott and Mathers were both skilled and knowledgeable magicians, but the other early members of the Order varied widely in the extent of their magical training. A structure in which all Order members could have a say in determining the Order's curriculum could easily have produced precisely the sort of watered-down version of the teachings as many of the later lodges in fact ended up adopting. An authoritarian structure, in which all teachings were handed down by the Order's rulers and were not subject to tampering, offered one way to avoid this risk.

Whatever their actual opinions, though, the Order's founders behaved as if they believed in the Secret Chiefs, and they made the presence of these beings central to the governmental structure of the Order. The authority of the visible Chiefs of the Order derived, explicitly, from the shadowy figures of the invisible Chiefs behind them. In this way, the Order's founders were able to legitimize the Order itself in the eyes of the magical community of their time, drawing on current mythologies in much the same way that kings of ancient times legitimized their rule by claiming descent from the gods. Nor should this be seen as nothing more than a cynical tactic of control. Mythologies of origin have played an important part in many lodge organizations, where they help to construct patterns of expectation and emotional response which can be critical to the success of initiatory work. The attempts of present-day Wiccans to construct a pedigree for their faith by reaching back into the mists of a mythologized prehistory derive from many of the same needs.

At the same time, the use of the Secret Chiefs as an element of the Order's system of governance was a disaster on a practical level, because it gave the top level of the leadership powers which could not be limited without disrupting the entire system of the Order. Mathers' dictatorial rule over the Golden Dawn in its last years rested entirely on his own claim to be acting under the command of the Secret Chiefs, from whom the Order's rituals, teachings, and right to initiate derived.[26] Within the Order's system, there was no way his authority to be challenged or limited, and no provision for establishing an alternative leadership in his place—barring new instructions from the Secret Chiefs. These did, in a sense, arrive in the end. The foundation of the major Golden Dawn successor groups, such as R.W. Felkin's Stella Matutina and Dion Fortune's

Fraternity of the Inner Light, followed on the emergence of new leaders who identified their own clairvoyant contacts with the Secret Chiefs of the Order. Meanwhile, the Order floundered through a series of political crises and schisms brought on, at least in part, by the fact that the existing structure could not legitimize any leadership but that of the Secret Chiefs—or those willing to claim to speak for them.

Conclusion: the legacy of the Golden Dawn

The Golden Dawn's transformation of the traditional lodge system, revolutionary as it was, thus was not without its risks. The Order managed to create, apparently for the first time in the history of the Western Esoteric Tradition, a fusion of collective and individual magical work in which the structure of the traditional lodge system blended seamlessly with the processes of personal spiritual transformation, and through which nearly every part of the wildly diverse legacy of Western magic was brought into a system workable on individual and group levels. Such a fusion, though, could and did create problems of its own, and in the case of the original Golden Dawn those problems played a significant role in wrecking the Order itself.

It was perhaps inevitable that the first group to attempt this kind of fusion would run into unexpected difficulties. The early stages of any kind of evolution are rarely smooth going. More important, at least from the perspective of the present, is the fact that the Golden Dawn's rites and teachings did not perish with the Order itself, and have become one of the central elements in the current renaissance of the magical arts. The Order's achievements have thus become the common property of magicians everywhere, just as its failures represent a lesson from which all students of the magical arts have something to learn.

Notes

1. Hamill, J., *The Craft: A History of English Freemasonry* (Crucible, 1986) is a competent overview of the subject.
2. Schmidt, A.J., *Fraternal Organizations* (Greenwood, 1990) gives details on these organizations and most other fraternal orders.
3. See Yates, F.A., *Giordano Bruno and The Hermetic Tradition* (University of Chicago Press, 1979).

4. *Ibid.*

5. Heisler, R., "John Dee and the Secret Societies," *Hermetic Journal* (1992, pp. 12–24).

6. Yates, F.A., *The Rosicrucian Enlightenment* (Routledge & Kegan Paul, 1972).

7. Heisler, R., "Introduction to the Hermetic Adepti," *Hermetic Journal* (1987, 35, pp. 34–41).

8. In discussing the basic techniques of fraternal initiation, I am placed in the awkward position of having to satisfy the demands of scholarship and of my obligations of initiation at the same time. As a member of several fraternal lodges I have been given ritual texts and other documents which are not publicly available, and I have also obtained—chiefly from used-book dealers—a number of rituals of orders, most of them extinct, of which I am not a member. In fairness to the orders involved, I have chosen not to give specific examples or citations from these materials. I should add that the interpretation of the lodge system given here, and particularly of the signs, grips, and words used in Degrees, is not taken from fraternal sources but is my own.

9. These are the presiding officers of, respectively, a Lodge of Free and Accepted Masons, a Lodge of Odd Fellows, a Camp of Royal Neighbors, and a Castle of Knights of Pythias, all currently active American fraternal orders.

10. There seems to be no biography as yet of this major Golden Dawn figure. Gilbert, R.A., *The Magical Mason* (Aquarian, 1983) gives a brief biographical note and some otherwise rare Westcott essays.

11. These are given in Regardie, I., *The Golden Dawn* (Llewellyn, 1971, Vol. 3, pp. 81–192).

12. *Ibid.*, Vol. 3, p. 148.

13. See, for instance, *ibid.*, Vol. 3, p. 125.

14. Those Flying Rolls not included in Regardie's *The Golden Dawn*, including Flying Roll X, may be found in Mathers, S.L.M. et al., *Astral Projection, Ritual Magic, and Alchemy*, (Destiny, 1987); Flying Roll X is on pp. 131–140.

15. *Ibid.*, p. 136.

16. Regardie, I., *Golden Dawn*, Vol. 3, p. 135.

17. *Ibid.*, Vol. 1, p. 185.

18. *Ibid.*, Vol. 3, pp. 287–289.

19. The original source for these is "Magister Pianco" (i.e., Baron Hans Heinrich von Ecker und Eckhoffen), *Der Rosenkreutzer in Seiner Blosse*

(*The Rosicrucian In His Nakedness*), an exposé published in 1781. They were reprinted in tabular form in Kenneth MacKenzie's *Royal Cyclopedia of Freemasonry*, and borrowed intact by the Societas Rosicruciana in Anglia as the basis for its own Grade system; this last was almost certainly the source from which the Golden Dawn borrowed. Manly Hall reprinted the table in his useful Hall, M.P., *Codex Rosae Crucis* (Philosophical Research Society, 1971, p. 13).

20. Regardie, I., *My Rosicrucian Adventure* (repr. as *What You Should Know About The Golden Dawn*, Falcon, 1985, see especially p. 100).
21. *Ibid.*, pp. 94–98.
22. The original bylaws of the Golden Dawn, as well as several later versions, are given in Gilbert, R.A., *The Golden Dawn Companion* (Aquarian, 1986, pp. 43–72).
23. See McIntosh, C., *The Rosicrucians* (Crucible, 1987, especially pp. 82–94).
24. This is the conclusion of Ellic Howe's waspish but well-researched Howe, E., *The Magicians of The Golden Dawn* (Aquarian, 1985).
25. Quoted in Mathers et al., op. cit., pp. 14–19.
26. See Mathers' manifesto of 1896, reprinted in Regardie, *What You Should Know About the Golden Dawn*, pp. 181–186.

Bibliography

Gilbert, R.A., *The Magical Mason* (Aquarian, 1983).
Gilbert, R.A., *The Golden Dawn Companion* (Aquarian, 1986, pp. 43–72).
Hall, M.P., *Codex Rosae Crucis* (Philosophical Research Society, 1971, p. 13).
Hamill, J., *The Craft: A History of English Freemasonry* (Crucible, 1986).
Heisler, R., "Introduction to the Hermetic Adepti," *Hermetic Journal* (1987, 35, pp. 34–41).
Heisler, R., "John Dee and the Secret Societies," *Hermetic Journal* (1992, pp. 12–24).
Howe, E., *The Magicians of The Golden Dawn* (Aquarian, 1985).
Mathers, S.L.M. et al., *Astral Projection, Ritual Magic, and Alchemy*, (Destiny, 1987).
McIntosh, C., *The Rosicrucians* (Crucible, 1987, pp. 82–94).
Regardie, I., *The Golden Dawn* (Llewellyn, 1971, Vol. 3, pp. 81–192).
Regardie, I., *My Rosicrucian Adventure* (repr. as *What You Should Know About The Golden Dawn*, Falcon, 1985, p. 100).
Schmidt, A.J., *Fraternal Organizations* (Greenwood, 1990).
Yates, F.A., *The Rosicrucian Enlightenment* (Routledge & Kegan Paul, 1972).
Yates, F.A., *Giordano Bruno and The Hermetic Tradition* (University of Chicago Press, 1979).

The method of judging questions according to Peter de Abano of Padua: a Medieval handbook of geomancy

Another discovery that would occupy my attention for years to come was this Latin essay on the traditional techniques of geomantic divination, which turned my geomancy readings from unproductive drudgery to clear and accurate constellations of meaning. I found it in an appendix to a French scholarly book on geomancy that turned up in the University of Washington library; I had just completed two years of Latin, so the translation offered few difficulties. I did a first rough translation in 1993, then revised it for publication in the Spring 1996 issue of Caduceus.

Introduction

Divination has always had an important role in the Hermetic tradition, although the types of divination which have been most used have changed several times over the tradition's history. Students of modern Hermetic systems will be familiar with the role played by the Tarot not merely as a divinatory method but also as a symbolic alphabet; astrology has had similar functions in Hermeticism since ancient times.

During the Middle Ages and Renaissance, though, one of the most important divinatory methods used by Hermeticists throughout the

Western world was geomancy. Like the *I Ching*, which it resembles in a number of ways, this system uses random actions to generate a set of binary digits: in the case of geomancy, single or double points, grouped in figures of four digits each. Four such figures, called the "Mothers," are produced by chance, and a total of twelve others—"Daughters," "Nephews," "Witnesses," a "Judge," and a "Reconciler"—are derived from these by a set of mathematical processes. These figures and their interactions are interpreted by the geomancer through a system of houses borrowed from astrological sources. (The whole procedure is given in detail in Channasson (1980), Regardie (1972), Skinner (1977), Skinner (1980), and in many other sources.)

During the Renaissance, the art of geomancy was among the most practiced of divinatory methods, and attracted the attention of Hermetic writers of the caliber of Cornelius Agrippa and Robert Fludd. The Hermetic Order of the Golden Dawn also included geomancy in its course of studies, but the version presented by Westcott and Mathers was a fragmentary one, copied verbatim from the works of the Jacobean plagiarist John Heydon. This has become the standard version used in the English-speaking world at present, with the result that most of the more interesting possibilities of geomancy have been almost completely neglected for a century or more.

The following is a translation of *Modo judicandi guestiones secundum Petrum de Abano Patavinum*, an anonymous text on geomantic divination found in a wide range of manuscripts from the fourteenth, fifteenth and sixteenth centuries. Unlike most other handbooks of geomancy, it deals solely with the interpretation of the geomantic chart once this has been produced by the standard procedures, and it gives details of interpretive methods which have long been forgotten in the English-speaking world. The text I have used for this translation is that edited by Thérese Charmasson (Charmasson, 1980, pp. 275–282), and is found in Munich ms. lat. 489, fol. 222–233. Words which have been added solely to fit the requirements of English usage have not been noted, but substantive additions have been placed in square brackets.

The method of judging questions according to Peter de Abano of Padua

Desiring to give true and certain judgement, according to the glorious and venerable science of geomancy, one first ought to invoke, supplicate, and entreat the clemency of omnipotent God, so that he may be able to extract the true signification of the figures, and open up by a true path the occult property of the twelve houses, and the Judge together with the Witnesses. In which judgment, nine things are to be considered:

—in the first place, the good or evil character of the figures.
—in the second place, to know what are the significators of the question.
—in the third place, if the first sign, which signifies the querent [the person seeking divination], occupies the house of the quesited [the subject of the divination].
—in the fourth place, if the first significator seeks conjunction with the other significator or on the contrary, if the significator of the quesited seeks conjunction with that of the querent.
—in the fifth place, to see whether a mutation is made in the question, that is, if either significator shifts out of its proper place, making a conjunction between itself and the other significator.
—in the sixth place, to see if there may be any translation between significators.
—in the seventh place, the good or evil character of the Witnesses and Judge must be considered.
—in the eighth place, the nature and signification of the sixteenth figure.
—in the ninth place, whether a thing lost will arrive quickly or whether hope will be cut off.

Of the good and evil character of the figures

The good or evil character of the figures is considered in this way. Now the good or evil of the four cardinal houses ought to be considered, namely which figures are benevolent, because if the figure in the first house is benevolent, a good beginning is to be presumed, whether from the goodness of the querent or otherwise; if the figure in the fourth house is good, a good end is to be rejoiced in; if the figures in the seventh and tenth houses are good, a good middle is to be hoped for, and the reverse has the opposite meaning. And if the fifteenth figure [the Judge] agrees with the fourth, the best end of all is not to be doubted, and the reverse has the opposite meaning.

Of the kinds of figures

Then it must be seen whether good figures are in aspect to the ascendant, because if they are in sextile aspect, that is, in the third and eleventh houses, it is good; if in trine aspect, that is in the fifth and ninth houses, it signifies better than all, and the reverse, when the ascendant is weakened.

Of the exaltations of the figures

Next, the exaltations of the figures must be considered. Now the figures of Mercury, Albus and Conjunctio, are exalted in the ascendant; the figures of Luna, Populus and Via, in the third; the figures of Venus, Amissio and Puer, in the fifth; the figures of Mars, Rubeus and Puella, in the sixth; the figures of the Sun, Fortuna Major and Fortuna Minor, in the ninth; the figures of Jupiter, Acquisitio and Laetitia, in the eleventh; the figures of Saturn, Carcer and Tristitia, in the twelfth; and when a good figure is in its exaltation, its good signification is doubled; if it is evil, its evil is doubled.

Of the association of figures

Likewise, it must be seen which figure benefits from its companions, and from which figures it arises. Now if a good figure is in good company, its good signification is completed and increased, and the reverse has the opposite effect, if it has an evil companion;[1] if on the other hand a good figure is created from good parents, this signifies complete good, while if it is created from one good and another evil figure, it remains in its own proper signification. And if it arises from two evil figures, it is tainted by them and is left mixed in character. If it is evil, all is reversed.

Of the mutation of a figure and its signification

It must also be known why a figure is said to change its fortune; this signifies that it happens that fortunate signs exercise their signification against the will of the querent, and signify the negation of the arrival of the thing desired. For example: if someone asks whether rains will come, and Laetitia is formed in the tenth house, which is the house of rains or drought, this Laetitia here signifies fair weather and lack of rain; Laetitia, therefore, changes its fortune, for although it is good, it becomes of evil signification, fair weather, when this be against the desire and will of the querent. For indeed any figure which has a signification against the will of the querent, whatever it may be, in that question is judged evil and the reverse in the opposite case.

Of knowing how to discover the significator

Now judgment in geomancy in no way can be given, if the practitioner himself does not know the places of the question, that is, the significators, which are known to signify the arrival or negation[2] of the question [that is, the quesited]. For indeed the significators are those figures which signify the querent and the quesited.

First house

Now the place of the querent's significator is the first house, since in the first house the querent is always considered, and note that someone is not the querent who asks in the place of another, but he for whom the question is asked is said to be the querent, whether he be present or not. For example: if I ask for N., as though it were he, not I but he is called the querent. And truly the other significator which signifies the quesited matter is considered now in one house, now in another.

Second house

If, for example, someone asks if he will profit, or if he will receive money from a debtor, or if something lost is in the house, or if his money will remain untouched, or if he will be enriched, all these are considered in the second house.

Third house

If on the other hand he should ask whether he is esteemed by a brother or sister, or whether he will die before a brother of his or a sister or a close relative, or of what sort his companions maybe in lodgings or on a journey, or if a journey will be short, or if it will be safe, or if his messenger whom he wishes to send will do what he ought to do well, all of this is considered in the third house; it is the other significator.

Fourth house

And if someone should ask whether he is esteemed by his father, or by his uncle, or by his father-in-law, or by any older member of his family, or if a patrimony ought to be increased or recovered, or if it be good to found a castle or a house, or if any work which has been started will come to an end, or if a thing has been lost in the place enquired about, or in what part of a house or ship or land or field is a thing which has been lost, or if a thing which has been lost will be found in a place hoped for, or if some building will fall down, or a plantation of trees come to bear fruit, or if a field will abound with produce, or if the price of seed will rise or fall in a quesited month or year, or if a particular tract of land is fertile, or if any matter will come to a good end; in all these questions, the fourth house is the significator.

Fifth house

And if someone asks whether he will have children, or similarly the querent asks whether she will conceive or give birth, or die during childbirth, or have complications, or what food will be served at a banquet, and of what flavor, and if the food be poisoned, or if the returns from the querent's property will be increased, or if he will live happily, or if a lawsuit or dispute which his carried on against him will be settled peaceably; the fifth house signifies all these things.

Sixth house

In the sixth house, these things are considered, namely whether the querent will be sick, or if an absent person is sick, and what caused him to fall sick; if he will be cursed by the medicine which has been selected; if small animals are fruitful or sterile or if they will be lost; if it is good to keep or hire a servant, or if he will run away or serve well, or if he will stay a long time with the querent, or what color the urine will be [this is a sign used in medical diagnosis].

Seventh house

In the seventh house, these things are considered: if the querent will take a wife; if a marriage will take place; if a marriage will be fortunate; if the querent will marry a particular woman; if he will regain a wife or a sweetheart or a lover; if he will be defeated by someone with whom he fights; if a woman be a virgin or if she has given birth, if a wife or sweetheart be lawful, if the querent will separate from his wife, if a particular horse will win a race, if the querent will be defeated in war or in a lawsuit; if his adversary will make peace or an alliance with him; if a business partner is honest; if a debtor intends to pay his debt; if an exile will return to his homeland; if he will be well in the land to which he goes; of what quality is the land to which he goes; and the quality of all opposites is declared by the seventh house.

Eighth house

In the eighth house, these things are considered: whether someone will die at a predestined point; if the querent will get possession of the remains of the dead; if in the land to which he goes he will be enriched; if his adversary has much money; if something reached the person to whom it was sent; if he will die as a result of a particular illness; whether something he fears has truly come upon him.

Ninth house

In the ninth house, these things are asked: if a particular person be Catholic, or if he have faith or if he be religious; if a wise man has skill [or a particular skill or knowledge]; if a long journey will be safe; if a church will be built; if the querent will receive church preferment [appointment to an ecclesiastical office]; if a church which has been begun will be completed; if a church will fall down; if the querent will not receive preferment, if he will be deposed from his position in the church, if a religious official will govern his subordinates well; if the church will receive goods; if the querent will receive favor in the church; if the treasury of the church will be increased; if the church will be honored with riches.

Tenth house

In the tenth house, these things are considered: if the querent will be king or a powerful man or an elected official; if he will be bailiff to a king or official, that is, will have land or people placed under him by the king; if the king will be honored in his kingdom or despised or if he will be deposed; if having been deposed he will regain the throne; if he will govern the kingdom well; if the kingdom will be at peace; if the kingdom will be increased; if the querent will have hope of gaining honors; if the querent will be honored; if he will be fortunate in his relations with the king or a prince or his particular lord; if the querent's teacher be faithful in all things; if the querent is esteemed by the king or prince or his lord; if his teacher knows the branch of knowledge which he has promised to teach; if the querent is esteemed by his mother; how his widowed mother will fare; if he will profit by a manual art; if the manual art about which he asks will be useful and lucrative to him; if on an appointed day it will rain, or what kind of wind will blow, or what kind of weather there will be.

Eleventh house

In the eleventh house, these things are considered: if the querent will be fortunate; if he will have friends; if a friend is useful; if the querent will be helped by a friend; if the friendship of a friend will endure; if a king or prince will have treasure, or if his treasury will increase; if the king's trib-ute [or taxes] will remain the same; if he will conquer land; from whom he will have tribute; if the querent will be a bailiff or a servant or a minister at the court of a king or prince; if a king or prince will forgive the querent and restore his [position, property, etc.]; if the querent will lose his posi-tion as bailiff or servant to a king or prince; if a thing hoped for will come to pass or if the querent will attain a thing hoped for; if by his service he will benefit his elders; if a thing which has been entrusted to someone will be safe, or if a thing which has been deposited will be reclaimed.

Twelfth house

In the twelfth house, these things are considered: whether the querent will have hidden enemies, or if the hidden enemies be dangerous, or if hidden enemies will defeat the querent; or how hidden enemies seek to harm the querent; and if a large animal which he wants to buy be good or vicious, or if he should sell it, if he will in truth profit from it, or if it is old or young; and if the querent will be captured or imprisoned, or if in that prison he will die, or if he will go into or out of debt or prison or slavery, and if he will be honorably buried, or what kind of sepulchre he will have, and if after his death he will have a good reputation or a bad one.

Of the occupation of figures

Occupation is when the sign of the querent occupies the house of the quesited. For example, someone asked whether he would be able to recover his house, which he had lost, and Albus was in the first house and shifted itself [i.e., also appeared] in the fourth, occupying the place of the quesited. And note that there is no kind of answer in this science better than this one, if the first sign be fortunate, seeing that the thing in question must be acquired, without doubt, if God wills.

Of the conjunction of figures

Conjunction is when one significator shifts itself into conjunction with the other significator [i.e., also appears in a house next to that of the other significator]. For example: someone asked whether his slave who ran away could be recovered, and Acquisitio was in the first house, and shifted itself into the fifth house, that is, in conjunction with the sixth house, which is the significator of the slave; from which one supposes that the slave will be recovered, because of the signification of this conjunction. And note that when the first significator shifts itself into conjunction with the other significator, this always means that the querent, through his own diligence and effort, will acquire the thing inquired about; and when the figure of the quesited goes to a conjunction with the significator of the querent, then this will mean that the querent, without diligence or effort on his own part, will have the thing inquired about.

Of the mutation of significators

Mutation is when both significators shift out of their own places, making a conjunction between themselves. For example, someone asked whether he would be able to have the woman he loved, and Carcer was in the first house and Puer in the seventh, signifying the woman; now there is a shifting of Carcer to the fourth house and Puer to the third house. This conjunction of significators outside of their own places means, therefore, that the querent will have the woman in question, but not in the proper place, that is, not in the place of the querent, nor in the house of the quesited; but because the conjunction is said to be made from the place of the querent, it denotes that the querent will have the woman near his own home.

Of the translation of figures

Translation is when one figure carries the disposition [of the matter] from one significator to the other. For example: someone asked whether he would be able to bring about his marriage,[3] and this is how the divination came out: Acquisitio was in the house of the querent and Laetitia was in conjunction with it, making a good translation to the seventh, since it was conjoined to it in the eighth [i.e., Laetitia also appeared in the eighth house and was thus in conjunction with the seventh house, the house of marriage], thus having disposition of the marriage, and because the ascendant [the first house] was acquisitive and fortunate, and because the figure Conjunctio was formed by [the combination of the figures in] the first and seventh houses, and because a trine aspect from the fifth house strengthened the ascendant, and even more because of the combination of all these, the marriage was brought about with ease.

Of the good or evil character of the Judge and Witnesses

The good or evil character of the Judge and Witnesses is considered thus, as experience shows: since the fifteenth figure [the Judge] is closer to the diviner than the others, it is therefore attributed to the Moon among the planets, since the Moon is closer to the Earth than the other planets. And just as the Moon in one lunation, by reason of the very swift speed of its course, passes through every sign and visits all of the planets, separating from one and applying to another; in the same way, the fifteenth figure comes into being out of the procreation and generation of all the figures above it. But since among these we first have the thirteenth and fourteenth figures [the Witnesses], the thirteenth figure is attributed to the planet from which the Moon is separating, and the fourteenth to the one to which it is applying; therefore if the thirteenth is good and fourteenth evil, this signifies that the matter about which the question is asked tends to the worse, and if the thirteenth is evil and the fourteenth good, the matter tends to the better, if the fifteenth supports their testimony. The good or evil character of the judge does not differ from that of the fourth house, because both of them signify the end of the matter in question; from which, if both of them be good, there can be no doubt of the best conclusion of the quesited matter, if God wills, and the reverse in the opposite case; and if one is good and the other evil, you may judge that the quesited matter will have a mediocre end.

Of the sixteenth figure

The sixteenth figure, of which the good or evil character must be considered, assuredly is created from the first and fifteenth figures. If it is good, and appears in another part of the chart, it signifies that, after the quesited thing is obtained in whatever position in the chart pertains to it, there will also be that good thing which arises out of the nature of the house in which the sixteenth figure is found. But if it be evil, all is the reverse.

Of the swift or slow conclusion of the question

Whether the arrival or denial[4] of the thing desired will take place sooner or later is considered thus: count the points of all sixteen figures of which I speak. Then if the number of points be ninety-six, because all the figures of geomancy are formed out of a total of ninety-six points, it is plain that the arrival of the conclusion will be swift, and neither slow nor doubtful; if it be more than ninety-six, it will be slow, and by as much as it is more than ninety-six, it will be that much slower; and if the tale of the points be less than ninety-six, so much more quickly the quesited matter seeks its end; and by as much as it is less than ninety-six, so much more quickly will the end arrive.[5]

Notes

1. "If it has a good companion" in the original.
2. The original has *adventus vel negotiatio,* which I have taken as a scribal error for *adventus vel negatio.*
3. The words *per translatorem,* "by a translator," were inserted in the text at this point.
4. Same as Note 2.
5. The original repeats "more than 96" and "slowly" in this last clause.

Bibliography

Agrippa, H.C., pseud., *Fourth Book of Occult Philosophy* (repr. Kessinger, 1992). Contains Agrippa's *On Geomancy* and Gerard of Cremona's *On Astrological Geomancy.*

Channasson, T., *Recherches sur une Technique Divinatoire: La Geomancie dans 1' Occident Medieval* (Librairie Droz, 1980).

Pennick, N., *Games of the Gods* (Weiser, 1989).

Regardie, I., *A Practical Guide to Geomantic Divination* (Samuel Weiser, 1972).

Skinner, S., *Terrestrial Astrology* (Routledge & Kegan Paul, 1980).

Skinner, S., *The Oracle of Geomancy* (Prism, 1986).

Geometries of the sword

The brightest star in the firmament of 1990s occult journalism, Gnosis
Magazine *provided students of Western esoteric spirituality with a lively mix
of in-depth articles and current news bearing on occultism. I became a regular
subscriber early on and finally submitted an article for the Summer 1996 issue
on Hermeticism. During the Summer of 1995, thanks to Joy Hancox' book*
The Byrom Collection, *I had encountered the extraordinary Pythagorean
swordsmanship of Gerard Thibault, whose massive work* Academie de
l'Espee (Academy of the Sword) *was to occupy my spare hours for most of
a decade thereafter. This was my first attempt to put Thibault and his Western
esoteric martial art in perspective. I hoped to attract the attention of people
interested in reviving Thibault's system as a living martial art; with a few
honorable exceptions, this hope was destined for frustration.*

Much of an American generation's first encounter with the concept
of esoteric spirituality came through the odd medium of Kwai Chang
Caine, the half-American Shaolin monk of the TV show "Kung Fu."
Behind his wanderings through the Old West lay the flashback images
of a Chinese temple where masters taught the secrets of the universe
along with those of flying sidekicks.

The latter, of course, were the immediate source of interest to my friends and me in the early 1970s, but part of Caine's attractiveness was that he wasn't just a martial artist. He could treat wounds, play the flute, meditate, dispense snippets of fortune-cookie philosophy, walk across rice paper without leaving a footprint, and nonviolently pound the stuffing out of a dozen cowboy-hatted heavies without working up a sweat. The man was a human Swiss Army knife, and it was a truism of the series that any garden-variety Shaolin monk was equally omnicompetent.

Television is television, of course, and plenty of the things that went into "Kung Fu" came straight from Never-Never Land. (The Shaolin Temple was destroyed a couple of centuries before Caine would have had the chance to study there, for one thing.) At the same time, the image of the esotericist as master of many trades is not all that inaccurate. Many religious traditions have a wide array of auxiliary arts—systems of art and craft which don't bear directly on the primary work of spirituality; but which have roles, sometimes important ones, in the broader structure of the tradition. A trained practitioner of one of these traditions is likely to have at least a nodding acquaintance with many of these arts.

The development of these auxiliary arts is particularly noticeable in Asian cultures, where large portions of the history of art, architecture, music, literature, medicine, and other disciplines revolve around the development of different monastic orders and religious sects. A properly trained Taoist priest in the modern period, for example, has studied not only philosophy, meditative practice, and ritual, but also calligraphy, music, landscape design, divination, and armed and unarmed combat.[1] In the Western world, much the same thing was once true in monastic circles: auxiliary arts ranging from Gregorian chant to brandy making, to say nothing of more esoteric practices such as the Art of Memory, were at one time common attainments of Catholic monks.

The student of the Hermetic tradition, on the other hand, has fewer options. At present, besides the almost forgotten traditions of lodge architecture and ritual art, there's a certain amount of literature and art that can be called Hermetic, as well as a fairly large legacy of often dubious medicine. For someone raised on Kwai Chang Caine, these are pretty slim pickings.

Still, the modern Hermetic tradition is shaking off 300 years of living in survival mode, when only the most crucial materials could be preserved in the face of almost universal indifference. At least for now, the survival of the tradition's basic practices and teachings seems secure, and the question of auxiliary arts may well be worth opening again. Some of these, of course, will be freshly invented, but there's also a case to be made for reviving arts that Were part of the tradition at an earlier time. The Renaissance, when Hermetic ideas and insights had perhaps their widest circulation in history, is one obvious place to look.

One place within Renaissance culture that may be less than obvious, but which contains some unexplored possibilities for the Hermetic tradition, is to be found in the arts of the sword. There, in the pages of a handful of early fencing manuals, can be traced the origin and flowering of a school of fencing based on Pythagorean geometry and Neoplatonic philosophy—a full-scale Hermetic martial art.

 ℅

In the year 1553, the press of Antonio Blado, *stampadore apostolico* to Pope Julius III in Rome, issued a new book on swordsmanship by one Camillo Agrippa.[2] This book, *A Tractate of the Science of Arms, with a Philosophical Dialogue*, provides the first definite date to a revolution then underway in the arts of combat in Europe.

For well over a thousand years before that time, both the form and the use of the sword in the Western world had remained all but unchanged; the only real difference between a *spatha* of the barbarian invasions and a broadsword of the time of Henry VIII was in the methods of forging and the quality of the metal. Modern historians of fencing tend to treat the swords of these periods as if they were vaguely sharpened steel clubs, which is unfair: the broadswords of the Middle Ages were superbly crafted instruments, and they retained the traditional shape because it worked, with ghastly efficiency. A solid blow from a well-made broadsword can cut a human body in half.

Pick up a broadsword, and there's no question of how it's meant to be used. Sweeping cuts from the shoulder, backed by the momentum of the whole body, gave it the power to drive past shields and batter through armor. The motions involved follow the natural motions of the human body, just like the round "haymaker" punches thrown by untrained fighters. Skill had a definite role in broadsword combat—another point that historians of fencing have tended to ignore—but strength, endurance, and raw courage were the paramount virtues in battle. The romances that were the favorite reading of the feudal warrior aristocracy celebrate mighty blows with the sword, not clever ones.

The new swordsmanship pioneered by Camillo Agrippa took a different approach. Agrippa himself was an architect, engineer, and mathematician, famous in his lifetime for erecting the great obelisk in the center of the piazza of St. Peter in Rome. He was also a close friend of Michelangelo, who provided illustrations for his book. He turned to questions of swordsmanship with the same spirit of inquiry that marked Renaissance culture as a whole.

Like so many other advances of that age, Agrippa's new swordsmanship had roots in one of the rediscovered treasures of classical culture. The recovery of Marcus Vitruvius Polio's *Ten Books on Architecture*, written around the beginning of the Common Era, had sparked a revolution in thought that did not stop at the limits of the architect's craft. To Vitruvius, geometry and proportion provided the master key to all forms of design; the best and most perfect proportions were those of the human body, worked out and applied according to the rules of geometry.[3] This same fusion of geometrical abstraction with the solid realities of the human form can be applied to combat as well, and Vitruvian ideas, which played a similar role in other facets of Renaissance culture, were central to Agrippa's new art of fencing.

The propositions of Euclid may seem far removed from the rough-and-tumble of combat, but there is (no pun intended) a point to the connection. The sword is perhaps the most geometrical of all weapons: a straight line moved through space to intersect another line or penetrate the surface of an opponent's body; each movement of a sword in combat is an arc or a line. Euclid had demonstrated centuries earlier that the shortest distance between two points is a straight line, and Agrippa's most important insight was that this idea should be applied to swordsmanship.

This involved a break with tradition on a larger scale than a first glance may show. The round motions of a cut, as mentioned above, follow the natural movements of the body, but to thrust in a straight line requires practice and careful coordination. At the same time, the shorter distance needed for a thrust to reach its target makes it quicker than a cut, just as the straight punch of a boxer will hit while a haymaker is still swinging through the air. The shift from cutting to thrusting thus put a premium on quickness, dexterity, and training rather than on simple force, and changed the entire context of swordsmanship.

In Agrippa's manual, following the principles of geometry, cuts with the sword's edge took a secondary role to thrusts with the sword's point.

The natural proportions and positions of the human body defined a new and more mobile stance, and new guards (the positions in which the sword is held before beginning an attack or parry) kept the sword's point always directed at the opponent, ready to thrust across the shortest possible space. The result was a new and extremely effective kind of swordplay, one that soon came to dominate the arts of combat across Europe. The Italian style of fencing, as it came to be called, was the ancestor of most subsequent styles of swordplay as well as of modern sport fencing.

A new kind of sword designed to suit this style, known as the rapier, followed quickly. Long and slender—many had well over a yard of blade alone—it was double-edged and had a swirl of metal bars about the hilt to ward off disabling attacks on the wrist. A precise weapon, designed to skewer rather than dismember, it was to the broadsword roughly what a hunting rifle is to a military assault weapon. The comparison is a precise one: the swords and swordsmanship used in warfare continued to rely on the cutting edge for another 350 years, until modern firepower rendered the last survivals of the sword utterly obsolete at the beginning of World War I.

CB

The cultural milieu of the Renaissance gave philosophical, religious, and esoteric connections to geometry that allowed Agrippa's practical insights to be developed in unexpected ways. The classical writings recovered by Renaissance humanists included most of the surviving works of Pythagorean and Neoplatonic philosophy, in which mathematical symbolism was wedded to mystical practice. These sparked a major revival of the esoteric geometry and numerology of Pythagoras and his successors, a revival central to much of Renaissance thought.[4]

The role of number mysticism and geometry in Renaissance esotericism is hard to overstate. Marsilio Ficino, whose fifteenth-century translations of Plato and the Hermetic writings jump-started the magical revival, was familiar with the new Vitruvian architecture and used its principles of proportion in his own esoteric writings. His younger contemporary Giovanni Pico de Mirandola, whose *Nine Hundred Conclusions* represent the first public manifesto of the new esotericism, devoted seventy-two of the Conclusions to mathematics and geometry. Many of the important publications of Renaissance esotericism, from the *De Harmonia Mundi* of Francesco Giorgi (1525) to the encyclopedic works of Robert Fludd a century later, draw extensively on Vitruvian concepts, using proportion and geometry as a key to the nature of the physical and nonphysical worlds.[5]

Nor was this borrowing a one-way affair. These magical traditions of geometry were incorporated into Renaissance art and architecture so thoroughly that an enormous range of Renaissance buildings show the hallmarks of Pythagorean thought; it can be said without much exaggeration that to the Renaissance architect, geometry was Pythagorean.[6] The revolution in swordsmanship set in motion by Camillo Agrippa was a natural subject for the same process. Though Agrippa's own work made no reference to the mystical implications of geometry, the fusion of the Vitruvian approach and the art of fencing opened the door to much more extensive developments along these lines.

CB

The year 1582 saw the publication of another major work on swordsmanship. *On the Philosophy of Arms and Their Dexterous Handling, and on Christian Attack and Defense* by Jeronimo de Carranza[7] was in its own way as revolutionary as Agrippa's work. Like its predecessor, it applied geometry to the subject of fencing, but it did so on a much wider scale.

Carranza's approach to swordsmanship, the foundation of what became the Spanish style of fencing, combined the linear thrusts of Agrippa with circular footwork. In training, a circle would be traced out on the ground, its diameter equal to the maximum length of an effective thrust. Standing at opposite edges of this circle, the combatants were just out of range of each other. Any movement across or around the circle offered the possibility of attack; Carranza traced out these movements and their possible counters in geometrical terms as relationships in space.

As the Spanish school developed, the subtlety and complexity of these analyses increased to a remarkable degree. In the writings of Luis Pacheco de Narvaez, Carranza's greatest pupil and the most famous of Spain's fencing masters, the responses to a given movement of the adversary depend not only on the movement itself, but on such things as the adversary's balance of humors—the four principles, identified with blood, phlegm, black bile, and yellow bile, that were central to

Renaissance medicine and psychology—and subtle variations in the quality of the motion.

To modern eyes used to the flashy movements and sport-fencing techniques of Errol Flynn and the various *Three Musketeers* movies, a duel fought in the Spanish style would be an odd spectacle. The combatants stood straight, feet close together and knees only slightly bent, facing each other side-on with right arms and swords extended. Their feet were in constant motion as they circled left and right, seeking an opening for a sudden thrust with the arm—the lunge had not yet been invented—or sidestepping an attack.

Modern historians of fencing have had a hard time believing that this manner of swordplay could have been of any use at all.[8] Nonetheless Spanish fencers had a reputation as lethal duelists throughout the sixteenth and seventeenth centuries, when this school was at its height. Their reputation carried weight even in cultural backwaters such as England, where Ben Jonson's Captain Bobadil in *Every Man in His Humour* talks constantly of the great Carranza. Even the stolid English master-of-arms George Silver, defender of the old broadsword, whose *Paradoxes of Defence* (1599) is one long diatribe against the "Italianated fight" then being imported into England, grudgingly admitted the effectiveness of the Spanish style of fencing.[9]

To what extent was this extraordinary system shaped by the Pythagorean traditions of geometry we've examined? It's difficult to tell; Spain was as strongly influenced by the esoteric revival of the Renaissance as any European country, but the presence of the Inquisition made Spanish Hermeticists more than usually concerned with staying out of sight. There is, however, one piece of evidence worth considering: the one book on the Spanish style that was written and published outside of Spain.

That book is an astonishing document, the most elaborate work on swordsmanship ever printed as well as one of the most lavishly produced books of an age in which printing often counted among the fine arts. It also, and more significantly, marks the furthest extension of Agrippa's geometrical approach to fencing, an extension that went beyond the published works of Carranza and Pacheco de Narvaez into an explicitly Pythagorean geometry of the sword.

Gerard Thibault, the author of this work, was a true man of the Renaissance: like Agrippa, an architect steeped in the Vitruvian tradition, but also a noted painter and physician as well as a first-rate swordsman of the Spanish style. In 1611, he took first prize in a fencing competition in Antwerp, competing against the acknowledged Dutch masters of the art, and went on to demonstrate his skill before Prince Maurice of Nassau in a celebrated exhibition lasting several days. He then set out to produce a definitive manual on fencing. *L'Academie de L'Espee*, produced with the support of the King of France, the Holy Roman Emperor, and an array of lesser luminaries, and illustrated by some of the best engravers of the period, took fifteen years just to print, and was finally published a year after the author's death in 1629.[10]

To Thibault, the true art of fencing was founded squarely and explicitly on the geometrical philosophy of Renaissance Pythagoreanism. The human body is a microcosm, a perfect reflection of the universe in its physical and spiritual aspects alike. In its proportions, its "Number, Measure, and Weights," it contains the harmony of the four elements and the seven planets. So too the positions and movements of fencing and the length of the sword must all be exactly derived from the proportions of the fencer's body in order to be harmonious and effective. Plato and Pythagoras, as well as Vitruvius, are brought into the discussion, along with references to the measurements of Noah's Ark and the Temple of Solomon—themselves derived from the mystical proportions of the human body.[11]

These same proportions define the complex pattern which, according to Thibault, governs footwork in combat. The circle of the Spanish school, its diameter redefined as the length of the human body from the feet to the highest reach of a hand above the head, is here inscribed in a square. A second square is inscribed within the circle, a set of diameters drawn across it, and a whole series of chords and additional lines defined by these are then drawn in. Every measurement of the diagram is related directly to some part of the body's dimensions, in a development of Vitruvian theories of proportion as complex as anything attempted in that age.[12]

In the training hall, the two combatants stood on opposite sides of a circle and moved from point to point around it as they fought. Just as in the Spanish school, a correct move kept the fencer safe from assault; an incorrect one left him open to a thrust or cut. Thibault's contention was that a proper mastery of these geometries, not strength or quickness, was the key to survival in the lethal environment of rapier fencing.

In the best Neoplatonic style, the realm of ideas was held to master that of space and time.

In its philosophical basis, as well as the scale and lavishness of its presentation, *L'Academie de L'Espee* invites comparison with the works of Thibault's contemporary, the great Hermetic encyclopedist Robert Fludd.[13] Fludd's ambitious attempts to bring all human knowledge into a Hermetically based synthesis derive from the same tradition, and show the same striving for a global view of the cosmos, as Thibault's work demonstrates in a less universal context. Both Fludd and Thibault also centered their work on the Vitruvian geometries and proportions of the Renaissance esoteric tradition, but used them as the basis for practical arts in a fusion of spirituality and craft that offers important lessons to modern Hermeticists.

At the same time, there is another similarity between these two writers. Both were part of the last flowering of Renaissance esotericism on the eve of the triumph of Descartes' "mechanical philosophy" and the Scientific Revolution. The works of Robert Fludd remained a source for the Hermetic initiates of later years; similarly, the geometrical patterns of Thibault's work were apparently studied with great care by at least one circle of eighteenth-century Masonic Hermeticists.[14]

In the mainstream of Western culture, though, these works went into eclipse. The Vitruvian swordplay of Thibault was treated as a useless irrelevancy by later fencers, just as Fludd's philosophy became an object of scorn to the banner-bearers of the Enlightenment.

૮8

Thibault's *L'Academie de L'Espee* is fascinating as a glimpse into one of the less obvious applications of Renaissance Hermetic thought. It may, however, have a more direct use for the modern Hermeticist. Thibault's work is thorough, to say the least, and can be supplemented by the even more extensive works of the Spanish masters from which his system derives. It's by no means inconceivable that these could be used to resurrect Thibault's way of swordsmanship as a Western esoteric martial art.

What would be the advantages of such a project? Issues of self-defense, which usually come up first when martial arts are discussed, are of minor importance here; the rapier isn't really a suitable means of self-protection on the streets of a modern city. What Thibault's art of the sword does offer is a physical movement discipline with close links to Hermetic philosophy and practice, something in very short supply in Western esotericism. Martial arts in other spiritual traditions have proven themselves as potent teaching tools, allowing the sometimes abstract insights of philosophy to be grounded in the most material levels of experience.

The revival of these geometries of the sword would require a substantial amount of work and would probably need to begin from a solid foundation of experience in surviving traditions of swordsmanship or other combat arts—a better foundation, certainly, than the present author has gained so far. Still, it offers some intriguing possibilities, and it may be that the time will soon arrive for this auxiliary art of the Hermetic tradition to play a part in the further growth of Western esotericism.

Notes

1. See, for example, Saso, M., *The Teachings of Taoist Master Chuang* (Yale University Press, 1978).
2. Agrippa, C., *Trattato di Scientia d'Armi, con un dialogo difilosofia* (Antonio Blado, 1553).
3. Vitruvius, *The Ten Books on Architecture* (Morgan, M.H., trans., Dover, 1960, pp. 72–75).
4. See Yates, F.A., *The Occult Philosophy in the Elizabethan Age* (Routledge & Kegan Paul, 1979) for this tradition generally.
5. Yates, F.A., *Theatre of the World* (University of Chicago Press, 1969) studies these developments of the Vitruvian tradition in detail.
6. See Yates, F.A., *Theatre of the World*; Taylor, R., "Architecture and Magic," in D. Frazer, H. Hibbard, and M.J. Lewine, *Essays in the History of Architecture Presented to Rudolf Wittkower* (Phaidon, 1967, pp. 81–109); and Hersey, G.L., *Pythagorean Palaces: Magic and Architecture in the Italian Renaissance* (Cornell University Press, 1976).
7. de Carranza, J., *De la Filosofia de las Armas y de su Destreza, y de la Agresion y la Defension Christiana* (n.p., 1582).
8. See, for example, Castle, E., *Schools and Masters of Fence* (Shumway, 1969, pp. 67–73).
9. Quoted in Castle, pp. 92–93. Silver's work is included in full in Jackson, L.L., ed., *Three Elizabethan Fencing Manuals* (Scholars Facsimiles & Reprints, 1972).

10. Thibault, G., *Academie de L'Espee* (Elsevier, 1628 [1630]). See also de la Fontaine de Verwey, H., "Gerard Thibault and His L'Academie de L'Espee," In *Quaerendo VIII.* (EJ. Brill, 1978).
11. See Hancox, J., *The Byrom Collection* (Jonathan Cape, 1992, pp. 204–205), where the introduction of Thibault's work is summarized.
12. Compare the plate from *Academie de L'Espee* reproduced in Hancox, p. 206, with plates from Robert Fludd's works in Godwin, J., *Robert Fludd* (Shambhala, 1979, especially pp. 47, 51, and 72).
13. For Fludd, see Godwin, op. cit., as well as Huffman, W.H., *Robert Fludd: Essential Readings* (Aquarian, 1992).
14. This group is the principal subject of Hancox's book, to which I am indebted for my first introduction to Gerard Thibault.

Bibliography

Agrippa, C., *Trattato di Scientia d'Armi, con un dialogo difilosofia* (Antonio Blado, 1553).
Castle, E., *Schools and Masters of Fence* (Shumway, 1969, pp. 67–73).
de Carranza, J., *De la Filosofia de las Armas y de su Destreza, y de la Agresion y la Defension Christiana* (n.p., 1582).
Godwin, J., *Robert Fludd* (Shambhala, 1979, pp. 47, 51, and 72).
Hancox, J., *The Byrom Collection* (Jonathan Cape, 1992, pp. 204–205).
Hersey, G.L., *Pythagorean Palaces: Magic and Architecture in the Italian Renaissance* (Cornell University Press, 1976).
Huffman, W.H., *Robert Fludd: Essential Readings* (Aquarian, 1992).
Saso, M., *The Teachings of Taoist Master Chuang* (Yale University Press, 1978).
Thibault, G., *Academie de L'Espee* (Elsevier, 1628 [1630]).
Verwey, H., "Gerard Thibault and His L'Academie de L'Espee," In *Quaerendo VIII.* (E.J. Brill, 1978).
Vitruvius, *The Ten Books on Architecture* (Morgan, M.H., trans., Dover, 1960, pp. 72–75).
Yates, F.A., *Theatre of the World*; Taylor, R., "Architecture and Magic," in D. Frazer, H. Hibbard, and M.J. Lewine, *Essays in the History of Architecture Presented to Rudolf Wittkower* (Phaidon, 1967, pp. 81–109).
Yates, F.A., *Theatre of the World* (University of Chicago Press, 1969).
Yates, F.A., *The Occult Philosophy in the Elizabethan Age* (Routledge & Kegan Paul, 1979).

Hermeticism and the utopian imagination

Part historical analysis and part polemic, this essay was a reaction against several pieces by Peter Lamborn Wilson, which attempted to borrow the prestige of the Hermetic tradition for his own brand of political and moral antinomianism. The words "utopian," "ludic," and "festal" featured heavily in these writings. The first explains the theme of the essay of mine that resulted; the second and third appear in an edged comment included below. The essay was accepted by Alexandria, *the same annual of esoteric studies in which one of Wilson's pieces was published, and appeared in issue #4 in 1997.*

"It was [Hermes], too, who in the east of Egypt constructed a city twelve miles long within which he constructed a castle which had four gates in each of its four parts. On the eastern gate he placed the form of an eagle; on the western gate, the form of a bull; on the southern gate the form of a lion, and on the northern gate he constructed the form of a dog. Into these images he introduced spirits which spoke with voices, nor could anyone enter the gates of the city except by their permission. Around the circumference of the city, he placed engraved images and ordered them in such a manner that by their virtue the inhabitants were made virtuous and withdrawn from all wickedness and harm. The name of the city was Adocentyn."[1]

The story of Adocentyn in the Latin version of the *Picatrix*, a standard text for the Hermetic magi of the Renaissance, provides a first point of contact between Hermeticism and the utopian tradition. These two movements of the Western spirit, the inner quest for transcendence and the outer quest for the good society, both have a place as powers of the hidden side of history, the skeleton-realm of ideas and visions which gives shape to the flesh of dates, times, events; and like most such powers these two have contacted and influenced each other at times. Adocentyn itself is a utopia, and an inspiration for other utopias; it has been echoed in other aspects of the Hermetic tradition, and some of those have taken on utopian aspects as well.

We live in a time in which ideals have become all but extinct in the collective life of Western society, a time in which pedaling in place and moment-by-moment crisis management have usurped the role of serious discussions about where we are headed and whether any sane person would want to go there. In such an age, the attractive power of the utopian imagination can be real, and those of us who turn for insight to Hermeticism and related systems of Western esoteric thought may be drawn to seek images of a better future by using these as a basis for utopian explorations.

There's much to be said for a project of this sort. At least once before in the history of the West, during the late Renaissance, Utopian ideas with roots in the Hermetic tradition seized the Western imagination and took a significant role in shaping the collective destiny of society. Futurologist Frederick Polak has suggested that the waning of utopian thought may be one of the more worrisome signs of our own age, reflecting a broader failure to conceive any positive image of the future at all.[2] If he's right, utopian visions based on the current revival of Western esoteric thought just might have an unexpected influence over our common fate.

As with anything else, though, these positive potentials have their downside. The history of the connections between Hermeticism and utopian thought is anything but straightforward, and is made even less so by the fog of partisan rhetoric and plain confusion which always seems to surround the coasts of utopia. Nor are the risks involved wholly abstract. Utopian thinking, to put the matter with maximum bluntness, has proven to be a fertile source of disasters as well as hope—a point we'll return to later—and Hermetic wisdom doesn't seem to grant any particular immunity to the consequences. The journey to Adocentyn may be worth making, but if history is any judge the road there may not be easy to find.

Some pitfalls of language

The first obstacle that has to be faced in this doubtful journey comes out of the terms of the discourse itself. Several centuries of journalistic usage have reduced the word "utopian" to little more than a synonym for "very good," "improbable," or—wistfully—both at once. Even taken in a more precise sense, the utopia is too often confused with two other, older images of the ideal society in Western thought: the Arcadian tradition, which grounds human happiness in a flight from the social realm into a world governed wholly by Nature, and the millenarian tradition, which looks to a final irruption of the transcendent into the world of social experience as a solution to the problems of suffering and evil. Over against these is the utopian tradition proper, which envisions human society as perfectible on its own terms, through human action and understanding, as expressed in some system of social arrangements.

These three currents of thought have touched and influenced one another in countless ways, and produced a substantial crop of hybrids; still, the distinction among them is real. It's in this sense that "green" utopias such as Ernest Callenbach's *Ecotopia* deserve the name, despite their intensely pastoral imagery; their forests and meadows are maintained by political and institutional arrangements which are inconceivable in the primal innocence of Arcadia. It's in this sense, too—admittedly not the one he had in mind—that Karl Marx's criticism of competing systems as "utopian socialism" hits the mark; the visions of Owen, Saint-Simon, Fourier, and the like all required some amount of human effort for their fulfillment, while that of Marx relied wholly on impersonal social forces, the nineteenth-century rationalist approximation of God. Marxism is thus millenarian, not utopian, and the communist paradise of its prophetic tradition shares the defining characteristics of all millennial realms: in theory, inevitability; in practice, indefinite postponement.

These same confusions have played themselves out in the contacts between Hermeticism and utopian thought as well. There's a substantial amount of Hermetic "utopianism" that is, properly speaking, nothing of the kind. When a figure such as Giordano Bruno is described as a utopian thinker despite the fact that he wrote nothing even vaguely utopian—his closest approach to it, the mythic cosmological reform of *The Expulsion of the Triumphant Beast*, limits itself to a general denunciation of the religious arrangements of his time and a desire that men would be more virtuous—it's obvious that the terms being used have been diluted nearly to the point of meaninglessness.[3] Similarly, there's a large amount of Hermetic "utopian" thought that is pure millenarianism, depending on a *deus ex machina* rather than any more concrete (or more likely) proposals for the reform of human society.

These considerations are partly worth noting as a help to clarity, but they have a more practical use as well. It's of no great importance here if vague optimism or a wish for social change is redefined as "utopian thought," although it does tend to confuse communication. Nor is the overlap between utopia and Arcadia a significant problem; the Arcadian tradition is all but extinct as an active force in Western thought at present, for the simple and melancholy reason that untouched natural environments no longer exist on our planet.

Millenarianism, though, is another matter. Millenarian traditions remain alive and powerful today—in traditional religious forms, in folk legends of the UFO type, and in a range of half-veiled forms from the survivalist myth of nuclear apocalypse to the Omega Points and evolutionary leaps posited by many currently popular thinkers. This is potentially a serious matter, because—it's hard to say this gently—millenarian thinking has quite probably produced more misery and failure than any other single phenomenon in the history of human thought. The appalling end of the Solar Temple movement is only one of the most recent examples.[4] Relying on supernatural intervention as a fix for earthly problems is one of history's classic recipes for disaster, but it's a seductive idea, and one which can take more than the ordinary amount of clear-headedness to avoid.

Conflicts between Hermetic and utopian thought

The confusions of language, though, don't make up all the potholes on the road to Adocentyn. A second set comes from the awkward point that the basic presuppositions of Hermetic philosophy offer little in the way of support to overtly utopian projects.

Central to Hermeticism, as to most traditions of Western esoteric spirituality, is a keen recognition of the difference between what Plato called the realms of Becoming and Being—the world of social and sensory experience bound by space and time, on the one hand, and the world of absolute reality transcending space and time on the other. Human consciousness, in the Hermetic vision, touches both these realms and has the potential to mediate between them, but the distinction remains. The geometrical metaphor is at once traditional and exact; be it ever so carefully drawn, no circle on paper can claim to be identical with *the* circle, the circle-archetype in the realm of ideals.

The same argument can be made even more forcefully in the case of utopia. From a Hermetic perspective, the ideal of justice cannot be converted into any specific system of laws or customs, nor can it be embodied in a concrete community. The same is true of any other ideal which may be chosen. Within the context of Hermeticism, then, to speak of a perfect human society is a little like discussing a heavy, orange thought. Societies, like circles, are concrete and imperfect reflections of ideal patterns, and the Hermetic tradition gives very little encouragement to the claim that a circle can be made perfectly round if only the right kind of paper and compasses are used to draw it.

In keeping with this, the Hermetic tradition historically hasn't been an especially prolific source of utopias or of utopian thinking. To the extent—an important one—that Hermeticism has roots in Plato, it can lay a limited claim to the ideal states of the *Republic* and the *Laws*; even so, it's too often forgotten that Plato's were neither the only nor the first utopias in classical thought, and that utopian writings in the ancient world came to be associated not with Platonism but with Stoic philosophy.[5]

The same pattern continues through the later history of the utopian tradition. The revival of Platonism, Hermeticism, and magical and alchemical traditions during the Renaissance gave rise to a handful of utopias—Campanella's *City of the Sun* and Andreae's *Christianopolis* are the best known of the very few examples—and to one significant burst of utopian politics during the first half of the seventeenth century.[6] By contrast, Renaissance humanism produced a far more substantial crop of utopias, among them the work of Sir Thomas More which gave its wry name—*ou topos*, "nowhere"—to the entire genre. The early years of the "mechanical philosophy," the newborn scientific materialism that overcame the Hermetic "chemical philosophy" in the struggle to define reality for the post-medieval West, were rife with utopias and utopian projects; and the zenith of the utopian tradition in the West during the eighteenth and nineteenth centuries, a period which saw thousands of utopias written and hundreds attempted in the form of actual communities, drew its inspiration not from Hermeticism or any other esoteric tradition but from the unlimited optimism of the Enlightenment's cult of reason.

A certain amount of questionable logic has crept into considerations of this last point, and it's as well to clarify matters here. The fact that people involved with esoteric spirituality were also involved with utopian schemes—as a certain number were—does not in itself redefine those schemes as esoteric, any more than the fact that (say) a number of Satanists enjoy playing volleyball would make volleyball Satanic. To point out, for example, that Transcendentalists of the stature of Bronson Alcott participated in abortive communal experiments, or that several important nineteenth-century French occultists were deeply involved in socialist politics, simply proves that these were men and women of their own time, caught up in many of the same interests and enthusiasms as their more orthodox neighbors. Claims of a closer connection between the traditions need to be backed by evidence of specific links between Hermetic thought and utopian practice—and these are few and far between.

Hermeticism and the political sphere

The same point can be made even more forcefully about claims that Hermeticism is itself political in nature, or defines some particular political stance. Claims of this kind have ranged from straightforward definitions of some such stance as "Hermetic politics," through a spectrum of more or less paranoid conspiracy theories, to subtle analyses of the political potential of Hermetic thought.

The first two of these can be dismissed fairly easily. It's true that some Hermeticists have been active in the political arena (although a great many more have not); it's equally true that some of their activities have been more or less secret in nature, at least at the time. The difficulty here is that the positions taken by politically inclined Hermeticists (and Hermetically influenced politicians) fall all over the ideological spectrum, from the alchemical anarchism of Gerrard Winstanley through the socialism of Eliphas Levi, past the stolid English middle-of-the-roadism of Dion Fortune, to the reactionary absolutism of the eighteenth-century *Orden des Gold- und Rosencreuz* and the overt fascism of Julius Evola. It's hard to see how views this divergent can be turned into anything approaching a consistent position, much less the sort of monolithic conspiracy trumpeted by former Golden Dawn chief C. M. Stoddart (among many others) and parodied to death by Robert Shea and Robert Anton Wilson in their tremendous satire *Illuminatus!*

There are deeper matters caught up in the question of Hermetic politics, however, which cannot and should not be passed over so easily. In an age as dominated by mass phenomena as the present, a tradition such as Hermeticism which focuses its attention on the individual rather than the mass may, paradoxically, be more relevant to political life than many more overtly political approaches. There's a real sense in which the journey of the individual from a dependence on mass consciousness to a personal knowledge of the Transcendent is a—and perhaps *the*—supremely political act.

At the same time, this approach to Hermeticism has pitfalls of its own. These can be seen most clearly, perhaps, in Joan Couliano's brilliant if problematic *Eros and Magic in the Renaissance*, which attempts to read the entire system of Renaissance Hermetic magic as a deliberate technology of psychopolitical manipulation. This essay is not the place for a full examination of the achievements and failures of this remarkable work, but a few points need to be made.

The core assumption of Couliano's argument is that the language of Renaissance magic can be converted precisely into the language of modern psychology—that, for example, *eros* can be understood as libido in the Freudian sense, the *pneuma* as the subconscious, and so forth. This equation allows magic to be seen in terms which make sense to the modern mind—as psychological manipulation grounded in a canny grasp of the motivating force of human desires—and forms the basis for his unsettling suggestion that modern methods of advertising and public relations are unknowingly following in the footsteps of the Renaissance magi.

The problem is that this equation can be defended only by doing a good deal of violence to the actual context of these ideas in Renaissance thought, and by excluding those factors—above all the transcendent and transpersonal powers central to Hermetic theory—which have no place in the modern vision of the universe. Couliano's central definition of the relationship between *eros* and magic, for example, claims that "all erotic phenomena are simultaneously magic phenomena in which the individual plays the role either of manipulator or of the manipulated or of the instrument of manipulation."[7] This corresponds closely to some modern attitudes on the subject. On the other hand, an identity between love and manipulation is worlds away from the Hermetically-inspired Renaissance conception of *eros*, which is well-documented from Ficino onwards, and plays a central role in such works as Giordano Bruno's *The Heroic Frenzies*. That conception identified love as one of Plato's four divinely caused states of madness; all understood as participation by the whole self in a realm of transcendent power—not as manipulations carried out through a passive medium by the deracinated and isolated ego.[8]

Couliano's interpretation—like most other modernizing interpretations of Hermetic thought—imposes the typical modern understanding of means and ends on a tradition which understood that distinction in a very different light. As the Hermeticists of the Renaissance saw it, the state of erotic desire, of participation in the divine power of *eros*, was itself an end, not simply a means to the end of sexual activity. In magic, similarly, the participation of the magus in transcendent power was the real work, the *ergon*, of magical practice; the ostensible goal of that practice was a *parergon* or side-effect, however valuable in its own right.

In politics, finally and crucially, the same point holds true. It may be that the study and practice of Hermeticism leads to certain political effects; still, these are not the point of the exercise. The aspect of life we may as well call the "spiritual" is precisely that which deals with ultimate ends. To treat it as a means to some other end is to banish it, and dress up that other end in spirituality's cast-off clothing. The results are far too familiar: on the one hand, all the overt and covert pathologies of power; on the other, the sanctimonious justification of the abuses of an oppressive order, or its inverse, the religious irreligiousness of "socially aware" denominations or their more avant-garde equivalents, in which religious language has become nothing more than a slightly dowdy way of talking about political ideology.

Building nowhere somewhere

Questions of means and ends are also involved in the last set of obstacles in the way of Hermetically based utopian projects. Utopias have many possible uses, ranging from simple entertainment and wish-fulfillment through satire and social criticism to deliberate attempts to design and construct a new society. This last purpose, however, has dominated the utopian imagination in modern times, and it's hard to argue against it at first glance; if you have a workable plan for a better society, or think you do, why not try to put it into effect?

This approach has ancient roots. The first utopian theorist of whom any trace survives, Hippodamus of Miletus, was involved in the founding of an actual community, the Panhellenic colony of Thurii. Plato's own utopian schemes, in their turn, formed the foundation of Plotinus's celebrated attempt to create a philosophers' city called Platonopolis.[9] The list of similar projects proposed or attempted since then, seeking the perfect society down nearly every imaginable road, is enough to stagger the mind.

If sheer energy were enough to win the struggle, this vast outpouring of effort and imagination might be expected to have brought utopia into being long ago. It has not, and with one significant exception, the long history of utopian communities is a history of almost unrelieved failure.

The one exception is monasticism. Religious communities of this very specific sort exist in most of the major world religions, and have flourished in a wide array of social and environmental contexts. Even the pressures of the consumer economy have had only limited success against the monastic way of life. There are several potent sources of strength in the monastic utopia: membership is voluntary, and depends on assent to a given set of beliefs, values, and rules of life; intensive devotional or meditative practices done as a group build deep bonds within the monastic community; rules of poverty and celibacy, all but universal in successful monastic systems, cut away exactly those issues—money, sex, and family—which drive most interpersonal conflicts.

The essence of the monastic utopia, then, is a radical simplification of life. On its own terms, it works brilliantly; so long as it can recruit new members to replace those that die, a monastery can exist and function indefinitely. On the other hand, the monastic system excludes so much of value in ordinary human life that, for most people, it can hardly be called utopian. However successful it may be, it's of limited value as a guide to broader approaches.

Outside of monasticism, the record of utopian experiments is bleak. The average lifespan of those which actually get past the drawing board is about three years. The specific factors in each individual breakdown vary with situations, and with scale—small communes have different breaking points than national regimes—but the pattern of failure is consistent enough that it's worth looking for a deeper cause.

There are any number of approaches to this question, but one drawn from issues of Hermetic philosophy raised earlier may not be out of place. The entire utopian project can be seen as an attempt to bridge the gap between the ideal and the concrete, and the results of the attempt may well count as a kind of experimental evidence in favor of Plato's division between the realms. The more a utopian system relies on ideal factors to handle practical difficulties, the more certain it is to break down at precisely these points.

Charles Fourier's system of utopian socialism is a case in point. Fourier's complicated theories postulated a state of Harmony as the natural endpoint of human social evolution, in which "passional attraction" would end all social woes and make possible a life focused around dining ("gastrosophy") and orgiastic sex, interspersed with modest periods of work at frequently changing tasks. In the nineteenth century these theories were immensely popular, and dozens of Fourierist "phalansteries"—collective settlements intended as the nuclei of the new order—were established in Europe and America. All of them went under after fairly brief lives. The idealized force of passional attraction proved to be too weak to motivate the constant hard work necessary to found and run a new community, and nothing else was available to do the job.[10]

Fourier and his followers, in particular, never quite seemed to grasp the difference between a little puttering in the garden and the more than full-time job of subsistence farming. The same problem appears elsewhere; it's one of the constants of utopian history that utopians tend to massively underestimate the amount of effort and skill needed to maintain what modern people consider a comfortable standard of living. As a result, utopian plans routinely have people consuming far more in the way of goods and services than they produce. On paper, this produces a highly attractive ludic and festal quality to utopian life; put into practice, it forces utopian experiments either to accept extreme poverty, to find some way to parasitize on the larger society or to go under as soon as the money runs out.

Another example of ideal factors as a point of utopian breakdown can be found in far too many of the alternative religious movements of the last fifty years. Here the ideal is, as often as not, akin to Plato's vision of the philosopher king: the personal spiritual qualities of the movement's leader are seen as justification for his or her absolute control of the community's decision-making process. The results are as predictable as they are unpleasant.

These kinds of difficulties can be addressed, of course; a community can develop practical ways to meet collective economic needs or to keep a rein on the behavior of its leadership. The problem is that the more this is done—the more the ideal is replaced with the pragmatic—the more the utopian community begins to resemble the unreformed world outside its borders. The history of the few successful utopian communities, like that of successful revolutions, is a history of compromise which starts with ideals and ends with a restoration of the status quo; the transition which turned the Oneida Community into a suburban development mirrors the one which replaced the tsars with commissars.[11] It's worth keeping in mind that the existing order of any society has evolved as it has for good reason; it represents whatever collective compromise people make between the desire for freedom and the fear of responsibility, and it will tend to reestablish itself with a fair degree of exactness after the turbulence of disaster or idealism has passed. It might even be said that, in this sense, we get exactly the society we deserve.

Breakdown along the fault lines of the ideal, and absorption into the larger society through pragmatism, form the Scylla and Charybdis of the utopian voyage. The rhetoric of failed utopias is a chronicle of excuses for either, or sometimes both at once. The attempt to bring the ideal society to physical birth will no doubt continue, but the results of the attempt to date may suggest that the real value of utopia may well lie elsewhere.

Three roads to Adocentyn

The various obstacles we've examined may seem to add up to a dismissal of the entire utopian project, at least from a Hermetic standpoint. They do not—but they do, certainly, call into question the assumption that a Hermetic approach to that project can be made successfully in a naive manner. The failure of utopian experiments is not the only sign that a confusion of the worlds of Being and Becoming is, to say the least, problematic; the disastrous history of millenarianism and the difficulties which follow on a political interpretation of Hermeticism can be traced to the same root.

To do away with this confusion and make use of the utopian imagination from within a traditional Hermetic perspective involves a significant change of focus, and it requires that utopia remain exactly where the word implies—nowhere. It may seem quixotic to try to imagine an ideal society in the knowledge that it can neither exist nor fully express its own ideals, but this paradox is the paradox of human consciousness, the reconciler of irreconcilable worlds. Nor is this strange exercise useless, for it leads in directions which have a good deal to offer. Three of those directions will be examined here. One of them will be familiar to many readers, the other two less so: one because it has largely been hidden away in the specialist literature, the other because its connections to the Hermetic tradition—and to the utopian imagination—have gone all but unnoticed in modern times.

The utopia of contemplation

Plato, who gave so much to the Western esoteric traditions, apparently devised the first and most important of these directions of utopian thought. A passage from the end of Book IX of the *Republic* puts it best:

> I understand, [Glaucon] said. You mean the city whose establishment we have described, the city whose home is in the ideal, for I think that it can be found nowhere on Earth.
>
> Well, I said, perhaps there is a pattern of it laid up in heaven for him who wishes to contemplate it and in so beholding to constitute himself its citizen. But it makes no difference whether it exists now or ever will come into being. The politics of this city only will be his and of none other.[12]

The hierarchical society of the *Republic* with its rigid class structure of philosopher kings, warrior auxiliaries, and underlings, has often been taken as Plato's own prescription for an actual state. It may have been that; the society of the *Laws*, which is unquestionably designed for practical ends, shares many of the same authoritarian features that modern readers find objectionable in the *Republic*. It was also, however, an attempt to represent the ideal of social justice, as Plato saw it, through the medium of the human imagination. That is its crucial role, and as a "pattern laid up in heaven," it is intended to serve not as a blueprint for practical social change but as a focus for thought and meditation, and as a model for the inner ordering of the self.

So far, so good; but to go on as Plato does, and suggest that the contemplator of this imaginary city becomes its citizen, involved in its politics and subject to its laws, is to touch on something potentially explosive.

Citizenship in Plato's time was anything but an abstraction. It's worth thinking about what it might mean to be a citizen, not of a Greek polis, nor of some modern nation-state, nor yet (in the facile modern phrase) of the world—but *of the Ideal*. What are the rights of such a citizenship? What are the responsibilities?

Plato's own understanding of the city of absolute justice may or may not be appropriate to Hermeticists today, who have seen many of its features parodied in the totalitarian states of our own era. The process of critical thinking and examination of ideals which is central to the dialogue has not lost its relevance, though, nor has the metaphor which tests justice in the self by projecting it onto the larger screen of a society. It may well be that process and metaphor can be best combined in the present time by the creation of new utopian images as reflections— again, as always, imperfect—of Plato's "pattern laid up in heaven."

The utopia of the craftsman

A second direction for Hermetic utopianism first took shape, like so much else Hermetic, in the hothouse environment of the Italian Renaissance, and like so much else it drew its inspiration from the recovery of an ancient manuscript. The manuscript was a copy of the *Ten Books on Architecture* of Marcus Vitruvius Pollio, and the movement that took its starting point from this find was one of the most intriguing facets of the Hermetic movement of that age.

Vitruvius, a practicing builder and engineer with a pedestrian command of Latin, was an unlikely source for a Hermetic revival; one more easily imagines him wearing the Roman equivalent of a John Deere cap than an adept's starry headgear. He drew extensively on older traditions, though, and gave a good deal of space to systems of architectural proportion which derived the bases of form and measurement from the human body. The humanists of the Renaissance took this in a sense far deeper than Vitruvius apparently meant it; they linked it with medieval number symbolism, surviving scraps of Pythagorean lore, and the traditional analogy that related human and cosmic forms as macrocosm and microcosm. They came to see architecture, engineering, all forms of craft as a deliberate reflection of ideal proportions and geometries in material form.[13]

The impact of this vision on the arts and architecture of the Renaissance is only now beginning to be traced by scholars, as former fringe subjects such as Hermeticism make their way further into the academic mainstream. Some of its effects went in unlikely directions—for example, the application of Vitruvian ideas to personal combat led to the birth of rapier fencing and ultimately to a school of swordsmanship which can only be described as a Hermetic martial art.[14] It's in architecture, though, that this movement came within reach of utopia. Several important architectural treatises exist which describe the siting, plan, and buildings of an ideal city based on Vitruvian geometries. The most fascinating of them, Filarete's *Treatise on Architecture*, expands this into a full-blown narrative of the founding of the imaginary city of Sforzinda, from the location of the site to the construction and decoration of the buildings within it.[15]

It's important to realize that these treatises were not simply a reflection of the practices of their time, as, for example, Vitruvius's work seems to have been. They were conscious attempts to reorient architecture toward the ideal while still keeping a firm grasp on practicalities. The cities and buildings they describe are not intended to be built; they were intended to suggest what could be built, to explore the possibilities of the builder's art, and in a way to tackle one facet of the utopian project on its own. The actual buildings designed by these same architects handled the further step of grounding some of these possibilities in practice.

Such explorations aren't limited to the field of architecture, of course; they can be used in the context of any craft. The appalling ugliness of so much modern building suggests that architecture might well be a good place to start, and the work of architects and designers such as Buckminster Fuller and Paolo Soleri show that the concept of the ideal city is still alive in current thought. The architectural visions of a modern Hermeticism could draw on new materials, and on philosophical and geometric perspectives drawn from a much wider range of sources than the Vitruvian revival of the Renaissance had to hand. It's intriguing to think about what a Hermetically-inspired ideal city of the present might look like, and how that image and the ideals undergirding it might best be communicated.

The utopia of secrecy

The third direction we'll be examining, like the second, has its roots in the Renaissance, although its origins were English rather than Italian.

It reached its full development centuries after the Vitruvian revival had faded out with the suppression of Hermetic thought at the end of the Renaissance. To speak of it at all is to enter a territory awash in ironies, some historical, some innate to the phenomenon itself.

The historical ironies are worth tracing first. Imagine—as an exercise in alternative history, perhaps—that the Hermetic tradition had given rise to an extensive, semi-secret movement just at the point in history when Hermeticism itself was being forced underground; that this movement had proliferated, taken on new forms, developed extensive systems of theory and practice; that it had grown to a size unmatched by any other manifestation of Hermeticism in history, and become a major channel for the diffusion of Hermetic ideas into mainstream Western culture.

This isn't actually alternative history, of course. That movement—the fraternal lodge movement of the eighteenth and nineteenth centuries—existed, and still exists, if on a scale much smaller than it once did. The connections between Freemasonry, which is one part of the movement, and the Hermetic tradition have been explored by a few scholars in recent years, but the wider context of Hermetic influence on lodge organizations remains a nearly untouched field.[16]

The lodge system combines a method of group organization rooted in medieval guild structures with a system of ritual and symbolic expression derived from Renaissance Hermeticism. The murky process of interaction by which these two diverse factors came together in seventeenth-century Britain isn't relevant to the present discussion, but the resulting hybrid is. On the organizational side, the lodge system is a pragmatic structure of governance, evolved over centuries in a wholly practical context to meet the requirements of collective activity. On the symbolic side, the lodge system is a structure of iconic communications, in which emblems expressing a set of ideal concepts—ethical, in the case of Freemasonry, Odd Fellowship, and similar fraternal lodges; mystical or magical, in the case of occult lodges such as the Hermetic Order of the Golden Dawn—are combined with ritual to shape the perceptions and actions of lodge members in specific ways.[17] In terms of the Platonic division, the organizational side is oriented to the world of Becoming, the symbolic side to that of Being.

Pervading both, and shaping the essential character of the whole system, is the defining factor of secrecy. It's fair to say that without secrecy the entire lodge system would lose much of its point. The secrets involved are rarely of any importance in themselves: a set of gestures, words, and images; the ordinary business of the lodge; confidences received from lodge members; in occultist lodges, a set of teachings and practices which are more often than not taken from publicly available sources. The act of making these secret and of keeping them secret is what is crucial.[18]

The use of secrecy creates a liminal space, a "space between the worlds," which corresponds exactly to the liminal space of human consciousness. Like the private world of thoughts, it observes, but it is not observed; it mediates between two worlds—in this case, the world of ordinary social life and the world of symbolized ideals. This liminal quality is reinforced in both spatial and temporal terms: spatially by the use of a specific and highly formalized meeting space, temporally by the lodge's ritual opening and closing and by the simple fact that a lodge only exists and functions during its meeting times. The lodge cannot absorb or be absorbed by the surrounding social context without ceasing to be a lodge. It exists in opposition to the rest of the world, an opposition veiled in secrecy.

The dominant role of secrecy in the lodge system creates a whole dance of nested ironies if, as here, there's an attempt made to talk about the nature of the system. It's precisely the act of not-saying that defines the thing discussed. Still, the liminal role of secrecy is also at the heart of the lodge system's role as the subtlest of all the Hermetic tradition's contributions to the utopian project. In most fraternal lodges and many occultist ones, the specific ideals which are central to the lodge symbolism define—sometimes very explicitly—a utopia, and this definition is the basis for standards of behavior within the lodge. The lodge thus models itself on the utopian vision, and in its turn the lodge itself becomes a model for life in the world outside it, mediating in the liminal space of secrecy between the utopian vision and the world of everyday life. The lodge itself is not a utopia, then, but it exists in a constant relationship with the utopian imagination. Like monasticism, it forms an interface between the ideal and the real by a radical simplification, but it does this without demanding a surrender of human meaning to the ideal.

The utopian role of the lodge system is, perhaps, clearest in cases where lodges have intervened in the larger social context, from the small-scale charitable work common to surviving lodges in the present to startling episodes like the Grange's war against railroad monopolies in late nineteenth-century America. It can be seen in its inverse form, as a kind of dystopia of secrecy, in the case of the Ku Klux Klan, itself a lodge organization of the classic type built up around its own repellent "ideals." These outward expressions of the system, though, don't exhaust the possibilities of the utopia of secrecy. The Invisible College of seventeenth-century England, itself a body deeply involved with the origins of the lodge system,[19] and the magical lodges which have been so significant a part of the Hermetic movement in recent centuries, may suggest others. How these potentials might be put to use in the current Hermetic revival, though, is a matter for individuals and groups to search out on their own.

Ultimately, in its focus on the hidden and the unspoken, the lodge system's utopia of secrecy expresses an insight with deep echoes in Hermetic thought and important lessons for the Hermetic utopian project. What is unseen and intangible is not necessarily powerless; the city of Adocentyn is closest, perhaps, when it is nowhere at all.

Notes

1. Quoted in Yates, F.A., *Giordano Bruno and the Hermetic Tradition* (University of Chicago Press, 1964, p. 54).
2. Polak, F.L., "Utopias and Cultural Renewal." In Manuel, F.E., ed., *Utopias and Utopian Thought*, (Houghton Muffin, 1965, pp. 281–295).
3. Bruno as utopian appears in the otherwise excellent Manuel, F.E. and Manuel, F.F., *Utopian Thought in the Western World*, (Harvard University Press, 1979, pp. 222–242).
4. See the collection of Solar Temple papers in Kinney, J., et al., "The Solar Temple Dossier." *Gnosis* (1995, 34, pp. 87–96).
5. See Ferguson, J., *Utopias of the Classical World*. (Cornell University Press, 1975).
6. Manuel and Manuel, *Utopian Thought in the Western World*, 261–366, surveys the movement.
7. Couliano, I.P., *Eros and Magic in the Renaissance*, (Cook, M., trans., University of Chicago Press, 1987, p. 103).
8. The Platonic source of the four kinds of madness is *Phaedrus* 244–250. This interpretation of Eros can be found throughout the literature of the Renaissance; its specifically magical implications can be traced from Ficino's writings through Agrippa's *Three Books of Occult Philosophy* and provides the proper context—*pace* Couliano's interpretation—for the

erotic imagery of Bruno's *De vinculis in genere*. See Ficino, M., *Three Books on Life* (Kaske, C. and Clark, J., trans., Renaissance Society of America, 1989); Agrippa, H.C., *Three Books of Occult Philosophy*, (Freake, J., trans., and Tyson D., ed., Llewellyn, 1993, especially 616–628); Yates, F.A., *Giordano Bruno and the Hermetic Tradition*, (University of Chicago Press, 1964, pp. 275–290); as well as Bruno, G., *The Heroic Frenzies* (Memmo, P. and Hill, Jr., C., trans., University of North Carolina Press, 1964). Compare also Plotinus 4.4.40, with its insistence that the magician must act from within the universe as a participant.

9. Recounted in Porphyry's *Life of Plotinus*. See Plotinus, *Enneads*, (MacKenna, S., trans., Larson, 1992, p. 9). For Hippodamus, see Ferguson, *Utopias of the Classical World*, 48–50.

10. The standard English-language collection of Fourier's writings is Fourier, C., *The Utopian Vision of Charles Fourier* (Beecher, J. and Bienvenu, R., trans. and eds., Beacon, 1971). For the attempts at putting his system into practice, see Kesten, S.R., *Utopian Episodes* (Syracuse University Press, 1993).

11. There is an extensive literature on the Oneida Community. For an overview of its history, see Lockwood, M. "The Experimental Utopia in America." In Manuel, F.E., ed., *Utopias and Utopian Thought* (Houghton Muffin, 1965, pp. 183–200).

12. Plato, *Republic* IX, 592 (trans. R. Hackforth).

13. There are several studies of the Vitruvian tradition in Renaissance Hermeticism, but the best starting place is Vitruvius himself; see Vitruvius, *Ten Books on Architecture*. Yates, *Theatre of the World*, and Hersey, *Pythagorean Palaces*, are solid overviews.

14. This development of the tradition is the subject of Greer, J.M., "Geometries of the Sword." *Gnosis* (1996, 40, pp. 50–55).

15. Filarete, (Antonio di Piero Averlino), *Treatise on Architecture* (Spencer, J., trans., Yale University Press, 1965). See also Alberti, L.B., *On the Art of Building in Ten Books* (Rykwert, J., Leach, N., and Tavernor, R., eds., MIT Press, 1988).

16. The non-Masonic developments of the lodge tradition remain all but unnoticed by scholars. Carnes, M.C., *Secret Ritual and Manhood in Victorian America* (Yale University Press, 1989), and Clawson, M.A., *Constructing Brotherhood* (Princeton University Press, 1989), are among the few significant studies; each is burdened with an interpretive apparatus (respectively, psychological and Marxist) that obscures more than it illuminates. Clawson does deal usefully with the role of Hermeticism in the origins of the tradition.

17. See Greer, J.M., "The Hall of Thmaa: Sources of Golden Dawn Lodge Technique." *Golden Dawn Journal* (1995, 3, pp. 121–144). for a more extensive analysis of lodge technique in the context of the Hermetic Order of the Golden Dawn.

18. My understanding of the role of secrecy in this context draws on an essay by Earl King, Jr. See King, Jr., E., "On Having and Keeping Secrets." *Caduceus* (1995, 1.3, pp. 18–24).

19. See Yates, Giordano Bruno.

Bibliography

Agrippa, H.C., *Three Books of Occult Philosophy* (Freake, J., trans., and Tyson D., ed., Llewellyn, 1993).

Alberti, L.B., *On the Art of Building in Ten Books* (Rykwert, J., Leach, N., and Tavernor, R., eds., MIT Press, 1988).

Andreae, J.V., *Christianopolis: An Ideal State of the Seventeenth Century* (Held, F., trans., Oxford University Press, 1916).

Bruno, G., *The Expulsion of the Triumphant Beast* (Imerti, A., trans., Rutgers University Press, 1964).

Bruno, G., *The Heroic Frenzies* (Memmo, P. and Hill, Jr., C., trans., University of North Carolina Press, 1964).

Campanella, T., *The City of the Sun: A Poetic Dialogue* (Danno, D., trans., University of California Press, 1981).

Carnes, M.C., *Secret Ritual and Manhood in Victorian America* (Yale University Press, 1989).

Clawson, M.A., *Constructing Brotherhood: Class, Race, and Fraternalism* (Princeton University Press, 1989).

Couliano, I.P., *Eros and Magic in the Renaissance* (Cook, M., trans., University of Chicago Press, 1987).

Ferguson, J., *Utopias of the Classical World* (Cornell University Press, 1975).

Ficino, M., *Three Books on Life* (Kaske, C. and Clark, J., trans., Renaissance Society of America, 1989).

Filarete (Antonio di Piero Averlino). *Treatise on Architecture* (Spencer, J., trans., Yale University Press, 1965).

Fourier, C., *The Utopian Vision of Charles Fourier: Selected Texts on Work, Love, and Passionate Attraction* (Beecher, J. and Bienvenu, R., trans. and eds., Beacon, 1971).

Greer, J.M., "The Hall of Thmaa: Sources of Golden Dawn Lodge Technique." *Golden Dawn Journal* (1995, 3, pp. 121–144).

Greer, J.M., "Geometries of the Sword." *Gnosis* (1996, 40, pp. 50–55).

Hersey, G.L., *Pythagorean Palaces: Magic and Architecture in the Italian Renaissance* (Cornell University Press, 1976).

Kesten, S.R., *Utopian Episodes* (Syracuse University Press, 1993).

King, Jr., E., "On Having and Keeping Secrets." *Caduceus* (1995, 1.3, pp. 18–24).

Kinney, J., et al. "The Solar Temple Dossier: Documents and Background on the Tragedy." *Gnosis* (1995, 34, pp. 87–96).

Lockwood, M., "The Experimental Utopia in America." In Manuel, F.E., ed., *Utopias and Utopian Thought* (Houghton Muffin, 1965, pp. 183–200).

Manuel, F.E., ed., *Utopias and Utopian Thought* (Houghton Muffin, 1965).

Manuel, F.E. and Manuel, F.F., *Utopian Thought in the Western World* (Harvard University Press, 1979).

Plotinus, *The Enneads* (MacKenna, S., trans., Larson, 1992).

Polak, F.L., "Utopia and Cultural Renewal." In Manuel, F.E., ed., *Utopias and Utopian Thought*, (Houghton Muffin, 1965, pp. 281–295).

Pollio, M.V., *Ten Books on Architecture* (Morgan, M.H., trans., Dover, 1960).

Yates, F.A., *Giordano Bruno and the Hermetic Tradition* (University of Chicago Press, 1964).

Yates, F.A., *Theatre of the World* (University of Chicago Press, 1969).

Pythagoras and Western magic

Another piece of mine from Caduceus, *this was the product of two years' study of what remains of classical Pythagorean tradition, part of the research that led in one direction to my translation of Gerard Thibault's* Academie de l'Espee *and in another to* The Sacred Geometry Oracle. *It was published in the Fall 1997 issue.*

Nowadays, Pythagoras of Samos is usually remembered as the discoverer of the so-called "Pythagorean theorem" on the relationship of the sides of a right triangle—a theorem that was known in Babylonia more than a thousand years before he was born.[1] Behind his place as a footnote in the history of geometry, however, looms a larger and substantially stranger reputation. He has been credited with major discoveries in mathematics and musical theory as well as geometry, and has a crucial place in the development of Greek philosophy; in fact, the word "philosopher" itself was apparently his invention.[2] At the same time, the school he founded was at least as much a religious sect as it was a philosophical movement, with teachings about reincarnation, ethical precepts and a sizable collection of ritual taboos binding its members. Furthermore, Greek and Roman writers—in tones that range from reverence to mockery—reported claims that Pythagoras himself performed miracles, foretold the future, and recounted his own previous lives dating back to before the Trojan War.[3]

It's little wonder that modern historical scholarship has veered awkwardly about when dealing with Pythagoras and his place in the history of ideas. For most of the last three centuries, the usual approach to the man and his thought has been to dismiss everything unacceptably magical about him as an encrustation of legends from the declining years of classical civilization.[4] In this way, Pythagoras has been squeezed into an early but honored place in the line of progressive thinkers that forms the origin myth of the modern world. In recent years, discomfort with this sort of mythic history has given rise to another, equally mythic, in which Pythagoras is pictured as a shamanic figure, an inheritor of archaic traditions from the Greeks' Indo-European roots or a borrower of practices from the Greek world's less civilized neighbors.[5] Both these views, of course, take for granted the same historical mythology of progress; the quarrel is simply whether magic belongs to the early parts of the story, as a primal inheritance not yet outgrown, or later on as a sign of a society-wide loss of nerve, one more aspect of the ancient world's failure to live up to modern expectations.

The critical problem with both these images, though, is that the early classical Greek magic that can be glimpsed through the lens of the early Pythagorean school can be adequately explained in neither way. As the evidence shows clearly enough, archaic magical practices were indeed involved in the Pythagorean phenomenon, but these were not simply being handed down unchanged. They were being reshaped and reinterpreted in terms of a new language, the language of philosophy— and this was happening during the years in which that new language was first being created.

The high magic of the ancient world was thus neither an outdated relic from past ages or a late product of cultural decline. It came into being in the first flowering of classical culture, as part of the same broad impulse, and it continued to develop in scope and sophistication throughout the centuries when the classical world was at its height. In the same way, and at the same time, as the tools of reasoned discourse were first being applied to the human experience of the natural world to create something akin to science, they were also being applied to a range of other human experiences to create the foundations of the high magic of the West.

In that development, the role of Pythagoras was a crucial one. He seems to have been the first major figure in the intellectual history of the

West to combine magic and philosophy, and a number of the elements that were central to his own synthesis—including a mystical analysis of number focused on the first ten natural numbers, the use of the pentagram as a magical symbol, theories of reincarnation and of cosmic harmony, and others—have remained part of the core of Western high magic ever since.

Life and travels

Pythagoras was born around 570 BCE,[6] to an engraver named Mnesarchos and his wife Pythais, on the island of Samos off what is now the coast of Turkey. Samos at that time was near the height of its wealth and influence as one part of a thriving belt of Ionian Greek settlements on the eastern shores of the Aegean. The years of Pythagoras' birth and early childhood were the years when construction began on the great Temple of Hera at Samos, which Herodotus ranked as one of the three greatest engineering projects in the Greek world. The great lyric poet Anacreon was a Samian, and Pythagoras' contemporary; on the mainland a short distance away was the city of Miletus, where Thales and Anaximander were founding the first major tradition of Greek natural science during Pythagoras' youth. Trade links and political contacts linked Samos with Egypt, the city-states of Phoenicia and the rich kingdoms of Asia Minor.[7] It was a propitious setting for the birth and youth of a philosopher.

Of his early life, no real information survives, although it's clear that he received the normal Greek schooling of the time—*gymnastike*, athletic training, and *mousike*, instruction in literature, music and the arts. Like most men of his time, he studied with a number of teachers in his youth, but only one of them seems to have left a lasting impression.

This was Pherecydes of Syros, according to ancient testimonies the first Greek ever to write a book in prose rather than verse. Tradition recounts that he had studied secret writings from Phoenicia. Whether this is true or not, the handful of surviving quotes and summaries of his book, *The Seven-Hollows Mingling Of The Gods* or *Origin Of The Gods*, reveals a vision of the cosmos at odds with most of the myths and speculations of mainstream Greek culture.[8] Three divine powers existing from eternity—Chronos or Time, Zan or Zas (an alternate form of Zeus), and Chthonie, the earth-principle—are said to govern the universe in Pherecydes' account. Chronos creates fire, water, and air from his seed, mingles them in five "hollows" or "nooks" from which a generation of gods is born, and then fights a battle with the serpent-god Ophioneus, winning the crown of heaven and casting Ophioneus into the sea. Zas weds Chthonie and gives her a robe embroidered with lands and seas, and she takes the name Ge ("Earth"); the robe also appears on a winged oak tree, which may be another manifestation of Chthonie. There was undoubtedly much more that has not survived.

This mythic cosmogony was not the only basis for Pherecydes' later reputation. A story repeated in numerous sources reports that once, upon drinking water from a well, he predicted that there would be an earthquake within days, which duly happened; one wonders if he had learned that turbidity or dissolved gases in groundwater can predict seismic activity. Similarly, he was said to have seen a ship making for harbor, commented to his companions that it would not reach land safely, and looked on as a cloudburst followed and swamped the ship. A solstice-marker on Syros was also credited to him. All this sounds very much like the work of a perceptive student of nature, but any attempt to classify Pherecydes as some sort of proto-scientist must also deal with the mythic vision of his book, and with the fact that Pherecydes was also apparently the first Greek to teach the doctrines of reincarnation and the immortality of the soul.[9]

According to one ancient writer, it was after hearing Pherecydes speak on these latter themes that Pythagoras decided to become a philosopher rather than an athlete.[10] The story may be apocryphal, but the impact of Pherecydes' ideas on his student was substantial enough to give it some degree of plausibility. Certainly, there is every reason to think that Pythagoras retained a good deal of affection for the older philosopher; during the latter's final illness, years later, it was Pythagoras who cared for him and arranged for his burial when he finally died.

Aurelius Augustinus, the same writer who described the effect of Pherecydes on Pythagoras' career plans, also commented that Pythagoras was "not contented with the philosophy of the Greeks, which then hardly existed or at any rate was most obscure."[11] To a young man hungry for learning, the merchant fleets that linked the harbor of Samos with the ends of the ancient world offered one obvious way to go past the limits of his own culture. It was a way that people from the Greek world had begun to take in significant numbers in the generation or two before Pythagoras. Polycrates, an important citizen of Samos who would make himself ruler of the island a few years later, had traveled to

Egypt and was a friend of the Egyptian Pharaoh Ahmes-sa-neith, whom the Greeks called Amasis; Pythagoras asked Polycrates for a letter of introduction, got it, and set out on the first of his journeys. According to his biographer Iamblichus, he was then twenty-two years old.[12]

Accounts of his journeys vary from biographer to biographer, but most agree that he spent time studying in Egypt and Babylon. What exactly he learned there is anyone's guess. Both these ancient civilizations were in the last years of their existence, and it's fairly clear that in Egypt, at least, much of the cultural and scholarly richness of the past had already been lost. Attempts to trace precise details of Pythagorean lore to Egyptian or Babylonian sources have had equivocal results.[13] It seems likely, though, that much of what Pythagoras later taught came from materials he gathered in his travels.

It should also be noted, though, that certain mystical strains in Greek culture had much to contribute to the Pythagorean synthesis. The movement known as Orphism was central here. There are any number of scholarly questions and disputes about the nature, sources, and history of the Orphic movement, and it's not even certain that Orphism as such existed during Pythagoras' time.[14] Certainly, though, there were a range of mystical teachings in circulation when Pythagoras was born, many of them associated with the mystery initiations of the Greek world. Porphyry describes a visit by Pythagoras to at least one of these, the Cretan mystery of the Idaean Dactyls, and later writers point to a number of identities between Orphic and Pythagorean traditions.[15]

His wanderings finally brought him to Crotona in what is now southern Italy, where he spent most of the last half of his life. There he founded a *hetairia*—a half-religious, half-political body—around his teachings, which apparently held political control over most of the Greek colonies in Italy for much of a century. At some point around 500 BCE, apparently as a result of political troubles, he moved from Crotona to Metapontum, where he died a short time later.

Pythagoras as shaman?

Egyptian, Babylonian, and Orphic or proto-Orphic teachings played important roles in Pythagoras' education, if the biographers are to be believed, and there is some plausibility to the claim. Certainly, echoes of all these elements can be found readily, from the earliest records onward, in the system of thought that went under his name. Some of his more enthusiastic biographers credit Pythagoras with an even wider range of travels, studies, and initiations, but this seems to be more an attempt to have him corner the market on wisdom than anything else; in this category must be placed Iamblichus' claim that Pythagoras studied under the Druids, for example.

The same sort of enthusiasm in a modern context has decked Pythagoras out with the attributes of a shaman, and as this point of view still commands a certain amount of respect it is probably necessary to deal with it here in detail. It has been pointed out, with some supporting evidence, that several of the tribal peoples to the north and east of the Greek homeland seem to have practiced something not too much unlike shamanism of the classic Siberian type; it has been suggested, with somewhat less justification, that certain Greek myths that can be linked to these peoples are fundamentally shamanistic in nature; it has been claimed, finally, that a handful of figures in the early history of Greek philosophy make more sense if they are reinterpreted as "Greek shamans," and some sweeping claims have been made on this basis.[16]

The problems with these claims are twofold. On the one hand, the word "shamanism" has come to be used with quite a bit of recklessness in recent years, even—in fact, especially—in academic circles. Properly speaking, it refers to a group of highly specific traditions and practices common to many of the native peoples of Siberia and the Americas.[17] Those traditions and practices are far from universal. There are plenty of magicians, healers, ritualists and diviners around the world, in and out of tribal cultures, who do their work in radically different ways. For their part, the figures lumped together as "Greek shamans"—although some of them do indeed seem to have been involved with magical practices—have only a small fraction of the characteristics that define shamans in the most accurate sense of the word.[18] To paper over the very substantial differences with a single term is to dilute that term itself to the point of meaninglessness; if "shamanism" means anything magical in the broadest sense, why not simply use the word "magic" instead?

The other side of the difficulty lies in the notion that these "shamanic" traditions in ancient Greek culture have to be traced back to non-Greek peoples in order to explain their existence. It's hard not to see the unspoken assumption at work here, which is that magical practices were foreign to the Greeks. With this assumption, though, we are back in the realm of modern mythology. From the Renaissance onward, attempts have been made to force the ancient Greeks onto a Procrustean bed of pure rationality, but these simply won't work; abundant evidence shows that magical practices were as deeply embedded in ancient Greek culture as they have been in all other human societies, including our own.[19] It is certainly true that important figures in the history of Greek philosophy seem to have been involved with magical practices, but there is no need to call on shamanism to explain that fact. The magical traditions of Greek culture are ample explanation all by themselves.

This point has implications central to our theme, though, because these Greek magical traditions are themselves linked, clearly and directly, to the currents of Greek mystical spirituality that underlay Pythagoras' own achievement. For example, Orpheus, the "father of initiations" and eponymous founder of the Orphic movement, was equally the dominant figure in the legendary lore of ancient Greek magic. Throughout the history of the classical world, his name was quite literally one to conjure with.[20] Equally, the powers of the underworld who were central to the mystery cults were the powers most often invoked in Greek magical workings.

We happen to know a fair amount about the latter because ancient Greek magicians had the archeologically useful habit of writing their spells on thin sheets of lead and dropping them into wells, springs, fresh graves, and other points of access to the underworld. As a result, more than 1500 of these *katadesmoi*—"binding tablets" is a good English equivalent—have been uncovered over the last several centuries. The similarities between the language of these texts and surviving Bacchic and Orphic literature are unmistakable, and it's unlikely to be an accident that the earliest binding tablets discovered so far, at Selinus in Sicily, were deposited in a temple with important links to the mystery cults.[21]

Attempts have of course been made to raise the usual modern barricades between religion and magic in these cases, but here again this can't be justified by the evidence. On the contrary, it's clear—just as with the Egyptian and Babylonian traditions Pythagoras apparently studied—that the Greek traditions that went into the making of the Pythagorean synthesis were ones in which magic, mysticism, and religion were blended to the point of fusion.

The miracles

It's in this context that the miracles attributed to Pythagoras in the ancient sources need to be assessed. These are, in their own way, a crucial part of the story. Very few historical figures of ancient times were credited with so many wondrous deeds, but a thread of the miraculous runs through the biographies of many of the central figures of our story; by itself these tales prove nothing, but they can serve as markers for patterns of thought and action that carry much more in the way of meaning.

What were the miracles credited to Pythagoras? To modern eyes, at least, they make for odd reading. According to his biographers, he appeared at the same hour of the same day in two towns more than a hundred miles apart. He tamed a savage bear by the power of his voice and converted it to vegetarianism, and instructed an ox to give up eating beans, a commandment it kept for the rest of its life. While walking on the seashore, he came across fishermen hauling in full nets and correctly predicted the exact number of fish they had caught. While he was crossing a river with a group of friends, the river itself called out "Hello, Pythagoras." He called an eagle down from the sky to be petted, and bit a poisonous snake to death. He recounted not only his own past incarnations but those of other people as well. He calmed storms, stopped high winds and banished a plague; and when he stood up among the spectators at the Olympic Games, the people around him saw that one of his thighs was made of gold.[22]

Strange though these accounts may seem, they follow patterns that can readily be traced elsewhere in Greek culture. Quite a number of figures in the classical world, in fact, were credited with such a mastery of wild animals, of the forces of nature, and of the fabric of space and time; notable among these is Orpheus himself; whose lyre-playing called wild beasts and rivers to heel. Near-contemporaries of Pythagoras such as Empedocles of Acragas were credited with similar feats, as were several later figures such as Apollonius of Tyana and Jesus of Nazareth. Also worth considering is the intriguing comment of Apollonius Paradoxographos that Pythagoras "first studied mathematics and numbers, but later also indulged in the miracle-mongering of Pherecydes."[23]

The common feature of all these accounts is that they were attributed to people who were involved with magic. Miracles such as these, in fact, were the stereotypical powers of the most respected class of magician in the classical world, the *theios aner* or "divine man."[24] Every important figure in the history of Greek and Roman magic is the subject of similar or identical tales, although few of them collected legends in such profusion. When miracle stories of this sort appear in accounts concerning a classical figure, therefore, it's worth looking into the possibility that the figure in question either was a magician or was thought to be one.

Certainly, Pythagoras was thought to be a magician, by later Pythagoreans as well as by their enemies. Was he one? Until recently, as mentioned earlier, most scholars rejected this idea with a good deal of heat, claiming that these legends and their uncomfortable implications were the product of the "decadent" thought of later centuries. In point of fact, though, accounts of the miracles of Pythagoras were widely known in the Greek world by the early fourth century BCE, little more than a century after his lifetime.[25] They can be found among the very earliest references to Pythagoras and his teaching. It's hard to imagine that such claims would have gathered so quickly around him unless there was something to attract them. This is not to say that Pythagoras necessarily performed any of these miracles; what it does say, and clearly, is that he was seen—in his own lifetime, or very shortly thereafter—as the kind of person who could be expected to do so, or in other words that he was seen as a magician.

Another kind of evidence points in the same direction, from a very different standpoint. Near the end of the sixth century BCE, when Pythagoras was probably still living, the philosopher Heraclitus accused him of manufacturing a wisdom of tricks and swindles out of other people's learning.[26] This language is striking, for it echoes the standard rationalist dismissal of magic in ancient Greek writings—the claim that magic was all a matter of trickery and outright fraud. In the later literature on Pythagoras, this same sort of argument appears at much greater length; a story recounted by Hermippus, for example, has Pythagoras faking a descent into Hades with the assistance of his elderly mother![27] Here again, it's hard to imagine such accusations clustering around Pythagoras unless there was something to attract them, and as we've seen, there's good reason to believe that that "something" was magic.

The Pythagorean teachings

To turn to the teachings of Pythagoras themselves, though, is to venture onto slippery ground. A few points are generally admitted—the idea that he taught some form of reincarnation, for example, is too widely attested to be challenged by more than a few modern scholars, and it's agreed equally that his teachings had a substantial ethical element, and dealt in some way with numbers. Beyond such generalities, though, matters become difficult.

The crux of the problem here, as with the related teachings of Orphism and the mysteries, is the secrecy practiced by the first generations of Pythagoreans. The earliest public account of Pythagorean teachings appeared in the writings of Philolaus of Crotona in the late fifth century BCE, which survives only in fragments quoted by other authors. The few fourth-century sources—Aristotle's book *On the Pythagoreans*, the writings of the Pythagoreans Philolaus of Crotona and Archytas of Tarentum, and a handful of others—have suffered a similar fate. As a result, the total corpus of surviving evidence for the original Pythagorean teachings could be made into a fairly slim pamphlet. On this scanty foundation, a succession of modern writers have built up various edifices of speculation, or simply brushed the whole matter aside as unimportant or undecidable.

Still, neither of these extremes is necessary. The surviving evidence does point in certain directions with a fair degree of clarity, and it's possible to trace at least some of the outlines of the Pythagorean teachings in their early forms. Some of these forms almost certainly go back to Pythagoras himself; others are likely to have been evolved later on; all of them are relevant to the Pythagorean tradition as it developed in later centuries, and to the important links between that tradition and the origins of Western high magic.

We can outline what is known about the early teachings under three headings: the *bios Pythagorikos* or Pythagorean disciplines of daily life, the *akousmata*, and the mathematical sciences on which Pythagoras' later reputation came to rest.[28]

The *bios Pythagorikos*

To the ancient Greeks, the most striking feature about the early Pythagoreans was the distinctive way of life they followed, and which they claimed to have received from Pythagoras himself. "Pythagoras was especially revered for this," comments Socrates in Plato's Republic; "his followers even now use the term 'Pythagorean Way of Life,' and they stand out among the rest of men."[29] The more sardonic eyes of Athenian comic playwrights noted the same sense of distinction, and made regular use of it; the wandering Pythagorean ascetic, grubby, threadbare and arrogant, is a stock figure of the Middle Comedy.

These comic portrayals, in fact, provide among the best outlines of the *bios Pythagorikos* in ancient writings. Pythagoreans appear in them as barefoot, longhaired, shabbily dressed, and stiff with dirt because their way of life forbids them from using the public baths. They will not touch meat or wine and live on vegetables and plain water. They follow such an ascetic life, the playwrights suggest wryly, because this is the best they can manage. When one character in a play by Aristophon announces that he has been to the underworld and seen that the Pythagoreans alone are permitted to feast with Pluto, another retorts that Pluto must be a very easy-going god if he dines with such ragamuffins.[30]

How much of this ascetic stance actually originated with Pythagoras himself is hard to say for certain, but there is good evidence that much of the *bios Pythagorikos* dates back to the earliest phases of the movement. Many of the same characteristics mocked by the poets of the Middle Comedy are also identified as Orphic customs, and many of them are also reflected in the *akousmata*, which certainly come from the oldest stratum of Pythagorean tradition. While the extreme poverty mentioned in the comic portrayals was at least partly a function of their context—the Pythagoreans in fourth-century Athens were refugees from the final collapse of the political side of the movement—many of the other features are likely to be original.

One thing that apparently does not belong to the earliest forms of the tradition, though, is the vegetarianism that was mentioned (and mocked) over and over again in comic references. The *akousmata*, as we'll see, establish a wide range of food prohibitions; certain kinds of fish and certain animal organs, as well as beans, are not to be eaten. This implies, however, that other kinds of meat are not forbidden, and in fact there is a substantial body of early references that picture Pythagoras and the early Pythagoreans as eaters of meat.[31] What prompted the change is anyone's guess, but it's possible that contacts between Pythagorean and Orphic circles in the years after Pythagoras' death are involved.

The *akousmata*

A second element of the earliest stratum of Pythagorean teaching is a collection of brief, enigmatic maxims or sayings called *akousmata*, "things heard," or *symbola*, "symbols" or "passwords." These can be grouped into two broad classes, which correspond to a large degree with the other two elements of the traditions surveyed here: one, the larger of the two, passes on rules for daily life closely linked to the *bios Pythagorikos*, while the other communicates fragments of a wisdom tradition that includes myth, proverbial lore, cosmology, and certain elements of the mathematical sciences. To the first class belong *akousmata* such as these:

> *Do not wear a ring with the image of a god.*
> *Do not eat from a whole loaf of bread.*
> *Do not roast what has been boiled.*
> *Do not eat heart or brains.*
> *Do not speak in the dark.*
> *Do not step over a yoke.*
> *Do not sit on a bushel.*
> *Do not stir the fire with a knife.*
> *Do not travel by the public highways.*
> *Abstain from beans.*
> *Abstain from those fish which are sacred.*
> *Put on the right shoe first, but wash the left foot first.*
> *Enter temples and perform sacrifices barefoot.*
> *Do not help a person to unload, only to load up.*

To the second, smaller class, belong these:

> *The Isles of the Blest are the Sun and the Moon.*
> *The sea is the tears of Cronus.*
> *The Great and Little Bears are the hands of Rhea.*
> *The planets are the dogs of Persephone.*
> *The most just thing is to sacrifice.*
> *Old age is decrease; youth is increase.*
> *A friend is a second self.*
> *The truest thing is number.*
> *The Oracle at Delphi is the tetraktys, which is the song the Sirens sing.*[32]

Most of these are baffling at first glance, but there are several keys that unlock their meanings. First of all, as scholars have been pointing out since the third century BCE, a good many of the *akousmata* of the first kind closely parallel popular superstitions and the precepts of Greek oracles and mysteries. Like the Orphics, the Pythagoreans adapted these traditional rituals of purity for new roles as part of a lifetime discipline, and enshrined them in maxims of a kind well suited for oral transmission.

Second, a number of *akousmata* of the second kind appear to be remnants, similarly suited for an oral tradition, of a very specific kind of lore. The sayings that link the Sun and Moon with the Isles of the Blest, for example, or polar constellations with the hands of the goddess Rhea, draw connections between the visible heavens and the structures of Greek mythology—connections that are highly reminiscent of the starlore of Babylonia, which Pythagoras is said to have studied. These *akousmata* may well be the remnants of a much more developed system of mythic astronomy using Greek images in place of Babylonian ones.

Finally, it's by no means certain that the *akousmata* should be read only in terms of their most obvious meanings. As early as 400 BCE, Anaximander of Miletus had already written a book exploring hidden interpretations in the *akousmata*.[33] The discovery of the Derveni papyrus, an allegorical commentary on Orphic poetry from the fourth century BCE, shows that the same sort of interpretation was going on in Orphic circles within a century or so after Pythagoras' death.[34] Later still, the *akousmata* were generally explained by various schemes of moral allegory: for example, the prohibition against stirring the fire with a knife was said to mean that one should refrain from stirring up the anger of powerful men, and that against eating hearts was interpreted as an injunction not to worry excessively.

Many of these interpretations show the unmistakable marks of late classical philosophy and religious thought, but it's quite possible that even in the beginning there was a hidden dimension to the meaning of the *akousmata*, one concealed under the proverbial Pythagorean silence. What that dimension might have comprised is impossible to guess, but the possibility of its existence opens up unexpected doors. In magical traditions rooted in the Pythagorean movement, certainly, the same sort of enigmatic communication on multiple levels came to play a central role.

Pythagorean mathematics

Finally, there is the matter of the mathematical sciences in early Pythagoreanism. Later accounts made the four sciences of the medieval quadrivium—arithmetic, geometry, music, and astronomy—central to Pythagoras' achievement; as the theorem bearing his name bears witness, the same habit of interpretation remains in place in our own culture. This approach to the early Pythagorean tradition has some validity, but it becomes misleading if taken in any simplistic way. There is a fair amount of evidence that Pythagoras and the early Pythagorean school devoted much of their efforts to the study of number, and to the ways number and numerical relationships serve as deep patterns for music and astronomy, but it's equally clear that these efforts went in directions that have little to do with mathematics in the typical modern sense of the word.

The mathematical sciences, in something like their modern sense, were adopted wholesale by later figures in the Pythagorean tradition, and this has done a good deal to cloud the point. It's perfectly true, for instance, that such later Pythagorean figures as Nicomachus of Gerasa (active in the second century CE) have important roles in the history of ancient mathematics, but it's by no means certain that Pythagoras himself did. Certainly, the earlier and more reliable sources say very little about this aspect of his work, and his name does not appear among classical lists of famous mathematicians until after the Pythagorean revival of the first few centuries of the common era redefined him in its own terms.[35]

What sets the Pythagorean approach to number apart from mathematics in the modern sense is that it treats numbers as symbols, with meanings that go beyond pure quantity. From a Pythagorean perspective, the difference between two numbers—say, 1 and 2—was not simply that 2 is twice as large as 1. Each of these numbers is at the center of a cluster of symbolic meanings; it has its own character, its own personality, and its own relationships to the world of human experience.

It was from this standpoint that the early Pythagoreans, as well as many of their philosophical descendants in later times, pursued the study of number. A certain amount of mathematical knowledge in the modern sense did come out of their inquiries, especially in number theory and music. Still, it's a mistake to see this, as some modern writers have done, as evidence for a "scientific" attitude in the Pythagorean movement. There are many ways to use numbers in human thought, and many of them—including those central to the Pythagorean approach—have little in common with the sense of number as an abstract quantity that seems like sheer common sense to so many people today.

Surviving references, many of them from Aristotle's lost work *On the Pythagoreans*, tell us something about what their symbolic understanding of number was like. We learn among other things that all numbers are born from the interaction of limit and the unlimited, opposite powers that are equivalent in some sense to odd and even, unity and plurality, male and female, and a range of other polarities. One, which is not a number but the source of all number, is mind and being; 2 is opinion; 4, the first square number, is justice, being equal times equal; 7 is opportunity, and also the virgin goddess Athena, because it is neither a factor nor a multiple of any of the other numbers from 2 to 10. 10 itself is the number of perfection and embraces the whole nature of number.[36] Numbers beyond 10 were of far less importance, and since the number 10 is itself the sum of the first four numbers—1 + 2 + 3 + 4 = 10—the entire world of number, and the perfection of the whole universe, is contained in the numbers 1 through 4.

This became the basis for the central Pythagorean diagram, the *tetraktys*. Like most of their mathematical patterns, it was typically laid out on the ground with pebbles, in the form shown below:

```
          0

        0   0

      0   0   0

    0   0   0   0
```

"What is the Oracle of Delphi?" asks one of the most significant of the *akousmata*, and answers: "The *tetraktys*, which is the song the sirens sing." What song that was, fortunately, is preserved in later documents, which point out that the tetraktys contains within itself the proportions governing the basic harmonies of music: from 1 to 2, the octave; from 2 to 3, the perfect fifth; from 3 to 4, the perfect fourth; and the difference between fifth and fourth, which is a single whole tone.[37] These same musical intervals, in turn, give rise to the "music of the spheres"—one of the most enduring of all Pythagorean concepts, the idea that each of the planets produces by its movement a musical tone that can be heard by the wise, bringing mathematics, music, and cosmology into a single unity.

A saying preserved in several of the sources describes the *tetraktys* as "the fount and root of visible Nature." What other connections Pythagoras may have found between this pattern and the natural world is anyone's guess, though texts from the Pythagorean revival of later centuries have plenty to offer. The same blending of symbolism, science, and philosophy that appears in the *tetraktvs*, however, is equally common all through the surviving remnants of early Pythagorean thought.

Conclusion

These, then, were the teachings—or some of them—that Pythagoras passed onto his students in the years after his arrival in Crotona: a fusion of Greek mythology and mystery teaching, Babylonian mathematics and starlore, and Egyptian theology, transformed by the presence of Greek philosophy in one of its earliest forms but still deeply rooted in the mythic world of its sources. All of these characteristics, each of these specific sources, and a fair number of the core ideas of the synthesis Pythagoras created from them, would go on to become central features of the tradition of Western high magic.

For all that, magic itself is the one thing that cannot be proved to exist as a subject of teaching in the earliest phases of the Pythagorean tradition, As we've seen, Pythagoras himself was understood as a magus from a very early period on; all the sources from which his synthesis was drawn have magic as a central element; the tradition in its later forms was as often as not part and parcel of explicitly magical systems. There is even evidence that Pythagoras himself and his Thracian disciple Zalmoxis both underwent symbolic journeys to the underworld, journeys that were interpreted by later skeptical writers as hoaxes but may well have originally had a serious ritual context.[38] Of magical teachings by Pythagoras himself, though, the only trace from before the common era is a mocking description by the comic playwright Timon, quoted by Diogenes Laertius:

> Pythagoras, who often teaches
> Precepts of magic, and with speeches
> Of long high-sounding diction draws,
> From gaping crowds, a vain applause.[39]

What those "precepts of magic" might have been the surviving evidence does not even allow us to guess. As a result, it may well be that—barring the discovery of new documentary information—the original expressions of Western high magic may remain a permanent mystery.

Notes

1. Neugebauer, O., *The Exact Sciences in Antiquity* (Princeton University Press, 1952, p. 35).
2. This claim appears in Iamblichus' hagiographical biography of Pythagoras—see Guthrie, K.S., comp. and trans., *The Pythagorean Sourcebook and Library* (Phanes, 1987), 70—but is generally accepted by modern scholars.
3. The primary sources for the life of Pythagoras include four ancient biographies, collected in translation in Guthrie (1987), and a wide range of other sources; very few classical figures are as well-attested. See Diels and Kranz (1951–1952) for collected testimonia.
4. This approach still remains standard in most histories of philosophy and mathematics. See also Philip, J.A., *Pythagoras and Early Pythagoreanism* (University of Toronto Press, 1966).
5. For Pythagoras as shaman, see especially Burkert, W., *Lore and Science in Early Pythagoreanism* (Edwin L. and Minar Jr., trans., Harvard University Press, 1972).
6. The dates of Pythagoras are conjectural, based on contradictory material from ancient sources. The dates used here are those proposed by de Vogel, C.J., *Pythagoras and Early Pythagoreanism* (Van Gorcum, 1966); see also the discussion in von Fritz, K., *Pythagorean Politics in Southern Italy* (Columbia University Press, 1940, 47–67). The following account of his life is largely based on the biographies by Porphyry and Diogenes Laertius, taking into account issues raised by Burkert (1972), de Vogel (1966), Kingsley, P., *Ancient Philosophy. Mystery and Magic: Empedocles and Pythagorean Tradition* (Clarendon, 1995), and Philip (1966).
7. Philip (1966), 173–175; see also Herodotus, Book 3.
8. For Pherecydes, see especially Schibli, H.S., *Pherekydes of Syros* (Clarendon, 1990), which includes the known fragments of and references to his work.
9. Based on the reconstruction in Schibli (1990), 128–129.
10. Quoted in Schibli (1990), 159.
11. *Ibid.*
12. This is implied (although not stated) by the chronology in Iamblichus; see von Fritz (1940), 47–49.
13. Most of these, such as the writings of R. A. Schwaller de Lubicz and his disciples, tend to mistake the possibility of a Pythagorean interpretation for proof that this interpretation is valid. See de Santillana, G. and

von Dechend, H., *Hamlet's Mill* (Davide R Godine, 1977) for similar logical mistakes in a more academic context.

14. See especially Burkert (1987) and Dodds, E.R., *The Greeks and the Irrational* (University of California Press, 1951).

15. For Porphyry, see Guthrie (1987), 126; for later parallels, see Kingsley (1995).

16. See, among others, Meuli (1935), Dodds (1951) and Burkert (1972).

17. Eliade (1964) remains the standard work on the subject.

18. Philip (1966) 159–162.

19. See Faraone (1992) and Kingsley (1995) among many others.

20. Guthrie, W.K.C., *Orpheus and Greek Religion* (Methuen, 1952, pp. 17–19).

21. For *katadesmoi*, see Gager (1992). For the temple at Selinus, and its relation to the earliest known binding tablets, see Gager (1992), 117 and 13 8–142, and Kingsley (1995), 242–244.

22. Sources for the miracles attributed to Pythagoras include the biographies by Porphyry (23–30) and Iamblichus (61, 134 and 140–143), as well as writings by Aelian, Plutarch, and others. See the summaries in Burkert (1972), 141–147, and Kingsley (1995), 289–316.

23. Apollonius, *Marvelous Stories* 6, quoted in Schibli (1990).

24. For the distinctions among classical concepts of the magician, see Smith, M., *Jesus the Magician* (Harper & Row, 1978).

25. See Burkert (1972), 137–147, and Kingsley (1995), 289–316.

26. Heraclitus B81, quoted in Diogenes Laertius; see Guthrie (1987), 142.

27. Quoted in Diogenes Laertius; see Guthrie (1987), 152.

28. The outline of Pythagorean teaching given here is largely based on Philip (1966) and Burkert (1972), which reach nearly opposite conclusions on the basis of much the same evidence. Philip's Pythagoras is a proto-philosopher, Burkert's a shaman; most of the divergence between these two images can be resolved readily by recognizing Pythagoras as a magician, and thus intermediate between the two. I have also taken note of the criticisms in Kingsley (1995).

29. Republic 600a.

30. For Pythagoreans in the Middle Comedy, see Burkert (1972), 198–201.

31. Burkert (1972), 180–185.

32. The *akousmata* appear in numerous sources. See Burkert (1972), 166–192; a standard collection may be found in Guthrie (1987), 159–162.

33. See Kingsley (1995), 112–126, and Burkert (1972), 166 and 172.

34. Kingsley (1995), loc. cit.

35. See Philip (1966), 76–133.

36. Burkert (1972), 465–482; see also Porphyry, in Guthrie (1987), and Waterfield (1988).
37. See, for example, Guthrie (1987), 317–319. For a later and far more complex version of the same symbolism, see Nicomachus (1994).
38. Primary sources are Diogenes Laertius, Guthrie (1987) 152, and Herodotus 4.96. See also Burkert (1972), 154–159.
39. Diogenes Laertius, in Guthrie (1987), 150.

Bibliography

Barnes, J., ed. and trans., *Early Greek Philosophy* (Penguin, 1987).

Burkert, W., *Lore and Science in Early Pythagoreanism* (Edwin L. and Minar Jr., trans., Harvard University Press, 1972).

Burkert, W., *Ancient Mystery Cults* (Harvard University Press, 1987).

De Santillana, G. and von Dechend, H., *Hamlet's Mill* (Davide R Godine, 1977).

De Vogel, C.J., *Pythagoras and Early Pythagoreanism* (Van Gorcum, 1966).

Dodds, E.R., *The Greeks and the Irrational* (University of California Press, 1951).

Faraone, C.A. and Obbink, D., eds., *Magika Hiera: Ancient Greek Magic and Religion* (Oxford University Press, 1991).

Guthrie, K.S., comp. and trans., *The Pythagorean Sourcebook and Library* (Phanes, 1987).

Guthrie, W.K.C., *Orpheus and Greek Religion* (Methuen, 1952).

Kingsley, P., *Ancient Philosophy. Mystery and Magic: Empedocles and Pythagorean Tradition* (Clarendon, 1995).

Minar, B.L., *Early Pythagorean Politics in Practice and Theory* (Waverly, 1942).

Neugebauer, O., *The Exact Sciences in Antiquity* (Princeton University Press 1952).

Philip, J.A., *Pythagoras and Early Pythagoreanism* (University of Toronto Press, 1966).

Schibli, H.S., *Pherekydes of Syros* (Clarendon, 1990).

Smith, M., *Jesus the Magician* (Harper & Row, 1978).

Von Fritz, K., *Pythagorean Politics in Southern Italy* (Columbia University Press, 1940).

The forgotten oracle

My second article for Gnosis, *this was an introduction to geomantic divination meant to attract the interest of students of the occult and was duly published in the* Gnosis *special issue on divination in 1998.*

Of the various methods of divination that have been part of the Western esoteric tradition down through the years, the art of geomancy has received the least attention in modern times. Nowadays, the subject is so poorly known that references to geomancy typically have to do with feng shui or ley lines rather than with the system of divination to which the term originally applied.

To some extent, this obscurity is surprising since geomancy was among the most popular divinatory methods during the great Hermetic revival of the Renaissance. Henry Cornelius Agrippa and Robert Fludd, two of the most important writers of that revival, both produced works on the subject. So did John Heydon, that master plagiarist of English Renaissance occultism, whose *Theomagia, or the Temple of Wisdome* contains a treasure of half-jumbled geomantic lore rarely touched since his time.

Astrology, with its much more extensive vocabulary of symbols, always played a more important part both in divinatory theory and in the symbolic discourse central to so much of Hermetic thought and practice. Still, geomancy also had a significant role in both these areas; it made use of a great many astrological elements for its own purposes, and it may have been more commonly used as a means of ordinary divination. The reason isn't hard to find. The erection of a horoscope in the days before computers required a substantial amount of time and a solid grasp of fairly complex mathematics, whereas a geomantic chart could be set up in moments by anyone willing to learn the simple and undemanding process involved.

Like the rest of the Renaissance Hermetic tradition, geomancy went into eclipse with the coming of the Scientific Revolution, and was preserved only by small coteries of Hermetic students during the two centuries that followed. Like much of the rest of the tradition, it was dusted off by the adepts and antiquarians of the late nineteenth-century occult revival. The Hermetic Order of the Golden Dawn, in particular, made geomancy an important part of its course of studies, and it was by the way of this connection that geomantic divination has gained most of what exposure it has had in recent times.

Unfortunately, the version of geomancy practiced by the Golden Dawn was fragmentary at best. The order's founders were borrowers for the most part rather than creative thinkers, and their treatment of geomancy shows some of the less impressive aspects of the pack-rat mentality that pervades too much of the Golden Dawn material. The entire Golden Dawn-lecture on geomancy was based on a few out-of-context sections extracted from Heyclon's three-volume *Theomagia*.

In their original context, these, sections provided a general overview of certain aspects of the reading, and were meant to be supplemented and clarified by the much more extensive discussions in the remainder of the text. On their own, these fragments of the complete system provide a badly distorted image of the way a geomantic chart is read. In the Golden Dawn documents, the interpretation of a geomantic chart is presented as a matter of looking up cut-and-dried, arbitrary meanings from a set of tables: a sharply limiting approach at best, and one which offers far too little scope for the intuition of the diviner—which is, after all, the crucial factor in the whole process.

What makes these failings particularly burdensome is the fact that practically all later works on the subject have taken the Golden Dawn system (with or without acknowledgment) as their basis, with little or no reference to the other readily available sources—Agrippa and Heydon are only two of these—much less the extensive manuscript literature dating from the Middle Ages and Renaissance. The Golden Dawn "look-it-up-in-the-tables" approach has remained universal in modern books of geomancy. The result has been the continuing eclipse of geomancy as a divinatory art.

Fortunately, the older methods have survived in detail in the medieval and Renaissance literature, and I have had the opportunity to work with this material and its practical methods for several years. My goal in this article is to present these methods as clearly as possible.

The sixteen figures

Geomancy is one member of a large family of divinatory methods founded on what modern mathematicians call binary or base-2 numbers. The most famous member of this family is the *I Ching* or *Book of Changes*, the oldest and most important of the divinatory systems of China. (It may be worth noting that the basic concepts of binary mathematics were first introduced to the West by way of early translations of the *Book of Changes*.) The principle underlying the whole family, though, can be seen in the simple divination process of flipping a coin. Certain random or quasi-random events can be used to produce one of two definite results; if meaning is assigned to the results, a clear answer can be found to any question.

In geomancy, four binary events—odd or even counts, generated through the processes of divination—make up a figure; there are thus $2 \times 2 \times 2 \times 2$ or sixteen possible figures, which make up the basic units of meaning. Each figure is made up of four lines, each of which can have one or two dots: a "head," corresponding to the element of fire; a "neck," corresponding to air; a "body," corresponding to water; and "feet," corresponding to earth (see Diagram 1).

Constructing the chart

It's possible to do a basic kind of geomantic divination by simply generating one figure through some random method—tossing a coin four times is as good as any—and reading the result as an answer. In traditional geomancy, a somewhat more complex procedure was used. Although this takes a little more time, it allows the figures to give a great deal more information than a simple yes or no.

THE SIXTEEN FIGURES OF GEOMANCY

PUER (BOY)	AMISSIO (LOSS)	ALBUS (WHITE)	POPULUS (PEOPLE)
Rashness, violence, energy, destructiveness. Generally unfavorable except in matters of love and war.	Transience and loss, things outside one's grasp. Favorable for love and for situations in which loss is desired, but very unfavorable for material matters.	Peace, wisdom, purity; a favorable figure, but weak. Good for beginnings and for business ventures.	Multitude, a gathering or assembly of people. Good with good, evil with evil; a neutral figure, neither favorable nor unfavorable.
FORTUNA MAJOR (GREATER FORTUNE)	CONJUNCTIO (CONJUNCTION)	PUELLA (GIRL)	RUBEUS (RED)
Great good fortune, inner strength. A figure of power and success, favorable for any form of competition.	Combination of forces or people; recovery of things that have been lost. A neutral figure, neither favorable nor unfavorable.	Harmony and happiness; a favorable figure in nearly all questions.	Passion, power, fierceness, and vice. Evil in all that is good and good in all that is evil.
ACQUISITIO (GAIN)	CARCER (PRISON)	TRISTITIA (SORROW)	LAETITIA (JOY)
Success, profit and gain; things within one's grasp. Favorable in nearly all matters.	Restriction, delay, limitation, imprisonment. An unfavorable figure.	Sorrow, suffering, illness, and pain. An unfavorable figure except in questions relating to building and the earth.	Happiness and health. A favorable figure.
CAUDA DRACONIS (TAIL OF THE DRAGON)	CAPUT DRACONIS (HEAD OF THE DRAGON)	FORTUNA MINOR (LESSER FORTUNE)	VIA (WAY)
A doorway leading out. Favorable for losses and endings, but an unfavorable figure in most questions. Brings good with evil and evil with good.	A doorway leading in. Favorable for beginnings and gain, neutral in other questions. Good with good, evil with evil.	Outward strength, help from others. Good for any matter in which a person wishes to proceed quickly.	Change, movement, alteration of fortune. Favorable for journeys and voyages.

The first step is to generate four figures through a series of binary processes. In medieval Europe, the standard method involved making a line of some random number of dots across smoothed sand or earth with a wand or, in a pinch, across parchment with a pen. The dots were then counted; an odd result gave a single dot, an even result two dots, and this was taken as the head of the first figure. Another line was made to produce the neck, another for the body, and so on; a total of sixteen such lines had to be drawn to produce the first four figures, the Four Mothers.

The next four figures, the Four Daughters, are generated from the Four Mothers. The First Daughter is produced by taking the head of each of the Four Mothers in order: thus, the head of the First Mother becomes the First Daughter's head; the head of the Second Mother becomes the First Daughter's neck; the head of the Third Mother becomes the First Daughter's body, and the head of the Fourth Mother becomes the First Daughter's feet. In the same way, the necks of the Mothers produce the Second Daughter, their bodies the Third Daughter, and their feet the Fourth Daughter.

At this point, a third process comes into play to create what the medieval handbooks called the Four Nieces and what modern geomancy usually terms the Four Nephews. The First Niece is generated from the First and Second Mothers by adding the points of each of the Mothers' lines in order and using the resulting odd or even numbers to determine the lines of the Niece. Thus, if the head lines of the first two Mothers are both single points (adding to 2) or both double points (adding to 4), the head line of the First Niece will be a double point. If one Mother has a single point for a head and the other a double (adding to 3), the Niece's head will be a single point. The process then continues down to the neck, the body, and the feet. In the same way, the Third and Fourth Mothers produce the Second Niece, the First and Second Daughters the Third Niece, and the Third and Fourth Daughters the Fourth Niece.

This additive process then goes to work on the Nieces, giving rise to the Witnesses. The Right Witness is created in exactly the same way from the First and Second Nieces and the Left Witness from the Third and Fourth Nieces. Finally, the Judge is created by adding together the two Witnesses according to the same process. Because the Four Mothers and Four Daughters are made from the same set of points, the Judge—which is descended from both—will always be made of an even number of points and so only eight of the sixteen figures (Amissio, Populus, Fortuna Major, Conjunctio, Carcer, Acquisitio, Fortuna Minor, and Via) can appear as Judge. This provides a check on the accuracy of the calculations; if a figure with an odd number of points turns up as Judge, there is an error somewhere in the chart.

First steps of interpretation

At the end of this process, the complete geomantic chart has been produced, and the mechanical part of geomantic divination is finished.
What remains is the interpretation of the chart, where the patterns that
have come out of this first phase become bearers of meaning.

The first and most important step in interpreting a geomantic chart is
based on the relationships among the Witnesses and the Judge. Of these,
the Judge itself is far and away the most significant, and it's possible to
get a fairly clear idea of the basic outlines of the reading by taking the
Judge alone as a guide. If the question which has been asked can be
answered with a yes or no, a favorable figure means yes, an unfavorable
one no. A more complex question often finds its answer in more specific
details of the meaning of the figure which appears as Judge.

The two Witnesses add another level of meaning. A favorable Judge
derived from two favorable Witnesses is made more positive still, while
an unfavorable Judge derived from two unfavorable Witnesses is the
worst possible sign. A Judge, favorable or unfavorable, which is produced from one favorable and one unfavorable. Witness takes on a
middle significance, representing a situation in which good and ill are
combined. A favorable Judge coming from this combination often means
success, but with difficulty and delay; an unfavorable Judge from the
same situation often means failure, but with some mitigating factors.

A favorable Judge that derives from two unfavorable Witnesses
becomes unfavorable, although not extremely so; it often means a seemingly unfortunate turn of events which comes out for the best in the
long run. An unfavorable Judge derived from two favorable Witnesses
becomes somewhat favorable although it can often mean a success
which has negative consequences in the end. In all cases, the meaning
of the figures themselves should be carefully studied, as these provide
the context in which these indications take shape.

There is also an element of time in these relationships. The Right
Witness is said to represent the past of the question, the Left Witness
the future, while the Judge represents the situation in its broadest sense,
including past, present, and future. Thus, for example, a favorable
Judge derived from an unfavorable Right Witness and a favorable Left
Witness represents a turn for the better, in which past difficulties are left
behind. The same Judge derived from a favorable Right Witness and
an unfavorable Left Witness stands for a situation in which past and
present successes will be paid for with future trouble.

The twelve houses

The information given by the Witnesses and the Judge is often enough to provide a clear response to the question. In other cases, though, it's useful to get a more detailed view of the situation or to see how specific issues are affected by the pattern of forces at work in the reading. Here the figures are read in terms of their, placement on the twelve geomantic houses. (As in astrological charts of the Renaissance, the houses are set out in a square rather than in a circle.)

These twelve houses, like so much else in geomancy, ultimately come out of astrological lore, and like the houses of an astrological chart they serve to map out the parts of human life that are affected by the forces in the reading. The twelve geomantic houses have slightly different meanings from their modern astrological equivalents, though. The following list of house rulerships comes from the medieval handbooks on geomancy, and can be used as a general guide:

First House. The querent, or the person about whom the divination is performed.
Second House. Goods, material wealth, gain.
Third House. Brothers and sisters, the querent's neighbors and environment, short journeys.
Fourth House. Father and mother, inheritances from parents, land, any hidden thing.
Fifth House. Children.
Sixth House. Servants, employees, domestic animals, illness.
Seventh House. The querent's spouse or lover, relationships, marriage, partnerships, quarrels, any unidentified person.
Eighth House. Death, inheritances (other than from parents).
Ninth House. Religion, learning, art, wisdom, long journeys.
Tenth House. Employment, position in society, people in positions of authority, and also the weather.
Eleventh House. Friends, sources of help, things desired.
Twelfth House. Enemies, suffering, difficulties, things feared.

Modern systems of geomancy tend to use some more or less complicated way of assigning the figures of a geomantic chart to these twelve houses, but the medieval method was simplicity itself. The first twelve figures of the chart—the Mothers, Daughters, and Nieces—are simply put into the twelve houses in the order of their creation.

Like the astrological houses, the geomantic houses follow a subtle but definite logic, and it's a useful exercise to try putting different questions into their proper place in the system until you can identify the house that goes with any given question. In this phase of interpreting a chart, this is exactly what needs to be done. The person for whom the divination is done, the querent, and the subject of the divination, the quesited, are each assigned to one of the twelve houses. The querent, as shown above, is always assigned to the first house, but the quesited may be found in any of the others, depending on its nature.

The geomantic figure which appears in the first house then is the significator of the querent, and the figure which appears in the house of the quesited is the significator of the quesited. The relationship between these two is the most important factor in this phase of interpreting the chart. Furthermore, if one or both of these figures also appear somewhere else in the chart—in the language of geomancy, if it passes to another house—that house plays an important part in the chart's meaning.

Relating querent and quesited

The medieval handbooks of geomancy give special names to the relationships that can occur between the two significators:

1. Occupation. The simplest of these, occupation, occurs when the same geomantic figure appears in the house of the querent and that of the quesited. This is the most positive relationship between significators, and means that the quesited matter is entirely in the querent's control.

2. Conjunction. Nearly as positive an indicator as occupation is conjunction, when one of the significators passes to a house next to the house of the other significator. If the querent's significator passes to a house next to the house of the quesited, this means the querent will need to take action to bring the matter to a successful conclusion. If the quesited's significator passes to a house next to the querent's, it means that the matter will take care of itself.

3. Mutation. Another positive indicator is mutation, where the significators of the querent and the quesited both pass to neighboring houses elsewhere in the chart. This indicates success, but by some unexpected chain of events.

4. Translation. A fourth positive indicator is translation, where a figure other than the two significators appears in houses next to those of both the querent and the quesited. Translation means that some outside factor intervenes in the situation to bring it to a successful conclusion. The nature of the figure which makes the translation has a great deal of importance here; an unfavorable figure can accomplish a translation just as effectively as a favorable one, but this means that the situation will involve some unpleasant experiences before it's resolved. A weak figure such as Albus or Populus, when it carries out a translation, often means that the matter is brought to a conclusion by some unlikely means, or even by what looks like a pure coincidence.

5. Lack of Relationship. The chief negative indicator in reading the twelve houses is a lack of relationship between the significators of the querent and the quesited. This simply means that the situation will not work out. Some indication of the reasons can be read from the nature of the two significators, which should always be considered in any case.

6. Aspect. A subtler category of interaction, which can have either favorable or unfavorable meanings, is found by reading the aspects between the significators. Aspects, like houses, were brought into geomancy from astrology and had to be modified in certain ways to fit the different nature of geomantic divination.

The most important modification is that aspects aren't read between the houses of the querent and the quesited. This is a function of the fixed relations of the different houses. The first house is always in a trifle aspect, which is favorable, with the fifth and ninth houses, and in a square aspect, which is unfavorable, with the fourth and tenth. To read these aspects as meaningful would imply, for example, that questions involving children would always get a favorable answer, while questions involving employment would always get an unfavorable one! For this reason, aspects between the significators occur only if at least one of them passes to a different house.

Four aspects are used in geomancy besides conjunction (which we've already examined): sextile, square, trine, and opposition.

The *sextile* aspect in astrology occurs when two planets, are at a 60-degree angle to each other. In geomancy, two figures are sextile when there is one house between them. This aspect is favorable.

The *square* aspect in astrology takes place when two planets are at a 90-degree angle to each other. In geomancy, two figures are square when there are two houses between them. This aspect is unfavorable.

The *trine* aspect in astrology occurs when two planets are at a 120-degree angle to each other. In geomancy, two figures are trifle when there are three houses between them. This aspect is favorable.

Opposition in astrology takes place when two planets are at a 180-degree angle to each other, on opposite sides of the sky. In geomancy, two figures are in opposition when there are five houses between them—when, in other words, they are in opposite houses in the chart. This aspect is unfavorable.

When one of the significators passes to another house and comes into an aspect with the other, this provides a favorable or unfavorable sign depending on whether the aspect itself is favorable or unfavorable. If the significators are also linked by occupation, conjunction, mutation, or translation, a favorable aspect will add to the positive nature of the reading. If the significators are connected by one of the major relationships, but there is also an unfavorable aspect linking them, the result is still favorable, but there will be trouble involved. When an unfavorable aspect is the only connection between the significators, though, the answer is negative.

The reconciler

Under certain circumstances, the indications of the Judge and Witnesses will seem to contradict those provided by the significators and their relationship. When this occurs, a sixteenth figure, the Reconciler, can be used to work out the overall meaning and set these factors into their proper context.

The Reconciler is generated from the figure in the first house and the Judge using the same additive process that creates the Nieces, Witnesses, and Judge. When the Reconciler is used in interpreting a chart, it is read in exactly the same way as the Judge, with the figure in the first house playing the part of the Right Witness and the Judge itself filling in for the Left Witness.

When combining the meanings of the Judge and Witnesses, the houses, and the Reconciler into a single interpretation, it can be useful to think of them as different "lenses" through which the same situation can be studied. The twelve houses provide more detail but with a narrower focus than the Judge, while the Reconciler gives a wide-angle view that places the entire reading in its broader context.

Whenever the interaction between two figures is crucial to the divination's meaning, the diviner can add the two figures in question to make a third figure, using the same additive process. The figure that results from this provides a snapshot of the relationship between the two parent figures and takes its broader context from the rest of the reading.

A Sample Divination

The querent is unhappy with her present job and hopes to find a better position elsewhere. The chart that results from the divination is pictured here.

The querent's significator is Fortuna Minor, which is a good sign to start with, as this figure's meanings include "help from others."

The significator of the subject (known as the *quesited*), since employment is a tenth-house matter, is Caput Draconis, another positive figure, but without a link between the significators this might represent a good job which remains out of reach.

The link is provided, however, by the mutation between Fortuna Minor in the second house and Caput Draconis in the third. Mutation typically implies that the goal the querent has in mind needs to be sought along unexpected paths; the house where the significator of the quesited occurs is often a guide to where those paths are to be found. Here the significator of the quesited passes to the third house, which represents the querent's siblings, neighbors, and nearby environment. This suggests that she would be well advised to talk to family members and neighbors about her job search and to follow up openings in her own neighborhood, rather than putting all her efforts into job agencies or the classified ads.

The mutation linking the significators is reinforced by two sextile aspects between them. Caput Draconis in the tenth house passes to the third house, sextile to Fortuna Minor in the first house, and Fortuna Minor passes to the fifth house, sextile to Caput Draconis in the third. (The apparent square between the tenth and first house doesn't count; remember that aspects aren't read between the significators in their own houses!) This suggests that her job search may be easier than she expects.

The Witnesses and Judge, finally, confirm these indications. The Witnesses are Caput Draconis and Albus, both favorable figures for beginnings and for gain. Combined, these produce Acquisitio, the best of the figures in material questions. The reading as a whole suggests that she will have little trouble in finding a new position suitable to her needs.

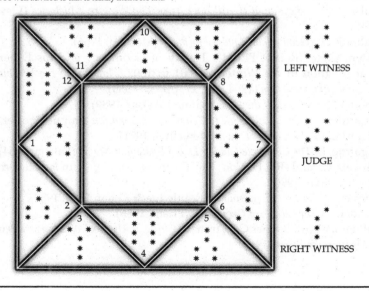

LEFT WITNESS

JUDGE

RIGHT WITNESS

Bibliography

Agrippa, H.C., *Three Books of Occult Philosophy* (Freake, J., trans., Tyson, D., ed., Llewellyn, 1993).

Agrippa, H.C., *Fourth Book of Occult Philosophy* (Kessinger, 1992). Contains Agrippa's *On Geomancy* and Gerard of Cremona's *On Astrological Geomancy*.

Anonymous, *Fasciculus geomanticus* (n.p., 1704). Contains Robert Fludd's *De animae intellectualis scientia, seu Geomantia: Tractatus de geomantia in quatuor libros divisus* and *De geomantia morborum*, with other geomantic texts.

Charmasson, T., *Recherches sur une technique divinatoire: La géomancie dans l'occident medieval* (Librairie Droz, 1980). Contains the text of *Modo judicandi questiones secundum Petrum de Abano Patavinum*.

Greer, J.M., "The Method of Judging Questions according to Peter de Abano of Padua: A Medieval Handbook of Geomancy," *Caduceus* (Spring, 1996, Vol. 2, No. 1, pp. 2–11).

Greer, J.M., "Medieval Methods of Geomancy, Part One," *Caduceus* (Summer, 1996, Vol. 2, No. 2, pp. 2–15).

Greer, J.M., "Medieval Methods of Geomancy, Part Two," *Caduceus* (Autumn 1996, Vol. 2, No. 3, pp. 26–39).

Heydon, J., *Theomagia, or the Temple of Wisdome* (For Henry Brome at the Gun in Ivie-Lane, and for Thomas Rooks at the Lambe at the east end of St. Paul's, 1664).

Hulse, D.A., *The Key of It All, Book Two: The Western Mysteries* (Llewellyn, 1994).

Jaulin, R., *La Géomancie: Analyse formelle* (Mouton, 1966).

Josten, C.H., "Robert Fludd's Theory of Geomancy and his Experiences at Avignon in the Winter of 1601 to 1602," *Journal of the Warburg and Courtauld Institutes* (1964, Vol. 27, pp. 327–335).

Pennick, N., *Games of the Gods* (Samuel Weiser, 1989).

Regardie, I., *A Practical Guide to Geomantic Divination* (Samuel Weiser, 1972).

Regardie, I., *The Golden Dawn* (Llewellyn, 1971).

Regardie, I., *The Complete Golden Dawn System of Magic* (Falcon, 1984).

Schwei, P., and R., Pestka. *The Complete Book of Astrological Geomancy* (Llewellyn, 1990).

Skinner, S., *Terrestrial Astrology* (Routledge & Kegan Paul, 1980).

Skinner, S., *The Oracle of Geomancy* (Prism, 1986).

Wilhelm, R. and Baynes C.E., trans., *I Ching or The Book of Changes* (Princeton University Press, 1967).

Osiris and Christ: powers of transformation in Golden Dawn ritual

In the traditions of the Hermetic Order of the Golden Dawn, the aspirant to the Portal Grade is expected to write a thesis on the rituals of the order as one of the requirements for that step in the ladder of initiation. Over the course of the late 1980s and early 1990s, as a solitary practitioner of that system of magic, I worked through all the formal requirements of the Grades, and the original draft of this essay was one of the results. When Chic and Sandra Tabatha Cicero put out a call for papers for an issue of their Golden Dawn Journal *on the magical pantheons, I submitted an expanded version of my Portal Grade thesis, the version printed here, and it was published in that journal in 1998.*

One aspect of Golden Dawn ritual that can easily baffle the modern student of the tradition is the fusion of Christian, Jewish, and Pagan imagery, which takes place constantly within all levels of the Order's ritual structure. Egyptian gods, Neoplatonic powers, and even such oddities as the Samothracian Cabeiri stand cheek by jowl with Cabalistic Names of God and mythic structures from Christian esotericism. Sometimes these various things are presented as different names or symbols for the same reality; more often, though, they simply coexist within the ritual work, and the connections between them are nowhere spelled out.

Some scholars, writing about the Golden Dawn from an academic perspective, have interpreted this habit as simple eclecticism, the same Victorian mania for clutter that produced so much atrocious art and architecture in the same period. To those who have worked with the Golden Dawn system, though, it's clear that deeper unities underlie the whole structure of the Order's ritual and magic. The system is effective and consistent in ways which a purely eclectic approach rarely achieves.

One of most important of these unifying patterns, one that runs through the entire labyrinth of Golden Dawn ritual, is the interaction between the images of Osiris, the Egyptian lord of the dead, and Jesus Christ, the Christian savior. These two figures both belong to the class of so-called "Dying Gods," deities whose deaths and resurrections are central to many religions. Some esoteric traditions have simply identified all such figures with one another. The Golden Dawn's approach, though, was subtler.

Both Osiris and Christ are used in Golden Dawn ritual, but in different places and in different ways. Neither one is an object of worship; in the Order's rituals, the only divinity who is actually invoked or worshiped is the abstract One of traditional Western magical philosophy, represented by the various Names of God used in the Cabala. Rather, Christ and Osiris each represent a pattern of forces—in the Order's terminology, a formula—which is used to structure consciousness in various ritual contexts.

In the rituals of the Outer Order, from Neophyte to Philosophus, Osiris is the primary figure; this is true in the magical work of these rituals as outlined in the Golden Dawn documents, but also, as we'll see, on a deeper level as well. The Portal Grade marks a transition, however; the symbolism of Osiris is central to its first half, but in the second, the figure of Christ takes over. This and the Adeptus Minor Grade are not Christian in any ordinary sense of the word, but the legends and imagery of Christ provide the dominant symbolism and much of the incidental detail for these ceremonies.

Understanding the role and meaning of these two figures will involve a journey down some strange bypaths. The Golden Dawn's use of Osiris and Christ rose from certain older patterns in the history of Western spirituality and magic; as with so many other things in the Order's work, the symbolism we'll be exploring has deep roots.

To understand that symbolism, it's necessary to turn back to ancient ways of looking at the world. In the process, some common assumptions that have structured the magical community's approach to questions of religion may prove to need revising, and some familiar images and ideas may take on an unexpected meaning.

The way of sacrifice

Osiris and Christ, as mentioned above, belong to a class of traditional divine figures that can be labeled "Dying Gods." At the root of the whole complex of these traditions is the concept of sacrifice, one of the oldest and most constant of all human spiritual ideas. Though it takes a bewildering array of forms, sacrifice centers on a single principle; its essence is exchange. This comes across most clearly, perhaps, in the sacrificial formula of Roman Paganism: *do ut des*, "I give so that you may give."

In every sacrifice, something is sent from the visible world of everyday life into the hidden world of powers beyond, so that something else may pass by the same channel out of the Unseen. Consider the sacrifices offered for fertility across the ancient world. Livestock of various kinds died before the altar, and certain portions of their bodies went up in fire to the local gods; the rest, sensibly enough, was cooked and shared out among the priests and worshipers. In exchange for the offerings, the powers behind the natural world sent sun and rain in season and kept disease from the livestock and the crops.

The same principle was used in less concrete ways. Sacrifices at the founding of a city, the naming of a child, or the coronation of a king brought forth a guardian spirit to give protection during vulnerable beginnings. More subtly, sin, disease, or ritual impurity—the three were not sharply differentiated, and modern research into the role of emotions in disease suggests that this seeming confusion has a point— were often understood as forces that drew the one affected by them out of the human world into the borderlands of the Unseen. Caught between the worlds, such people were seen as dangerous to themselves and the community alike, and had to be brought back into the human world; one common way to do this was by sacrifice. This is the origin of the sacrifices of purification that have such a large role in the Hebrew sacrificial rites, among many others.

To the modern mind, these ways of thinking about the world are likely to sound bizarre or worse. The principle behind sacrifice, though, is a principle of balance; the act of exchange between the worlds was seen as a way of maintaining the balance of the universe, and the rituals of sacrifice were thus central to the balance of the ancient world on many levels. The priests and philosophers of that world were by no means blind to the deeper implications of this principle, and some of the highest intellectual achievements of the ancients drew on it in ways we can only begin to trace today.

One role of the idea of sacrifice, though, is central to our theme. While the process of exchange central to sacrifice was not measured out on a tit-for-tat basis—one sacrificed a few cows in exchange for the birth of many more—the concept does imply that different scales of offering were needed to bring about different scales of divine response. From this came the idea that the most important divine actions, such as the creation of the world, could only have resulted from the sacrifice of a divine victim. Many creation myths—Norse, Babylonian, and Hindu, among others—thus came to tell of the origin of the world out of the sacrifice of a primal being; a tale of the same sort lies behind the Cabalistic account of Adam Cadmon.

Seed as sacrifice, sacrifice as seed

The traditions of sacrifice also made particularly deep connections with agriculture, the economic basis of ancient society. Time and the coming of new discoveries have both tended to blur the tremendous impact that the discovery of agriculture made on ancient cultures. At once a complex and evolving technology and a profoundly magical act, farming reshaped philosophy and spirituality just as it revolutionized the cycle of everyday life. In turn, traditional ways of thinking shaped the way that agriculture itself was understood.

The seed buried in the earth, then, was seen as a sacrifice, and—by the same principle of exchange that governs all sacrifice—it brought forth a response from the Earth. But that response, in turn, had to be brought all the way into the human world by a second sacrifice, the harvesting and threshing of the grain. This double sacrifice in which the grain was both victim and reward, was bound to the seasons of the year by the nature of the agricultural cycle; around it gathered calendar-lore and early astronomy, as well as an enormous amount of magical and ritual practice.

The thought of the ancient world tended to clothe itself in myth, and so this cycle of seed and sacrifice appears in one form or another throughout mythology and folklore. One example, drawn from Celtic sources, can be followed in the Scots ballad of John Barleycorn:

There were three kings come from the East,
Their fortune for to try,
And they ha' ta'en a solemn vow
John Barleycorn should die.
They took a plough and plough'd him down,
Cast clods upon his head,
And they ha' ta'en a solemn vow
John Barleycorn was dead.
But when the Spring came kindly on,
And show'rs began to fall,
John Barleycorn got up again
And sore surpris'd them all.
The sultry suns of Summer came,
And he grew thick and strong;
His head well armed wi' pointed spears,
That none should do him wrong.
The sober Autumn enter'd mild,
And he grew wan and pale;
His bending joints and drooping head
Show'd he began to fail.
His colour sicken'd more and more,
He faded into age;
And then his enemies began
To show their deadly rage.
They took a sickle, long and sharp,
And cut him at the knee;
Then tied him fast upon a cart,
Like a rogue for forgery.
They laid him down upon his back,
And cudgel'd him full sore;
Then hung him up before the blast,
And turned him o'er and o'er.
They next filled up a darksome pit

With water to the brim;
They heaved in poor John Barleycorn
And let him sink or swim.
They roasted o'er a scorching flame
The marrow of his bones;
But the miller us'd him worse than that,
And ground him 'twixt two stones.
And they ha' ta'en his own heart's blood,
And drank it round and round,
And still the more that they ha' drunk
Their joy did more abound.
So let us toast John Barleycorn,
Each one wi' glass in hand,
And may his great posterity
Ne'er fail in old Scotland![1]

This ballad presents the mythic image of the agricultural cycle in its most obvious form—seemingly, a form far removed from either the Golden Dawn rituals or the ancient myths on which those rituals drew. Appearances deceive, though. The story within this ballad, beneath its rustic clothing, is identical—in outline, and in many of its details—to the ancient Egyptian legend of Osiris.

The myth of Osiris

According to classical accounts, Osiris and his sister-wife Isis were King and Queen of Egypt in the earliest of times, the founders of Egyptian civilization and the inventors of farming. Osiris' brother Set, however, envied his brother and set out to kill him and seize the kingship for himself. He secretly arranged to learn the exact measurements of Osiris' body and had a richly decorated coffin made precisely to fit. Then, at a banquet, he offered to give the coffin to anyone who fit its measure. All the guests lay in it, one after another, but everyone was too large or too small. Finally, Osiris lay in the coffin, upon which Set and his henchmen shut the lid, nailed it, sealed it with molten lead, and cast it into the Nile.

Isis, grieving, went in search of the body of Osiris, and after wandering the world discovered that it had floated all the way to Byblos in Syria. There it had lodged in the branches of an acacia tree, which had then grown around it, lifting it into the air; the tree had been cut down and made into one of the pillars of the local king's palace. After various adventures, Isis reclaimed the body and returned with it to the Nile delta. There, with the help of Thoth the god of magic, she restored Osiris to life, and by him conceived a son, Horus.

Set, however, discovered their hiding place, and he and his henchmen attacked Osiris again, cutting him into fourteen pieces, which he then scattered across Egypt. Isis searched for them and found all of him but his penis, which had been eaten by a fish. Because of this lack, Osiris could not be restored to life, but instead was mummified and went into the otherworld to become lord and judge of the dead. Horus, however, grew to manhood, finished off the story (and Set) in the traditional manner, and became king.[2]

To describe this legend as "just" an agricultural myth is a little like describing *Romeo and Juliet* as a play about puppy love gone wrong. Much that is finest in Egyptian literature and art centers on this story. At the same time, the agricultural side of the myth cannot be doubted. The first death by burial amid the irrigating waters of the Nile is followed by the raising up of the body of Osiris and the birth of Horus, who in this context—Horus is one of the most complex of the Egyptian gods—represents the seed grain for the next season; the penis of Osiris has the same significance, and is swallowed up in the waters of the Nile just as Osiris himself had been. Thereafter, the body of Osiris is broken apart and passes into the otherworld. Many of the rituals of the cult of Osiris have to do directly with the plowing and harvesting of the fields, and devout Egyptians molded little statues of Osiris from earth and barley seed, watered these, and watched the resurrection of Osiris unfold as the seeds sprouted and grew. A number of these statues were found, withered but intact, in the tomb of Tutankhamen.

Symbols of the Dying God

The same pattern of sacrifice can be found in the myths of many other ancient cultures, more or less garbled by the transition from oral to written cultures, and thus from myth to literature. One version that played an important role in the traditions ancestral to the Golden Dawn was the Greek myth of Orpheus, the divine musician. The versions that have survived were rewritten for literary effect, but the tale still shows the marks of the older pattern: Orpheus descends into Hades, the realm of Death, and returns from it alive; later, he is killed and torn to pieces, though his head continues to sing and becomes an oracle of the gods.

The severed head that speaks is an important feature, one that came to Greece with the Greeks' Indo-European ancestors. Other Indo-European peoples use the same image quite often; the severed head of Bran son of Llyr, in the second branch of the Welsh *Mabinogion*, spoke for eighty-seven years after it was cut off its body; the severed head of Mimir, in the Norse *Ynglingasaga*, was kept by Odin as an oracular source of wisdom. It is an image we will see again in this essay.

Some of the Indo-European myths of divine sacrifice also give a different manner of death for the sacrificed god. Instead of being cut or torn apart, he is suspended in the air and pierced by a spear; typically, too, he dies once, rather than twice, in these legends. This probably derives from a symbolism of hunting or the slaughter of livestock rather than farming. The Norse god Odin's self-sacrifice on the world-tree Yggdrasil is a famous example:

> *I know that I hung   on the windy tree*
> *Nine full nights,   wounded with the spear,*
> *sacrificed to Odin,   myself offered to myself,*
> *On the tree—   where its roots run*
> *No one knows.*[3]

The Welsh, with a typically Celtic delight in the bizarre, had their sacrificial hero Llew Liaw Gyffes meet his death by the spear in a bathhouse beside a stream, with one foot on the back of a goat and the other on the rim of a cauldron. Other Celtic legends, not to be outdone, have their victims suffer three different deaths at once.[4] While this level of weirdness was equaled by few other mythologies, the spear and the suspended death are also themes that will appear again in our exploration.

A final image that is often found in Indo-European myths, although it has very ancient sources and can be found worldwide, focuses on the burial of the seed as a pattern of the transcendence of death. This image, which hearkens back to archaic customs of mound burial, has given rise to countless legends of sleeping kings and gods buried beneath the earth, waiting out the turning of the cycles of time to come forth again. The legend of the fate of Arthur, the "Once and Future King," is part of this complex of legends; so, critically, is that of Merlin sleeping in his cave. This, too, is an image we will see again.[5]

The astronomical sacrifice

The natural relationship mentioned above between the agricultural cycle and the seasons drew the symbolism of sacrifice into another of the major intellectual adventures of the ancient world. Astronomy and astrology, the twin quests to understand the movement of the bright points in the heavens and to interpret their meaning to dwellers on earth, had a profound effect on ancient thought, shaping attitudes toward time and destiny, and quite possibly giving rise to the entire concept of natural law. What the ancients lacked in telescopes and other equipment, they made up in patience and careful recordkeeping; the entire structure of modern astrology, and more of current scientific astronomy than modern scientists like to admit, are both founded on the knowledge gained over several thousand years by Chaldean scholar-priests who watched the heavens from mud-brick towers.[6]

Their discoveries, true to the ancient way of thought, were preserved in myths. The twelve labors of Hercules or his many equivalents—the Samson of Biblical myth, whose name comes from the Hebrew word for "sun," is one—represent the twelve signs of the Zodiac, through which the Sun moves in the course of the year. Other tales of Mars and Venus, Jupiter and Mercury—to this day, the names of planets as well as gods—tracked other movements across the sky. Many of these myths had the practical function of preserving calendar-lore, so that farmers could tell by a glance at the dawn, dusk, or midnight sky when it was time to plant crops or move herds.

One particular movement is of some importance in this context. The precession of the equinoxes, that slow wobble of the Earth's axis that causes the points of the equinoxes and solstices to creep slowly backward around the Zodiac, makes the stars and the seasons shift with respect to one another over long periods of time. Theoretically, the Sun stands at the beginning of the sign Aries on the day of the Spring Equinox; in fact, it is now much of the way through Pisces on this date. Around 4000 years ago, when many of the myths we now read were taking shape, it stood near the beginning of Taurus.

This gradual shift in the heavens had a profound impact on ancient myth and philosophy. The passage of the Spring Equinox through each of the constellations was held to mark an age of the world, at the end of which the whole pattern of time shifted. The passing of each age was marked in myth by the legendary sacrifice of the symbol of its sign;

thus the age in which Aries held the equinoctial point saw myths of bull sacrifice, which marked the passing of the age of Taurus, play an important part in mythology.

Perhaps the clearest expression of this is to be found in the religion of Mithraism, one of the mystery religions that rose toward the end of the classical world The great mythic event of the Mithraic faith, and one of the most common images in Mithraic art, was the taurobolium or bull sacrifice, in which Mithras is shown killing a great bull while various other figures and creatures stand nearby. This image baffled scholars until recently when it was shown to be a precise star map of the constellations around Taurus. It has been suggested, quite plausibly, that Mithras was identified with the hidden power that was seen as driving the process of precession, the unmoved mover behind the visible cosmos who slew the Bull of Heaven by ending its long reign at the primary station of the skies.[7]

The mystical sacrifice

The development of an astrological symbolism of sacrifice was far from the only transformation of the pattern we've been examining. Another was the development of a mystical dimension of mythology—that is, a way of understanding myth in which the death and resurrection of the god become the model for the transformation of the individual self. In terms of the Western tradition, the most important name in this context is that of Orpheus, the divine musician mentioned earlier.

In Greek tradition, Orpheus was the founder of a tradition of mystical knowledge and initiation, the Orphic mysteries. Very little is known for sure about these today, but classical writings preserve some of the teachings of the tradition. To the Orphics, soma, Greek for "body," and sema, Greek for "tomb," were one and the same; the human spirit was trapped in matter and could only regain its true stature by escaping from the physical world. Their teachings included number symbolism and traditions about the immortality of the soul, and focused on the idea that knowledge of the real nature of the self was the key to redemption from the material world. In a way, their beliefs represented a rejection of the old theory of sacrifice, for the Orphic vision sought not to balance the worlds of spirit and matter but to separate them once and for all.

A surviving Orphic myth expresses the same thing in symbolic language. According to this, Dionysus was the child of Zeus, the king of the gods, and Persephone, the queen of the underworld. He was hidden away in a cave from Hera, Zeus' jealous wife. However, Hera learned of the child and incited the Titans—the primal powers of creation, who existed before the gods—to kill him. They disguised themselves by whitening their bodies with gypsum, crept up on the child, distracted him with toys and a mirror, and then killed and dismembered him and ate the body. Zeus, learning of this, burned the Titans to ashes with a thunderbolt. From their ashes were created the first human beings.[8]

In this myth, most of the elements of the agricultural cycle can be traced out, at least in outline: the first death has been reduced to hiding an underground cave, but the second appears in its full form, complete with the eating of the body, which has its mundane image in the breaking and eating of bread. This is not the main point of the myth, however. To the Orphics, Dionysus represented the primal human soul, distracted by the toys and mirrors of the senses and then consumed by material life; the Titans represented matter, and the ashes from which humanity was born, partly Titanic, partly Dionysian, were the mixture of spirit and matter that makes up the human individual—and the human predicament.

The Orphic tradition is of critical importance for two reasons. First, it represents the first point of emergence in the West of the idea of individual spiritual transformation. The rites and theologies of the older sacrificial system were focused on the community, not the individual, and ideas such as personal freedom and the value of the individual had no role in them. The liberation sought by the Orphics, on the other and, was a liberation of the individual, motivated by the same ways of thinking that made Greece the birthplace of the concept of democracy.

The second reason for Orphism's importance is that most of Western spirituality has grown up from Orphic roots. Pythagoras, the first major esoteric teacher in the recorded history of the West, was an Orphic initiate, and classical accounts state that he took the basis of his system of mystical geometry and mathematics from Orphic sources. Orphic and Pythagorean influences, in turn, play important roles in the thought of Plato, and the whole range of Neoplatonic, Gnostic, and Hermetic traditions, which became the basis for Western magic, can best be seen as further developments on Orphic themes. So can—despite a long history of sometimes strident denials—another Western spiritual tradition that emerged in the same era: Christianity.

The Christian synthesis

For most of the last 2000 years, the barrier between Christianity and Paganism has been a kind of Berlin Wall through the middle of Western spirituality. Christians have defined their faith as uniquely good, and insisted, loudly, on the differences between their religion and every other religion in the world. In turn, modern Pagan revivalists have too often simply reversed the equation; one can read any number of Christian-bashing diatribes in the current Pagan and magical press, in which all non-Christian religions are seen as good while Christianity is uniquely evil.

What makes both these attitudes particularly misleading is that the supposed rigid barrier between Christianity and other religions simply isn't there. Despite the claims made for it, Christianity—even at its oldest and most basic levels—has roots in a wide range of classi-cal Pagan sources, roots that are at least as significant as Christianity's connections with Judaism. Nor are these Pagan materials simply bor-rowed and tacked on to a non-Pagan structure; they are central to the entire structure of Christian myth and theology, and they are worked together in a manner common to many other religions of the time. In fact, it would not be going too far to describe Christianity as the best surviving example of late classical Paganism.

In Christianity, practically every major theme of classical Pagan tradition appears, woven together into a single many-layered mytho-logical structure. The births of two miraculous children, John and Jesus, are announced by angels; one is born to a woman past menopause, the other to a virgin; John is born at the summer solstice, Jesus at the winter solstice. John, the elder, goes out into the wilderness, baptizes his fol-lowers with water, and speaks of one who will come to baptize with fire. Jesus appears, is baptized, goes into the wilderness to contend with the powers of evil, and embarks on his own career as a holy man. Mean-while, John is seized by an evil king and beheaded in a dungeon; the traditional date for this is August 29. Jesus travels about, performs mir-acles, and at Passover celebrates a meal in which he says that the bread is his body and the wine is his blood. He is then crucified and pierced with a spear; he dies, is resurrected, and ascends into heaven thereafter.

The old agricultural pattern is one of the more obvious elements of
this myth. Here the two deaths have been divided between two figures.
John, born at Midsummer and sacrificed just before the beginning of
Fall, the planting season in the Middle East, is the seed. Jesus, born at
Midwinter as the new crop grows, and sacrificed at the harvest just after
the beginning of Spring, is the ripe grain. It is thus the body of Jesus that
is eaten in the bread—one does not eat seed grain, after all. (The name
of Bethlehem, the town where Jesus was born, literally means "house of
bread" in Hebrew.)

Onto this a second, astronomical and calendrical level of symbolism
has been built. John, born of an old woman at Midsummer, is the
waning half of the year, and he descends into the Earth to die as the
Sun descends in the Heavens; "I must decrease," he says comparing
himself and Jesus, "but he must increase."[9] Jesus, born of a young virgin
at Midwinter, is the waxing half of the year and meets his death raised
up above the Earth as the Sun ascends in the Heavens. Jesus in the
midst of the twelve apostles is also the Sun amid the signs of the Zodiac,
while Mary and Martha—Mary comes from the Hebrew for "sea," and
Martha means simply "lady" or "mistress"—are Venus, sea-born goddess across the ancient world, as the evening and the morning star.

On a broader scale, Virgo the Virgin and Pisces the Fishes—the constellations of the equinoctial points in the age that began about the time
of the life of Jesus—appear in Christian myth as the Virgin Mary, on
the one hand, and the constant fish-symbolism of the New Testament,
on the other. Jesus himself is Aries, the sacrificial Lamb of God, the former place of the Spring Equinox that was sacrificed at the turning of
the ages. Christians who are "washed in the blood of the lamb" rarely
realize the roots of that phrase in the astronomical symbolism of the
Mithraic mysteries, where initiates were quite literally doused with the
blood of a freshly sacrificed bull; still, the connection is there.

Christian mysticism and magic

Along with the agricultural and astronomical levels, a mystical level to
Christian myth seems to have been present from the beginning. Trying
to grasp the nature of this part of the symbolism, though, leads quickly
into regions marked "off limits" for a very long time. The core of the
problem is that most of what survives of early Christian mysticism
has been given a label—Gnosticism—which means almost nothing,

but which has become an excuse for a remarkable level of scholarly shoddiness.[10]

Consider the case of the Gospel of Thomas, one of the documents of the "Gnostic" library uncovered in 1945 at Nag Hammadi in Egypt. A collection of sayings attributed to Jesus, it has generally been assigned to a date in the second century, comfortably distant from the life of Jesus, and labeled a "Gnostic" forgery. Unfortunately for this claim, sayings collections are recognized as the earliest form of Christian writings, replaced as early as 80 CE by the first narrative Gospels, and the sayings in the Gospel of Thomas are in many cases more complete and (according to modern "form criticism" methods) more authentic than their equivalents in the official Gospels. What makes this especially uncomfortable is that the Jesus of the Gospel of Thomas explicitly rejects the idea of an apocalyptic end of the world, the cornerstone of much later Christian theology, and teaches the essentially Orphic doctrine that knowledge of the self's true nature—not faith—is the key to salvation.[11]

Another discovery in Egypt offers an even more startling perspective on the question of Christian mysticism. The distinguished Biblical scholar Morton Smith has pointed out that the closest equivalents to many of the most basic elements of Christian faith and practice are to be found in Greek magical papyri that were discovered in Egypt at various times in the nineteenth century. One example is the formula of the Eucharist, in which the participants ritually eat the body and drink the blood of Christ in order to become part of the body of Christ. The closest equivalent to this formula outside of Christian contexts is to be found in the magical papyri, where magicians did exactly this to incorporate into themselves the power of a god. Based on these connections, and a great deal of other ignored data, Smith showed that the historical Jesus of Nazareth may well have been not a prophet, nor the expected Jewish Messiah, but a magician pure and simple.[12]

The exact form of the original mystical interpretations of Christianity is a matter for guesswork, despite these clues. One thing that does seem clear, though, is that the basic Orphic theme of the spirit as a prisoner in matter, and the Orphic rejection of sexuality and physical existence, were present in the Christian tradition from the beginning. At the same time, as we've seen, sacrificial imagery played a critical part in the symbolism of Christianity, and some of the ideas central to the new faith— particularly the dogmas of the Incarnation, which held that the creator of the universe was capable of inhabiting a human body and soul, and the Resurrection, which held that the physical body of Jesus had taken on immortality and divine power, bridging the two worlds Orphic thought sought to separate—pulled Christianity in a very different direction.

While the Orphic current remained dominant, these other patterns of thought were taken up by mystics, particularly in the Eastern Ortho- dox Church. There, even at present, one of the major points of church teaching is the idea of attaining the "resurrection body" or "glorified body"—a transformed body, material but without the limits of mat- ter, equivalent to the body Christ was believed to have had after his resurrection—during one's life through mystical practice. The primary practice used to achieve the resurrection body was a system of mystical prayer known as the Heart Prayer, which combined special methods of breathing and posture with the constant repetition of some variation on the words "Christ have mercy on me, a sinner"; this is still an extremely common practice among Eastern Orthodox monks and laypeople. The experiences of heat and light within the heart center, which this practice can generate, have led some scholars to compare it to kundalini yoga.[13]

In addition to this material, an enormous body of Pagan magical practices and beliefs was absorbed into Christianity from the earli- est times. Some of these were eliminated when the Christian church became respectable and took on the Roman government's hostility toward magic and magicians, but a great deal more came in later, in the early Middle Ages, when the church carried out what amounted to an immense salvage operation on what remained of classical Pagan culture.[14] From this period date many of the Christian "saints" who were lightly disguised Pagan gods and goddesses, and a whole range of overtly magical practices reworked to call on Christian names and powers. All of this remained part of the Christian synthesis until the magical Christianity of the Middle Ages was crushed between the twin wheels of Reformation and Counter-Reformation at the beginning of the modern age.

The Middle Ages thus mark the last flowering of mythological thought in the Western world. The ways of thinking and speaking about the world, which shape the myths of all ages, move through medieval culture, but those ways became increasingly closed to the West, shut first by the Aristotelian rationalism of the late medieval schoolmen and then, more completely, by the rise of materialist thought in the early modern period. The awareness of that loss runs through the culture of the Renaissance, showing clearly in its cult of the "ancient wisdom" of the Corpus Hermeticum and its obsessions with classical myth. After the Scientific Revolution ushered in the first versions of what could be called modern thought, these interests (and the awareness behind them) were largely consigned to the cultural underground of magic, where the remnants of Renaissance occultism mixed with radical religious beliefs and fringe science.

And it was from this underground, finally, that the Hermetic Order of the Golden Dawn emerged near the end of the nineteenth century.

The Golden Dawn

In the year 1887, three English Freemasons—Dr. William R. Woodman, Dr. W. Wynn Westcott, and Samuel Liddell Mathers—founded the Hermetic Order of the Golden Dawn. According to the official history of that Order, this action followed on the discovery of mysterious "Cipher Manuscripts" by Westcott, a correspondence with a Rosicrucian adept in Nuremberg, and the granting of a charter by that adept for the founding of the Order.[15]

This tale, with its heavy borrowings from Masonic legend and popular occult fiction of the time, has been more or less conclusively shown to be a fraud, and the manuscripts themselves date from 1875–1880 at the earliest.[16] Still, the dubious origins of the Order don't invalidate its system of magic, a system that combines and synthesizes in a fairly coherent manner nearly the whole body of traditional Western high magic.

The rituals of the Order have very much of the same quality. Their basic framework is derived from the traditional structure of fraternal lodge ritual, a topic I have explored elsewhere.[17] Their final form is a sometimes clumsy collage of tag-ends of occult wisdom, in which (to give just one example) figures in Egyptian robes representing the Samothracian Cabeiri quote lines from the Chaldean Oracles as they symbolically climb the Cabalistic Tree of Life! In between these two levels, though, is a third level of ritual meaning, and at this level something very different from either of the first two is happening.

Many lodge initiations, fraternal or magical, are constructed around the reenactment of a myth or a legendary story. In an obvious sense, this is true only in the Adeptus Minor Grade of the Golden Dawn, where the rediscovery of the tomb of Christian Rosencreutz as described in the Fama

Fraternitatis forms the center of the ritual. Other rituals within the Golden Dawn structure seem, at least on first glance, to be either a simple hodge-podge of symbols or repetitious climbings and reclimbings of the Tree of Life. Again, appearances deceive. The mythic structure of the Golden Dawn rituals exists on the level of the entire sequence of grade ceremonies, rather than that of individual grades, and the myth around which the whole structure is built is precisely the one we've been exploring. Nor are the connections between this myth and the rituals simply a matter of imagery; as the Golden Dawn's papers show, they were consciously developed into tools of transformative magical work on every level, in a manner few Western magical traditions have been able to achieve.

The journey of the candidate

The best way to outline this process is to follow the candidate through the whole sequence of the Golden Dawn's initiations. Here Osiris and Christ are the central powers, symbols of transformation around which the candidate's journey from Neophyte to Adept is directed.

In the Neophyte Grade, the candidate is brought into the hail blinded and bound. He—the male pronoun will be used here purely for the sake of convenience—is brought to the altar and pledges himself and then the sword of the Hiereus is brought against the back of his neck in a symbolic beheading. This phase is also a dismemberment; in the words of the Z-3 paper:

> (T)he Aspirant of the Mysteries is now, as it were, divided. That is, his Neschamah is directed to the contemplation of his Higher Self attracted to the Hegemon. His natural body is bound and blinded, his Ruach threatened by the simulacrum of the Evil Persona attracted by Omoo-Szathan, and a species of shadow of himself thrown forward to the place of the Pillars, where the Scales of Judgement are set ... Rarely in his life has he been nearer death, seeing that he is, as it were, disintegrated into his component parts.[18]

The candidate then enters the Path of Darkness to begin his search for light, and the rest of the Neophyte Grade centers on that search, the discovery of the light, and the establishment of the light once it is found. The whole pattern relates closely to that of physical death and near-death experiences, as well as to that of birth; in both cases, the breaking of an established pattern results in a journey from darkness to light.

The same pattern can be traced out, however, in the burial and germination of the seed, the first stage of the mythic pattern we've been following. The seed is separated from the plant on which it has grown, cast into the darkness of the soil, and from there strives upward into the light. The symbolism of beheading, dismemberment, burial, and quest, which we've seen in other myths of the type, is present here in detail.

As a reenactment of the Osiris myth, however, this sequence starts halfway through the tale. The first death of Osiris is not part of the Golden Dawn ritual pattern; rather, like the Orphic myth of Dionysos or the Christian legend of John the Baptist, the first death is the beheading/dismemberment. In one sense, then, the formula of the first half of the ritual sequence might best be called the Formula of Dionysos, rather than that of Osiris. Still, there is another sense in which the entombment of Osiris does indeed play a role. The candidate in the Neophyte Grade, the "Inheritor of a Dying World," enters the hall blinded and bound, and thus already symbolically dead. His tomb is the body, and more generally the world of material existence: as with the Orphics, *soma* equals *sema*.

In the four Elemental Grades that follow, the candidate sets out—in the words of the Zelator Grade—"to analyze and comprehend that light" which was revealed in the Neophyte Grade. In large part, these Grades simply extend and complete the symbolism of the Neophyte Grade; they play only a small part in the symbolism we are following here. Still, that part has an echo in the myths. The keynote of these Grades is journeying, and in them the candidate travels through the realms of the four elements and of the lower half of the Tree of Life. These rituals are marked by a series of "admission badges," most of them crosses, which are given to the candidate as he travels; counting the three badges given to the candidate in the Portal Grade, there are fourteen badges in all, the same number as the parts of the body of Osiris. Like Isis, then, the candidate must wander the world in search of the fragments of Osiris—but here Osiris is also the candidate himself.

This is made clear in the first half of the Portal Grade when the candidate recapitulates each of the elemental grades, and from the realm of each element brings a token to lay on the central altar. These tokens represent the candidate himself, in terms taken straight from the myths: "Equated and equilibrated," the Hiereus says at this point, "here lie the Four Elements of the body of Osiris slain." The knowledge lecture on the work between the Portal and Adeptus Minor Grades expands on this:

> As the unborn child, stage by stage, grows through the ancestral history of the race so the Candidate in the Portal by a single circumambulation for each, recalls his past Grades and, at the end of the first point regards their symbols on the Altar as parts of his body, and contemplates them as coming together in one place—the unity of his person.[19]

The scattered portions of the candidate's symbolic body, then, are gathered up in the elemental grades and brought together in the Portal. Placed on the altar, though, they are brought into equilibrium by the symbol of the cross. Freud was far from the first person to envision the cross as a phallic symbol—such ideas filled a whole literature of underground scholarship in the Victorian period—and in this sense the presence of the cross allows Osiris to be reassembled completely, as the Osiris of Egyptian myth could not be.

The cross, however, is also the defining symbol of Christianity, and its appearance here marks a change in symbolism. Up to this point the imagery of the rituals has been linked with Osiris, but now the imagery of Christ comes to the fore.

In the second part of the ritual, the body of Osiris is taken to the Altar of Spirit beyond the Veil—the Veil, which itself, in the words of the Portal ritual, is "the Veil of the Four Elements of the Body of Man, which was offered on the Cross for the service of Man." On that altar the elements of the body are offered up in fire, along with a paper bearing the magical name of the candidate, who thus offers himself up wholly to Spirit. It is at this stage, finally, that the symbol of the Rose Cross—core symbol of the Inner Order and synthesis of the entire magical tradition of the Golden Dawn—is first revealed to the candidate.

As the Neophyte Grade represents birth and death, the sequence of initiation from Zelator to Portal thus can symbolize both the process of growth by which the newborn child becomes an adult, and (in Western magical lore of that period) the process of purification in the after-death state, by which the soul between lives learns from its experiences.[20] For our purposes, though, these ways of approaching the rituals are less important than the archaic agricultural pattern we've been tracing. The seed that sprouted in the Neophyte Grade roots in the earth in the Zelator Grade, and through air, water, and the fire of the sun

grows to maturity in the Portal Grade. Next, in the ancient cycle, follows the harvest.

This is represented in the Adeptus Minor Grade, amid the framework of a symbolism we've already discussed. The candidate here is
judged, condemned, and crucified, and his body is marked five times
with the point of a dagger. He is then taken down from the cross and
brought into a tomb. All of this corresponds exactly to the Biblical
legend of Jesus, as well as to the sacrificial myth behind it. At this point,
though, a different element appears, for in the tomb is the figure of the
Chief Adept as Christian Rosencreutz, who speaks to the candidate and
exchanges implements with him before bidding him leave the tomb.
It is the Chief Adept, in the third point of the ritual, who rises from the
dead and proclaims the triumph of life.

The legend of Christian Rosencreutz is an example of the mythology
of burial discussed earlier; like Merlin in his tower of glass, the founder
of the Rosicrucian Order is at once dead and present, having passed
from physical activity into another, deeper order of being. Still, this
element of the ritual is an addition to the basic pattern, not a departure
from it. After the Adeptus Minor Grade comes the Adeptus Major, the
last Grade apparently worked in the original Golden Dawn system, and
there the myth has its proper conclusion.

The original version of the Adeptus Major Grade, which was
apparently written by Samuel Mathers, has not been published and
may have been lost. Two later versions, one by A. E. Waite and the other
by Robert Felkin, have survived.[21] These differ in details, but the basic
pattern (which probably dates from Mathers' own work) is the same
in both. The candidate, bound to silence, is brought into the Vault and
there laid in the Pastos like a corpse in the tomb. A vigil is kept outside,
and at intervals a gong sounds and sentences are spoken. Finally—after
six hours, in Waite's version—the candidate is raised from his symbolic
death and receives the secrets of the Grade.

Here the candidate takes the place of the Chief Adept of the Adeptus
Minor ritual and completes his passage through the myth of Christ. The
imagery used in both versions of the ritual has much to do with light
and darkness, just as in the Neophyte Grade, and this connection is
not accidental. If the Neophyte Grade is taken as birth, the two Adept
Grades discussed here are death and burial; if the Neophyte is death,
these Grades are incarnation and birth. A circle is formed from planting
to harvest and from harvest to planting.

The way of transformation

In the Golden Dawn system, then, the old mythology of the agricultural sacrifice is taken over and used as a framework for initiation. Some elements of the ancient synthesis are lacking—for example, despite the importance of the Equinoxes in the Golden Dawn, and despite the attention given to astrology and the celestial sphere in the Order's papers, the astrological symbolism we've seen in other sources seems to have made little impact on the Order's system. Nonetheless, the connections are clear and point out important parts of the process of ritual.

In this process, the figures of Osiris and Christ mark two phases of the initiatory work. They also represent, in turn, two stages in that path of inner transformation which is the focus and goal of the Golden Dawn system. The first stage, corresponding to Osiris, is marked by the dissolution of the self, while the second is the reintegration of the self in a higher form: the solve and coagula of alchemy, in which the keys to the Great Work are said to be contained. More precisely, in alchemical language, the Neophyte Grade is the nigredo or "black phase" of corruption and disintegration; the elemental grades correspond to the cauda pavonis or "peacock's tail," in which various colors (Cabalistically, the colors of the bow Qesheth) mark the different aspects and transformations of the materia; the Portal Grade, when the white sash is received by the candidate, is the albedo or "white phase," the coagulation of the Stone, while the adept grades represent the rubedo or "red phase," when the Stone takes on the attributes of the Sun.

All this can be understood in a psychological sense, as a process of change in the psyche through self-knowledge. Such an interpretation is a valid one, backed by many of the Golden Dawn documents, and it forms the basis for a range of more or less Jungian readings of the rituals. There's another way in which these symbols can be read, though. This second way deals not with the psyche alone but with the total human being on all levels, including the physical, and the transformation it seeks touches on every part of human experience and existence.

The clearest expression of this broader way of thinking about the rituals is found in a Golden Dawn paper entitled Flying Roll X, written by Samuel Mathers and circulated among the Adepti of the Order. Subtitled "Concerning the Symbolism of Self-Sacrifice and Crucifixion contained in the 5=6 Grade," this dense and often murky paper touches on a range of themes we've seen already, and applies them to the work of the magician in some startling ways.[22]

Central to this interpretation is the relationship between the different levels of the self: the *nephesh* or vital self, the *ruach* or ordinary conscious self, the *neshamah* or higher spiritual self, and the transcendent aspects of the self beyond the neshamah. Normally, in Golden Dawn teaching, the *ruach* is cut off from the higher levels of the self, and the chief task of the magician is to restore this connection.

This, according to Flying Roll X, is the chief practical meaning of the myth of the Dying God. The *ruach*, the ordinary self, must perfect itself through self-knowledge, and then offer itself up to the *neshamah* as a vehicle for the Higher. The center of the personality, in other words, must shift from the conscious self to a higher, spiritual self of which ordinary consciousness knows nothing. The prospect is a terrifying one—such a surrender of the self to the unknown is perceived as death, and often involves states like those of near-death experience—but this act of self-sacrifice on the part of the *ruach* brings about the rebirth of the wholeness of the self. Again, this acts on all levels:

> (O)nly after incurring that physical death, as it were, could the other divine parts suddenly come down and make it the resurrected or glorified body, which, according to the description, had after the Resurrection, the apparent solidity of the ordinary body, and the faculties of the Spirit body. Because if you can once get the great force of the Highest to send its ray clean down through the Neschamah into the mind, and thence, into your physical body, the Nephesch would be so transformed as to render you almost like a God walking on this Earth.[23]

The stress on the body of the resurrection in this passage points to one of the more unexpected of the Golden Dawn's borrowings, but it is not the only reference to Eastern Orthodox mystical techniques in the Golden Dawn material. In the Adeptus Minor ritual itself, the Chief Adept makes what may be an explicit reference to the Heart Prayer technique mentioned above:

> And let the humble prayer of thy heart be: "God, be merciful to me a sinner, and keep me in the pathway of truth."

It's possible that these things were borrowed from the Eastern Church at some earlier point in the development of the tradition that gave rise to the Golden Dawn.[24] The core symbols of the Rosicrucian movement of the late Renaissance—the heart as Sun, the phoenix in flames, the pelican wounding its own breast, the central image of the rose on the cross itself—can be read as references to the experiences caused by work with the Heart Prayer, but there doesn't seem to be any evidence that the Golden Dawn itself used this interpretation, or taught or practiced the methods involved. Nor, it's worth noticing, does the path of transformation outlined in Flying Roll X seem to have received much practical attention in the Order; as happened so often in the Golden Dawn's history, the deeper possibilities of the system were all but ignored in favor of play-acting and power politics.

Still, the approach to Christian myth and symbolism used throughout the Golden Dawn's magical system reaches toward a resolution of many of the conflicts and confusions surrounding Christianity at present. To the founders of the Golden Dawn, the myths of Christ were wholly compatible with those of Osiris, as well as those of other Pagan divinities, and the whole structure of Christian religion was understood as a variation on a set of themes common in the religions of the Western world. This understanding enabled the Golden Dawn to draw on useful features of Christian spirituality while discarding many of the less valid elements of that tradition—a project that might well be worth carrying on in the present.

In addition, the path of transformation illuminated by the Order's rituals offers a valid way for the modern magician. It blends the perspectives of the Orphic tradition with those of the older way of sacrifice, using Christian and non-Christian myth alike as the instruments of fusion. The work of inner transformation is described, in Golden Dawn materials, in ways that sound very much like the Orphic quest to transcend physical existence; when the Hierophant in the Neophyte Grade speaks of "earthly or material inclination, that has bound into a narrow place the once far-wandering soul," or when the new Hierophant in the Equinox ceremony describes the purpose of the Golden Dawn's work as "so to lead the Soul that it may be withdrawn from the attraction of matter," they use the language of more than 2000 years of Western esotericism. The answer that is offered by these rituals to the problems of human existence, though, is not the abandonment of the material world, but the transformation of matter through interaction with spirit: the ancient way of sacrifice made new.

In place of the blood sacrifices of an earlier time, the Golden Dawn Adept offers up his or her own self, transmuting matter into spirit and spirit into matter within the temple of the body, restoring the ancient pattern of exchange while opening up the higher possibilities of his or her ng. This vision is not unique to the Golden Dawn system—the Order's founders were pack rats rather than creators, and very little in their system is unique in any sense—but there are few places in the magical traditions of the West where the possibilities of this approach to the world have been as thoroughly set out for those who are willing to look.

Notes

1. This version of John Barleycorn—as with any folk song, there are scores of them—was collected at the Seattle, WA Folklife Festival in May 1992.
2. I have adapted this account from Plutarch's version in *De Iside et Osiride*.
3. *The Elder Edda, Havamal*, 139.
4. Llew's death is recounted in the "Tale of Math ap Mathonwy" in the *Mabinogion*. The triple death is found in a number of Scottish and Irish legends; see Stewart, R. J., *The Mystic Life of Merlin* (Routledge & Kegan Paul, 1986).
5. See R. J. Stewart's fascinating essay "The Tomb of a King" in Stewart, R. J., *The UnderWorld Initiation* (Aquarian, 1985, pp. 261–266).
6. The seminal work on ancient astronomical symbolism is de Santillana, G. and von Dechend, H., *Hamlet's Mill* (repr. David Godine, 1977), a masterly book weakened only by the authors' inability—epidemic among modern scholars of mythology—to realize that myth can have more than one purpose and speak of more than one part of human experience.
7. See Ulansey, D., *The Origin of the Mithraic Mysteries* (Oxford University Press, 1989).
8. The Orphic tradition is discussed in Warden, J., ed., *Orpheus: The Metamorphoses of a Myth* (University of Toronto Press, 1982), and explored sympathetically in Fideler, D., *Jesus Christ Sun Of God: Ancient Cosmology and Early Christian Symbolism* (Quest, 1993).
9. John 3:30.
10. See Davies, S.L., *The Gospel of Thomas and Christian Wisdom* (Seabury, 1983) for a discussion of the scholarly evasions surrounding the catchall category "Gnosticism," which serves essentially as a dumpster for unpopular evidence concerning the early years of Christianity.
11. The Gospel of Thomas may be read in Robinson, J.M., ed., *The Nag Hammadi Library* (Harper Collins, 1988, pp. 126–138). See also Davies, op. cit.

12. Smith, M., *Jesus the Magician* (Harper & Row, 1978).
13. The classic text of this tradition in Eastern Orthodoxy is the Philokalia. See *The Philokalia: The Complete Text* (Faber and Faber, 1983). See also Matus, T., *Yoga and the Jesus Prayer Tradition* (Paulist, 1984), a capable summary by a practitioner of both the Heart Prayer method and Hindu yogic traditions.
14. See Flint, V., *The Rise of Magic in Early Medieval Europe* (Princeton University Press, 1991) for an eye-opening study of the absorption of magic into Christianity. Meyer, M., ed., *Ancient Christian Magic* (Harper Collins, 1994) is another useful source.
15. The official version of the history of the Order is discussed in Gilbert, R. A., *The Golden Dawn Companion* (Aquarian, 1986, pp. 1–29).
16. See Howe, E., *The Magicians of the Golden Dawn* (Routledge & Kegan Paul, 1972).
17. Greer, J.M., "The Hall of Thmaa: Sources and Transformations of Golden Dawn Lodge Technique," in *The Golden Dawn Journal Vol. 3* (Cicero, C. and Cicero S.T., eds., Llewellyn, 1995).
18. Regardie, I., *The Golden Dawn* (Llewellyn, 1971, Vol. 3, p. 135).
19. Regardie, *The Golden Dawn*, Vol. 1, 185.
20. Compare, for example, this section of the initiatory sequence with material on reincarnation by Golden Dawn member W. B. Yeats; see Yeats, W.B., *A Vision* (Collier, 1966).
21. The Waite version of the Adeptus Major ritual is in Regardie, I., *The Complete Golden Dawn System of Magic* (Falcon, 1984, Vol. 7, pp. 127–158). The Felkin version is in Zalewski, P., *Secret Inner Order Rituals of the Golden Dawn* (Falcon, 1988, pp. 100–125).
22. Flying Roll X is included in Mathers, S.L. et al., *Astral Projection, Ritual Magic and Alchemy* (Destiny, 1987, pp. 131–140).
23. *Ibid.*, 136.
24. Regardie, I., *The Golden Dawn* (Llewellyn, 1971, Vol. 2, p. 227). I am indebted to Carl Hood Jr. for pointing out the Eastern Orthodox references within the Golden Dawn material.

Bibliography

Davies, S.L., *The Gospel of Thomas and Christian Wisdom* (Seabury, 1983).

de Santillana, G. and von Dechend, H., *Hamlet's Mill* (repr. David Godine, 1977).

Fideler, D., *Jesus Christ Sun Of God: Ancient Cosmology and Early Christian Symbolism* (Quest, 1993).

Flint, V., *The Rise of Magic in Early Medieval Europe* (Princeton University Press, 1991).

Gilbert, R. A., *The Golden Dawn Companion* (Aquarian, 1986, pp. 1–29).

Greer, J.M., "The Hall of Thmaa: Sources and Transformations of Golden Dawn Lodge Technique," in *The Golden Dawn Journal Vol. 3* (Cicero, C. and Cicero S.T., eds., Llewellyn, 1995).

Howe, E., *The Magicians of the Golden Dawn* (Routledge & Kegan Paul, 1972).

Mathers, S.L. et al., *Astral Projection, Ritual Magic and Alchemy* (Destiny, 1987, pp. 131–140).

Matus, T., *Yoga and the Jesus Prayer Tradition* (Paulist, 1984).

Meyer, M. ed., *Ancient Christian Magic* (Harper Collins, 1994).

Regardie, I., *The Golden Dawn* (Llewellyn, 1971, Vol. 3, p. 135).

Regardie, I., *The Complete Golden Dawn System of Magic* (Falcon, 1984, Vol. 7, pp. 127–158).

Robinson, J.M., ed., *The Nag Hammadi Library* (Harper Collins, 1988, pp. 126–138).

Smith, M., *Jesus the Magician* (Harper & Row, 1978).

Stewart, R. J., *The UnderWorld Initiation* (Aquarian, 1985, pp. 261–266).

Stewart, R. J., *The Mystic Life of Merlin* (Routledge & Kegan Paul, 1986).

Ulansey, D., *The Origin of the Mithraic Mysteries* (Oxford University Press, 1989).

Warden, J., ed., *Orpheus: The Metamorphoses of a Myth* (University of Toronto Press, 1982).

Yeats, W.B., *A Vision* (Collier, 1966).

Zalewski, P., *Secret Inner Order Rituals of the Golden Dawn* (Falcon, 1988, pp. 100–125).

Magic, politics, and the origins of the "mind-body problem"

After quarrels among the founders caused Caduceus: The Hermetic Quarterly *to fold in 1997, I started a similar quarterly.* Abiegnus: A Journal of the Western Esoteric Traditions *ran for two years, and I ended up writing two substantive pieces for it. This one, an exploration of the historical roots of modern consciousness, drew heavily on the studies I'd done earlier in the decade while completing a degree in Comparative History of Ideas at the University of Washington.*

Part One

The "mind-body problem," as it's usually called, is among the most persistent themes of debate in the intellectual history of the modern West. Like most of the really difficult issues of philosophy, the problem itself is simple enough to state. In Western cultures, most people experience themselves as a composite of two elements: a material body, on the one hand, and an apparently non-material mind, self, personality or soul—terms and conceptualizations vary—on the other. The problem is how to account for the relations and interactions between these two very different things.

The theories that have been proposed over the last 400 years have ranged all over the map, but two general approaches have predominated. The first approach postulates two realms of being, one mental, one material, and then finds some way to connect the two within the human organism. The other approach postulates that only one of the two realms is real, and then finds some way to derive the experienced reality of the second one from it.

These two approaches, which we can call dualism and reductionism respectively, have varied in popularity. In the early modern period, for example, dualist approaches predominated. At present, by contrast, the more common approach is a form of reductionism that defines mind as a side-effect (an "epiphenomenon," in philosopher's jargon) of the physical body's nervous system. This latter notion is commonly presented these days as simple common sense—but like most forms of "common sense," it relies on a whole series of assumptions which do not necessarily bear close examination.

There are some severe problems, practical and philosophical, with dualist and reductionist approaches alike. A whole literature has grown up to examine these problems exhaustively, though, and they need not be revisited here.[1] What has been less discussed is the way that both these stances, and the "mind-body problem" itself, are artifacts of history. Neither the problem nor its proposed solutions are built into the human condition; rather, they are products of specific transformations in the cultural history of the West.

The history of ideas does not, after all, take place in a vacuum. A theory or a system of thought commonly has a double life in society; it plays a part in the intellectual life of its time, but it may also serve as an ideological stance for interests that are far from intellectual in nature. The struggle between capitalism and Marxism that ended with the demolition of the Berlin Wall, for example, was about a great deal more than the relative merits of Adam Smith's economic theories compared to those of Karl Marx. So, too, the apparently abstract questions discussed above have served interests that are far from abstract. Equally, in turn, the conflict between interests and factions has had far-reaching effects on the way we perceive some of the most basic elements of the universe of human experience.

Between body and mind

One way to start looking at the origins of the "mind-body problem" is to consider some alternative ways of looking at the self. Human cultures are diverse, and there have been a dizzying number of ways that people have interpreted their own experience of themselves. One particular pattern, though, deserves attention here.

This is the model that makes mind and body two of a larger number of levels of the self. Most people with any sort of background in esotericism, Western or Eastern, are familiar with models of this kind; common examples include the Indian system of subtle bodies and chakras, borrowed by Theosophists in the late nineteenth century and now common to a wide range of traditions, and the various levels of the self traced out in Cabalistic lore.[2] Connected to this model, in a large proportion of the cases where it appears at all, is a concept generally called "vitalism"—the idea that biological life is somehow closely linked to an energy or subtle substance that is closely related to breath, and as often as not called by the same word.

The multiple-level model of the self and the theory of vitalism relate to the "mind-body problem," as it's usually posed, in a curious way. In traditions where these two approaches are used, the relation between mind and body is rarely seen as a problem at all, because it's precisely the level of vital energy that bridges the gap between ordinary consciousness and physical matter. In systems of medicine and physiology based on these approaches—both Indian Ayurveda and traditional Chinese medicine are good examples—vital energy is seen as the glue that holds mind and body together.

It's common in the modern West to treat such ideas with a good deal of scorn. One rarely encounters the term "vitalism" in modern scientific writings, for example, without finding the word "naive" in front of it. Still, naive or not, traditions based on these principles have a good deal to show for themselves. There is a very extensive literature on the extraordinary physical feats performed by those trained in "vitalist" disciplines, ranging from healing arts such as acupuncture through the various kinds of yoga to the Asian martial arts.[3] It might be suggested that a theory that enables human hands to shatter brick and stone may not be quite as naive as it sounds.

The implications of all this for the "mind-body problem" are intriguing. From the standpoint of these other traditions, certainly, there's something missing from the problem as it's usually stated. The bond that unites body and mind, the whole realm of vital energy, has vanished from the modern Western perspective.

But where did it go? And why?

The Great Chain of Being

This disappearance is a relatively new thing, historically speaking. The Western world, before the modern period, relied on models of the self closely in accord with the ones we've been examining. There were more than one of these models, but all shared the core assumption that mind and body were only two parts of a complex whole.

This shared assumption rested on Biblical authority and medieval Catholic theology, which defined body, soul, and spirit as the three main levels of the whole self. In the hands of medieval philosophers, though, all three of these levels were analyzed further. Much attention was paid to a threefold division of the soul, borrowed ultimately from Plato:[4] the rational soul, or what we would now call the mind, was accompanied by the animal soul—the seat of the passions and energy—and the vegetable soul—the seat of what we still call "vegetative processes" such as breathing, digestion, and growth. The two lower levels of the soul intertwined with the "vital spirit"—the familiar concept of life energy once again—and with the four humors, subtle substances that held the physical body in a state of health or, by their imbalance, brought about disease.[5]

Compared to modern ideas, this medieval concept of the self is striking both for its complexity and for its underlying unity. Each part of the whole self has its place in a spectrum between the highest spiritual self and the material body. Each one, to shift metaphor, is a link in a chain that joins spirit to matter without a break.

It's precisely in this latter metaphor that we approach one of the core concepts of medieval thought, the idea of the Great Chain of Being.[6] This is the idea that everything participates in a single hierarchy of being, from the throne of God down to the depths of formless matter. Everything in existence, no matter how strange it might be, has its own proper place in the Chain which nothing else can fill. Like the notes of the octave or the sequence of natural numbers—to both of which the Chain was often compared—each link of the Chain of Being was seen as relating to all the others according to common, universally true patterns. At the same time, the individual links were wildly diverse, as diverse as the universe of human experience itself.

This same habit of thought expressed itself with equal force in the politics and religious beliefs of the age. Socially, the Middle Ages had taken feudalism to its logical extreme, producing a system in which one kind of relationship—the bond of feudal subordination between lord and vassal—functioned at every level of society from serf to king. The result was a complex patchwork of local rights and obligations, united by an overarching structure relevant to all. The same pattern reflected itself in medieval Christianity, where the giddy profusion of local saints, festivities, and customs existed within a common framework of doctrine and ritual, and where ancient philosophy, Biblical authority, and lightly whitewashed Pagan practices coexisted with a high degree of comfort.[7]

Thus, the Great Chain of Being served as a philosophical model for the whole of the medieval world—or, from another perspective, the structure of the medieval world gave ideas such as the Great Chain of Being a good deal of appeal, especially to those who benefited from that structure. This is an example of the double life of ideas mentioned earlier. Whatever the intrinsic virtues of any idea, it also has the effect of justifying certain ways of organizing society and distributing power and resources. A philosophy that describes the world as a hierarchy, in which everything has its proper place, will tend to support and justify hierarchical political systems such as feudalism in which every person has his or her proper place. In order to overthrow such a system, in turn, it's often necessary to overthrow its favored philosophy. This is precisely what happened in the history of the early modern West.

Central to this process was the transformation of Europe from a feudal society in which wealth and power were a function of the control of real estate, to a mercantile, proto-capitalist society in which wealth and power came from control over money and trade. Advances in transport and communication fostered this shift, but it was far from a simple matter of technological progress. The catastrophe of the Black Death also played a role; so did conflicts within the feudal hierarchy, in which kings of several nations turned to the urban merchant class for help against the nobility. So did many other factors that had far less to do with political or economic power. The result was the tremendous cultural upheaval of the Renaissance.

Currents of change

Any attempt to outline the Renaissance in a few paragraphs would be an invitation to failure, and unnecessary to boot; there are many good studies on that age and the way it transformed the Western world.[8]

No such attempt will be made here. The situation that concerns us is the one that took shape toward the end of that period, when the wave of the Renaissance was receding across Europe and what historians call (awkwardly enough) the "early modern" period was beginning.

At that time, three broad currents of thought dominated the scene in Europe. One of these was based on what was left of medieval Christian tradition. Protestant Reformation and Catholic Counter-Reformation had left little of the old spirit of synthesis intact; the need to defend theological claims against the scathing attacks of rationalists and sectarian enemies forced all sides in the religious disputes of the time to harden their boundaries. Still, a more or less conservative Christianity still remained as a powerful intellectual force in most of Europe. Because of its connections with the medieval philosophical movement known as Scholasticism, it was often called the "Scholastic philosophy."[9]

The second current had more complex origins. In classical times, some traditions of thought argued for a view of the world based entirely on the evidence of the senses and the operations of logic. Some of these, particularly as reflected through the writings of Aristotle, became ancestral to a medieval school of philosophy known as Nominalism, which held similar beliefs.[10] In the Renaissance, Nominalist ideas spread in many directions and took a wide range of forms. All this ferment coalesced toward the end of the Renaissance with the rise of a new, radically materialist philosophy of nature, armed with an equally new experimental method that allowed questions about nature to be put to practical tests. We now call this new philosophy modern science; in the late Renaissance, it was called the "mechanical philosophy."[11]

Then there was the third current—that complicated blend of Cabala, Platonism, magic, and alchemy that we now call Renaissance Hermeticism.[12] The Renaissance discovery of ancient texts of magical philosophy, above all the books attributed to Hermes Trismegistus, sparked an explosive revival of magic. Over the next few centuries, philosophers of magic such as Marsilio Ficino and Cornelius Agrippa found ways to fit the whole body of Western occult tradition into a more or less cohesive whole. The resulting system was a major influence on Renaissance culture and remained influential, especially in England and Germany, as the Renaissance waned. Because of its heavily alchemical emphasis in the late Renaissance, its most common name at the time was the "chemical philosophy."[13]

These three currents—Christian orthodoxy, emergent natural science, and Renaissance Hermeticism—did not develop in isolation from one another, and many of the writers and scholars of the age held views drawn from more than one. It has even been argued, notably by the late Dame Frances Yates, that much of what became the mechanical philosophy had its roots in the Renaissance revival of magic.[14] Still, it's important to recall that these currents were recognized, during the period we're discussing, as three distinct movements of thought. To speak of the Scholastic, mechanical or chemical philosophies in any educated circle in sixteenth- or seventeenth-century Europe was to name things that everyone present would recognize at once.

A three-handed poker game

At the same time, it was to name things that tended to have very specific allegiances among the forces contending for power in that turbulent time. The three philosophies just described served as the intellectual bases for a sort of three-handed poker game, with theories about the nature of the universe as the chips, and political and social power as the ultimate stake.[15]

The Scholastic philosophy was supported above all by the aristocracy. Scholastic emphasis on hierarchy and tradition, in philosophical and religious contexts, had an obvious harmony with the claims of the nobility to a status they had held since the dawn of the feudal age. Equally, major educational and religious institutions in most parts of Europe were at once bastions of Scholasticism and integral parts of a political order still dominated by the nobility. The alliance was thus both logical and nearly unavoidable.

Similar considerations brought about a link between the mechanical philosophy and the rising power of the merchant classes. The new philosophy of materialist science rejected tradition as a basis for knowledge, just as the emerging capitalist system rejected it as a basis for the distribution of power and wealth; the mathematical focus of the new sciences made sense to men who relied on financial calculations to earn their living; the promise of unlimited technological advance held out by writers such as Francis Bacon appealed to classes which owed their existence to developments in transport and manufacturing technologies. Members of the merchant classes thus became important early proponents of the mechanical philosophy, just as they tended to favor religious currents—the Puritan movement in England, Jansenism in France—that downplayed the role of aristocratic pomp and ritual.

The third current, the chemical philosophy, had its own allies, from at least two different levels of society. On the one hand, the Hermetic tradition drew support from the very top of the feudal pyramid; many aspects of Hermetic teaching—particularly its use of solar symbolism—could be used (and were used) as ideological props for the expansion of royal power. Many of the royal courts of the late Renaissance accordingly became centers of Hermetic thought and practice.[16]

On the other hand, the chemical philosophy also had a good deal of support from a much more modest social level. The spread of printed books provided easy access to education to an increasingly large and important class of skilled craftsmen. Their interests ranged all over the intellectual map, but a substantial involvement in Hermeticism was an important trend.[17] Here the relevant factor may well have been the promise of power as a function of knowledge, and the innate egalitarian bias of a philosophy that valued inner attainment rather than outer wealth or rank.

It would be a massive oversimplification to pretend that any of these alliances was a uniform social fact. People's beliefs, then as now, can't always be reduced purely to political or economic factors; certainly, there were plenty of noblemen interested in the mechanical or chemical philosophies, just as there were merchants who held conservative religious beliefs or dabbled in alchemy and workmen and kings who looked on Hermeticism with horror. Still, there's enough truth to the broad alignments to make a very specific kind of sense of the poker game's aftermath.

The breaking of the chain

The three-way struggle outlined above might have ended in any number of ways; writers of the "alternate history" genre might easily trace any number of possible outcomes, each one with its own profound impacts on the modern era.[18] The way it did turn out was complex in detail but simple enough in outline. In effect, two of the players formed an alliance and squeezed out the third. The two that allied were the Scholastic and mechanical philosophies, or to put the same thing in a different way, the aristocracy and the new capitalist class; the one that was squeezed out was the chemical philosophy—along with its supporters at both ends of the social spectrum.

The way in which this process worked out, as a set of parallel transformations in the political and philosophical spheres, will be covered in the second article of this series. It may be worth pausing here, though, to glance ahead to the central factor that made an agreement possible between Christian traditionalism and the new natural sciences: a radical division of the universe into two realms, one of spirit, one of matter. This gambit allowed each of the two systems of thought to have its own territory, safe from intrusion by the other. The idea of an absolute distinction between matter and spirit came to function, in effect, as a demilitarized zone between the factions.

Philosophically, this settlement took its keynote from the work of Rene Descartes (1596–1650), whose theories divided mind and body so radically that the direct intervention of God had to be used to explain the apparent connections between them. Politically, it emerged first in England, as the tumults of the seventeenth century forced the feudal and mercantile elites to form an alliance against threats from absolutist royalty and working-class revolutionary movements alike.

The armed truce thus established was unstable at best, and finally collapsed for good around the middle of the nineteenth century. While it lasted, though, it shaped the consciousness of the modern West in ways that are still very much with us today.

Crucially, those effects include the modern West's blindness to magic, vital energy, and nearly everything related to them. The separation of the universe into two realms demanded the breaking of the Great Chain of Being and a systematic and corrosive neglect of those parts of human experience that once linked the ends of the broken chain together.

Notes to Part One

1. The critique of the dualist model dates back at least as far as William Blake, that of reductionism to the nineteenth century. See Roszak, T., *Where the Wasteland Ends* (Doubleday, 1973) and Sheldrake, R., *A New Science of Life* (Park Street Press, 1985).
2. The literature on Indian subtle-body traditions, even in Western languages, is too substantial even to summarize here. For one account of

modern Cabalistic teachings on the subtle bodies, see Greer, J.M., *Paths of Wisdom* (Lewellyn, 1996, pp. 54–64).

3. A wide range of this material is reviewed in Murphy, M., *The Future of the Body* (Tarcher, 1992).
4. The Platonic source for this division is *Republic* 435a–441c.
5. The medieval model of the human organism, which remained in use well into early modern times, has been recently explored in Tobyn, G., *Culpeper's Medicine* (Element Books, 1997).
6. See Lovejoy, A.J., *The Great Chain of Being* (Harvard University Press, 1936), in which the history of the concept is covered at length.
7. Flint, V., *The Rise of Magic in Early Medieval Europe* (Princeton University Press, 1991) is a good introduction to the medieval Pagan-Christian synthesis.
8. See the excellent annotated bibliography in Debus, A.G., *Man and Nature in the Renaissance* (Cambridge University Press, 1978, pp. 142–152).
9. The Scholasticism of the Middle Ages included strong components of what we would now call natural science and rationalism—a point often neglected in modern histories. See Gilson, E., *Reason and Revelation in the Middle Ages* (Scribner's, 1938).
10. See of Ockham, W., *Philosophical Writings* (Franciscan Institute Publication, 1957) for important early works in this movement.
11. The literature on the "mechanical philosophy" is immense, as might be expected. A good introduction is Dijksterhuis, E.J., *The Mechanization of the World Picture* (Oxford University Press, 1961).
12. Yates, F.A., *Giordano Bruno and the Hermetic Tradition* (University of Chicago Press, 1964) remains the best introduction to this movement.
13. See Debus, A., *The Chemical Philosophy* (Science History Publications, 1977).
14. See Yates, op. cit.; also Westman, R. and McGuire, J.E., eds., *Hermeticism and the Scientific Revolution* (University of California Press, 1977).
15. For the social dimension of the philosophical debates of the late Renaissance, see Jones, R.F., *Ancients and Moderns* (Washington University Press, 1961); Webster, C., *The Great Instauration* (Holmes and Meier, 1976); and Wightman, W.P.D., *Science in a Renaissance Society* (Hutchinson, 1972).
16. See, for instance, Hart, V., *Art and Magic at the Court of the Stuarts* (Routledge, 1994), and Evans, R.J.W., *Rudolf II and His World* (Claredon Press, 1973).
17. See Yates, F.A., *Theatre of the World* (Routledge & Kegen Paul, 1969) for a discussion of the role of skilled workmen and the breaking of traditional class barriers in the rise of late Renaissance Hermeticism.

18. The only attempt in this direction I know of is Anderson, P., *A Midsummer Tempest* (Tor Books, 1984), set in an alternate history in which every word written by Shakespeare is literally true. (This may also be the only fantasy novel written in modern times in which nearly all the dialogue is in iambic pentameter.)

Bibliography

Anderson, P., *A Midsummer Tempest* (Tor Books, 1984).

Debus, A., *The Chemical Philosophy* (Science History Publications, 1977).

Debus, A.G., *Man and Nature in the Renaissance* (Cambridge University Press, 1978).

Dijksterhuis, E.J., *The Mechanization of the World Picture* (Oxford University Press, 1961).

Evans, R.J.W., *Rudolf II and His World* (Claredon Press, 1973).

Flint, V., *The Rise of Magic in Early Medieval Europe* (Princeton University Press, 1991).

Gilson, E., *Reason and Revelation in the Middle Ages* (Scribner's, 1938).

Greer, J.M., *Paths of Wisdom* (Lewellyn, 1996, pp. 54–64).

Hart, V., *Art and Magic at the Court of the Stuarts* (Routledge, 1994).

Jones, R.F., *Ancients and Moderns* (Washington University Press, 1961).

Lovejoy, A.J., *The Great Chain of Being* (Harvard University Press, 1936).

Murphy, M., *The Future of the Body* (Tarcher, 1992).

Ockham, W., *Philosophical Writings* (Franciscan Institute Publication, 1957).

Roszak, T., *Where the Wasteland Ends* (Doubleday, 1973).

Sheldrake, R., *A New Science of Life* (Park Street Press, 1985).

Tobyn, G., *Culpeper's Medicine* (Element Books, 1997).

Webster, C., *The Great Instauration* (Holmes and Meier, 1976).

Westman, R. and McGuire, J.E., eds., *Hermeticism and the Scientific Revolution* (University of California Press, 1977).

Wightman, W.P.D., *Science in a Renaissance Society* (Hutchinson, 1972).

Yates, F.A., *Giordano Bruno and the Hermetic Tradition* (University of Chicago Press, 1964).

Yates, F.A., *Theatre of the World* (Routledge & Kegen Paul, 1969).

Part Two

Any quest for the historical origins of our current habits of mind-body dualism runs up against powerful psychological barriers. As we saw in the first part of this article, the basic understanding of reality most common in the Western world—the understanding that divides human experience into two separate realms, one of consciousness, the other of matter—is fairly recent as a historical phenomenon, and its origins are tied up closely with those of modern Western science.

Like the ruling ideology of any other culture, this latter has become thickly encrusted with myths. Since our society tends to put its mythology into historical form, the history of science has ended up dominated by a set of potent mythic images that have remained almost unquestioned until quite recently.

One recent and very acute study of the emergence of modern science has characterized this mythic context as the idea that "the new science [became] an essential, perhaps the essential, part of our culture largely because educated, literate Europeans ... perceived its self-evident truth and in in that moment of illumination embraced it," and comments: "We cannot write a history that presumes that the educated Western elite and the scientists they read possessed an inherent rationality that was superior to previous or contemporary rationality, which in turn made their new version of the natural world obviously correct."[1] This caution is all the more necessary because a very large number of histories of science take precisely this stance.[2]

For 300 years, in fact, the history of the Scientific Revolution has most often been presented as the record of a small number of brilliant and intrepid men who broke through centuries of superstition to create the first true science of nature. This is certainly one way to talk about the emergence of modern scientific thought, of course, but it's far from the only one—and like most mythic narratives, it tends to blur the complexity of real historical processes in favor of the simplicity that makes a good story. For all practical purposes, though, this story is the origin myth of the modern world.

Challenging a living myth can be a dangerous business, but it may also be a necessary one. The habit of thinking about ourselves as thinking minds inhabiting material bodies, rather than using more inclusive or less sharply divided categories, is arguably at the root of a number of the problems—social as well as psychological—that we face in the present time.[3] If, as I hope to show, that habit has its roots in the politics surrounding the Scientific Revolution rather than in anything more meaningful to us in the present, a good case could be made that it's high time we consider alternatives.

This article has a more modest goal, however. Its intention is simply to explore how we got where we are—how an unusual way of thinking about the nature of the self became common sense in the Western world, and stayed that way for some 300 years.

Part One of this article outlined the background to that change. In this section, we'll be examining the specific historical events that surrounded the birth of the modern way of envisioning the self. Our focus will narrow to a single country—England, where the historical process we're following passed through its critical stages—and to a single period, the late seventeenth century, when English society was shaken to its core by revolutionary change.

The world turned upside down

The English Civil War and the short-lived republic that followed it form a watershed in the history of the Western mind. To a remarkable extent, the habits of thought we think of as "modern" came into being in response to the upheavals, intellectual as well as political, of that period. This is hardly surprising. England was the first nation in the world to make the transition from an agrarian economy to an industrial one. The English Civil War marks the critical period when power on all levels of English society slipped out of the hands of the feudal aristocracy and into those of the rising capitalist class.

The historical background can be outlined simply. The English king, Charles I, had dissolved Parliament after a series of increasingly bitter political struggles, and for more than a decade ruled England as an absolute monarch. A combination of crises forced him to call a new Parliament in 1640, which proved no more biddable than its predecessor. When he attempted to dissolve Parliament again, it refused to disband. The result was war.

In the first part of the struggle the Royalist forces came close to victory, but the balance turned with the rise of Oliver Cromwell, a country squire turned Parliamentary general, and his New Model Army. Drawn mostly from the lower classes, rigorously trained and drilled, the New Model Army was the first truly modern army in Europe, and it proved unstoppable in the field. By 1645 the war was over, and Charles was a prisoner of Parliament; in 1649 he was executed.

By then, however, a new factor had entered the picture. The English Parliament, then as now, consisted of the House of Lords, made up of aristocrats and bishops, and the House of Commons, made up of elected representatives. At that time, however, and up to the nineteenth century, voting rights were restricted to men whose personal property was worth more than a fairly substantial sum. The House of Commons thus represented the rural gentry and the urban merchant and capitalist classes, rather than the "commons" in any broader sense. In order to recruit soldiers and win popular support, though, the Parliamentary party had presented its side of the struggle in terms of securing the rights and liberties of Englishmen of all classes. What the winning side discovered to its horror, once the fighting was over, was that the common people of England were more than ready to take such slogans literally.

The result was an extraordinary outpouring of radical political ideas.[4] A swarm of popular movements—Ranters, Levelers, Diggers, Seekers, Fifth Monarchy Men, Muggletonians, and many more—sprang up all through England, proposing unheard-of ideas such as voting rights for all men, free public education and health care, the abolition of class privilege, and the separation of Church and State. Some went further, calling for equal rights for women, rejecting Biblical religion altogether, equating Nature or Reason with God, or calling for the complete abolition of private property. To an astonishing extent, most of the themes of the next 300 years of radical politics came surging out all at once.

The extent of the threat this popular movement posed to the existing order should not be underestimated. Over a period of several months in 1647, Leveller agitators came within an ace of seizing control of the New Model Army itself. In a less dramatic but potentially more transformative action, Digger groups in a dozen places seized unoccupied land to establish what we would now call communes, free from the control of landlords and gentry.[5]

The threat to the New Model Army was suppressed by Cromwell late in 1647, largely by rounding up and shooting the more outspoken agitators; soon after, Cromwell himself seized power as Lord Protector and overwhelmed his opponents by sheer military force, and England entered a decade-long period of dictatorial rule as arbitrary as anything in Charles' reign. The Protectorate was little more than an armed truce, though, and when Cromwell died in 1658 the radicals came out in force almost at once.

During the next two years, England went through a repeat of the crisis of 1645–1649. Agitators reappeared in the army ranks, and pamphlets calling for drastic social changes circulated widely. The gentry and merchant classes were thus faced with a Hobson's choice. As an anonymous pamphleteer put it in 1660: "Can you at once suppress the sectaries and keep out the King?"[6] Across England, those men of property and influence who had once supported revolution decided that they could not, and chose the devil they knew. Accordingly, in 1660, Charles' heir returned from exile, taking the throne as Charles II, and England's experiment with the republican government was over.

The legacy of the Civil War years did not vanish with the new king's accession, though. Quite the contrary; though a Stuart sat on the throne, he was there because he had been summoned back by a vote of Parliament. Power had shifted decisively to the House of Commons and the classes it represented. This shift was sealed in 1688 when Charles II's successor James II, who tried to resume the absolutist ways of the earlier Stuarts, was overthrown and replaced with contemptuous ease.

At the same time, the gentry and merchants who had spearheaded the rebellion against Charles I were by no means as interested in radical change, or as unwilling to compromise with the aristocracy, as they had once been. Their brush with the Levellers had left a large fraction of them far more aware of the advantages of social order, and far more interested in finding some accommodation that would guarantee the stability of a system from which they also benefited.

"The Familistical-Levelling-Magical temper"

That accommodation took its form, to a great extent, in response to the forces it was intended to hold in check. The ideas of the Civil War radicals had many roots: radical Protestantism; a range of all-but-forgotten social ideas; the simple experience of living in a society where the word of a rich man in court outweighed the testimony of a dozen poor witnesses, and where the Enclosure Acts were already being used to break up rural society for the benefit of landowners. Another major source, though, was Renaissance Hermeticism. There was an esoteric component, an important one, to the radical thought of the Civil War period, and this played a crucial part in the aftermath.

The redoubtable Gerrard Winstanley provides one example out of many. The chief theoretician of the Diggers, Winstanley showed a solid familiarity with alchemical thought all through his famous series of political pamphlets, and used alchemical metaphors as the foundation for his economic theory.[7] He also recommended that astrology be taught in the universities.

The same recommendation was made by John Webster in his proposals for college reform in the 1650s; Webster also called for natural magic and alchemy to be put into the curriculum. Such proposals, significantly, led to Webster being labeled a Leveller. One opponent of Webster's ran together the views of the Family of Love, a radical Protestant sect, with Levelling and esoteric traditions, to accuse him of encouraging "the Familistical-Levelling-Magical temper."[8]

It would be easy to run off any number of further examples—the list of important figures among the radicals who were followers of Jakob Böhme, for example, or who were students or practitioners of astrology—but the point is made. What makes that point ironic is that an equally strong Hermetic presence, of a different kind, also existed at the other end of the social and political spectrum. As an excellent study by Vaughan Hart has demonstrated that the court of Charles I and his father, James I, had been rife with Hermetic influences.[9] The "court Hermeticism" associated with the Medicis of Florence, and with the Elector Palatine Frederick whose short reign may have given inspiration to the original Rosicrucian manifestoes,[10] had one of its last significant flowerings in that context.

Thus, Renaissance Hermeticism ended up associated with both of the losing sides of the Civil War years—with the absolutism of the Stuarts as well as with the popular radicalism of the Levellers. While it was not the only ideological threat faced by the post-Civil War compromise, it had a long if somewhat checkered history and some degree of intellectual respectability. In an age when philosophies had the same kind of political impact that economic theories do now, it could not simply be ignored.

Such concerns took on greater weight after 1688 when the threat of popular unrest was joined by the danger of a Stuart restoration backed by foreign troops. Across the Channel, the French King Louis XIV had revoked the Edict of Nantes, abolishing religious freedom in his realm; the absolutism England had shaken off with James II was resurgent on the continent, backed by a Catholic Church increasingly committed to a hardline stance. Until 1746, when the last serious Stuart rising under Bonnie Prince Charlie was crushed at Culloden, the new English order was at constant risk.

An ideology for England

The survival of the English political compromise, in fact, demanded an ideological and philosophical compromise as well. The victors of the Civil War had gone into that struggle, in very many cases, as supporters of Puritan religion and the mechanical philosophy of Descartes; the Royalist faction, largely aristocratic at least in leadership, tended to support the established Anglican church and the traditional Scholastic philosophy of Christian Aristotelianism.[11]

By the 1660s both sides were looking for something else—a new philosophical stance that would combine elements of both, providing a common ground for all sides while supporting the new social and political order. The need for such a new stance was widely recognized at the time, and there were possibilities being proposed as early as the 1650s.[12]

The old Scholastic philosophy in its pure form was unacceptable to the Puritans, and after 1688—since Scholasticism on the continent was largely a Catholic preserve—guilt by association with the Catholic Stuarts rendered it politically suspect. The mechanical philosophy in its pure form, as presented by Descartes among others, gave too little room to God and too much to matter for post-Civil War tastes; English writers of the 1650s and 1660s insisted that Cartesianism led directly to an atheism that smacked far too much of the Ranters and Levellers. A way had to be found to fuse the two.

And a way was found. That way nowadays bears the name of its most brilliant exponent, Isaac Newton, but at the time it drew on the work of many different writers, scholars, and publicists. Its political dimensions were clear from the outset and discussed openly at the time.[13] Its public face was the Royal Society, which had begun to take shape as an "Invisible College" as early as the 1640s, and which made no bones about its role as a support for the new status quo.

The new ideology took its keynote from older versions of the mechanical philosophy but veered off from them in a telling way. The mechanistic theories popular in the early seventeenth century had stressed that the only things that actually existed in the world known to the senses were matter and empty space. Atomic theories of matter, dating back to the ancient Greek thinker Democritus and publicized in classical times by the Epicurean school, had been dusted off and revived by a number of mechanical philosophers, among them Descartes and Pierre Gassendi.

These mechanistic theories tried to account for every kind of physical interaction in terms of the actions of solid particles in direct contact with one another. In some cases, this led to a certain amount of absurdity; in Descartes' theories, for example, the phenomenon of gravity had to be explained by postulating little corkscrew-shaped particles that emanated from the surface of the earth, screwed themselves into objects and yanked them downwards.

What the new English theories did was to take this framework and introduce one other ingredient—the existence of forces that could act at a distance, without the need for direct physical contact. Gravity was the classic example, but the effects of magnetism and static electricity were also explained in the same way. Such forces were a staple of older theories of the physical world; they had been banished from earlier versions of the mechanical philosophy, but the Newtonian system readmitted them in a limited way.

The reasons for this are highly revealing. In his published writings, Isaac Newton simply stated that his formulae explained how gravity worked, and refused to tackle the more troublesome question of what gravity itself was. In his private journals, and in the writings of many of the publicists who made use of his work to spread the new scientific gospel, things are put a little more clearly: gravity, and other forces that act at a distance, are manifestations of the will of God; the planets stay in their orbits because God keeps them there.[14] In effect, Newton and the other "natural philosophers" of the Royal Society had taken the cosmos of the mechanical philosophy—made up wholly of atoms and the void—and made it the lower story of a two-story universe. The upper story, in turn, was defined by the theology of the Anglican church, which had its roots in a watered-down and moralized Scholasticism. Thus, the Newtonian achievement was a matter of joining together two seemingly irreconcilable philosophical systems—combining a mechanical philosophy of nature with a Scholastic philosophy of religion. A consequence of this division, though, was that the universe had to be split into two radically different realms, one of matter, one of spirit.

Here, too, Descartes led the way; his mechanical philosophy had divided the universe into matter and spirit, leaving the latter in the hands of orthodox theology. The Cartesian system allowed almost no contact between the two worlds, though, and this was why the English thinkers saw Cartesian thought as halfway to atheism; what difference was there, they argued, between a God who has no influence on the universe and a God who doesn't exist at all? What the Newtonian synthesis allowed was a way for the spiritual world to affect the physical one. Metaphorically, it left a narrow stairway open between the two stories of the cosmos, so that traditional claims of divine power and influence could still be justified under the new scheme.

At the same time, access to that stairway had to be tightly controlled. Common to nearly all of the radical sects and movements of the Civil War years was a belief in the "Inner Light," the individual's ability to have personal experience of spiritual truth. That same quest for direct experience also motivated alchemists, magicians, and Hermeticists of all kinds; as the conservative Catholic reaction on the continent gained strength, too, its propaganda came increasingly to rely on claims of miracles, visions, and other personal contacts with the spiritual realms— mediated, to be sure, by the institutions of the Church.[15]

To admit that spirit could affect matter was to leave the door open for all these things, and even to the claim, shocking to respectable thinkers at the time but central to magical philosophy, that the equation could be made to work in reverse—that material actions could shape spiritual realities. While several of the important members of the Royal Society— Newton among them—were interested in alchemy and other Hermetic sciences,[16] the political situation militated against any stance that would provide ammunition to the radical sects.

The ghost in the machine

The solution to this problem was in some ways the critical ingredient in the whole Newtonian synthesis. This was the redefinition of God in rational terms. In place of the intensely personal and concrete God of earlier versions of Christianity—a God defined in terms of mythic acts and passions, miracles and mighty deeds—the Newtonian vision brought in a deity of pure reason whose main function in the cosmos was that of establishing and maintaining natural laws. This rationalized God was not entirely new; some Greek conceptions of divinity, especially those of Plato and Aristotle, also stressed reason as the central divine attribute. To the classical philosophers, though, this rational God was closed up in his own contemplations, free of contact with the messy world of matter. The Newtonian God, by contrast, was the guarantor of order in nature, the "clockmaker god" who established the gearwork of the universe, wound it up, and then let it run without miraculous interference.

The political subtext in all this is hard to miss, especially coming at a time when the concept of a government of laws was first being proposed as an alternative to royal absolutism and popular radicalism alike. There is a close parallel, in fact, between this new image of God and the new definition of monarchy in England after 1688, in which the king's first duty was to maintain the laws and the established religious and political order. Nor was this political dimension missed at the time; speeches and sermons all through the late seventeenth and early eighteenth centuries relied explicitly on Newton's physics and its associated theology as a justification for the post-1688 political settlement.[17]

What may be a little less obvious, but is of critical importance to our theme, is the effect of the same image of God on the image of the self. Whatever its broader relevance, the Hermetic idea that microcosm mirrors macrocosm is a psychological fact; each culture's idea of the universe is its image of the human writ large. By defining the universe as a collection of lifeless matter controlled from above by a rational God, the new natural philosophy fostered a definition of the self as a "ghost in the machine," a rational mind connected in some limited manner with an inert material body. As we'll see in the third part of this article, though, this image had further developments ahead of it, and those developments again had political roots.

Notes to Part Two

1. Jacobs, M., *The Cultural Meaning of the Scientific Revolution* (Temple University Press, 1988, p. 6). I have used Jacob's survey extensively here; see her "Bibliographic Essay," pp. 255–261, for additional sources.
2. This "triumphalist" perspective on the history of science is almost universal in works written before the 1970s and is still defended by a number of philosophers of science.
3. This thesis has been argued cogently by a number of writers in recent decades. See especially Roszak, T., *Where The Wasteland Ends* (Doubleday, 1972).
4. Hill, C., *The World Turned Upside Down* (Maurice Temple Smith, 1972) remains the standard text on the astonishing array of radical movements in England during the Civil War period.

5. For the Levellers and the New Model Army, see Hill, pp. 46–58. For the Diggers, see Hill, pp. 86–120.

6. Quoted in Hill, pp. 280–281.

7. There is a good-sized literature on Winstanley, and many of his works have been reprinted in modern times. See Wilson Hayes, T., *Winstanley the Digger* (Harvard University Press, 1979); Hill, op. cit., esp. pp. 86–120 and 313–319, and Winstanley, G., *The Law of Freedom and Other Works* (Penguin, 1973).

8. Hill, op. cit., p. 233. For the Webster debates, see also Debris, A., ed., *Science and Education in the Seventeenth Century: The Webster-Ward Debate* (Elsevier: 1970).

9. Hart, V., *Art and Magic at the Court of the Stuarts* (Routledge, 1994).

10. This is the thesis of Frances Yates' famous *The Rosicrucian Enlightenment* (Chicago: 1964).

11. This has been a point of contention recently, but Merton, R.K., *Science, Technology and Society in Seventeenth-Century Society* (Harper Torchbooks, 1970) and Webster, C., *The Great Instauration* (Duckworth, 1975) adduce solid evidence for the claim. See also Jacobs, pp. 73–76.

12. See Jacobs, pp. 84–104.

13. *Ibid.*

14. Most of Newton's discussions of religious issues are in his manuscript notebooks; like his alchemical work, they received little attention until quite recently. See Jacobs, pp. 84–91.

15. This same sort of argument was made by several important figures in the Cambridge Platonist movement of the 1650s and 1660s, who collected evidence of witches and ghosts in the hope of proving the reality of supernatural beings.

16. Newton's alchemical work has been usefully discussed by Teeter Dobbs, B.J., *The Foundations of Newton's Alchemy* (Cambridge University Press, 1975).

17. See Jacobs, pp. 105–135, and Gascoigne, J., "The Holy Alliance: Newtonian Natural Philosophy and Latitudinarian Theology" (Ph.D. dissertation, Cambridge University, 1981).

Bibliography

Debris, A., ed., *Science and Education in the Seventeenth Century: The Webster-Ward Debate* (Elsevier: 1970).

Gascoigne, J., "The Holy Alliance: Newtonian Natural Philosophy and Latitudinarian Theology" (Ph.D. dissertation, Cambridge University, 1981).

Hart, V., *Art and Magic at the Court of the Stuarts* (Routledge, 1994).

Hill, C., *The World Turned Upside Down* (Maurice Temple Smith, 1972).

Merton, R.K., *Science, Technology and Society in Seventeenth-Century Society* (Harper Torchbooks, 1970).

Jacobs, M., *The Cultural Meaning of the Scientific Revolution* (Temple University Press, 1988, p. 6).

Roszak, T., *Where The Wasteland Ends* (Doubleday, 1972).

Teeter Dobbs, B.J., *The Foundations of Newton's Alchemy* (Cambridge University Press, 1975).

Webster, C., *The Great Instauration* (Duckworth, 1975).

Wilson Hayes, T., *Winstanley the Digger* (Harvard University Press, 1979).

Winstanley, G., *The Law of Freedom and Other Works* (Penguin, 1973).

Part Three

At the dawn of the eighteenth century, as Part Two of this article showed, the worldview of Newtonian science—an understanding of the experienced world that defined it in terms of particles of dead matter obeying rational laws, overseen at a distance by an abstract, equally rational God—had become the dominant ideology in Britain and an important presence in the broader world of European scholarship and science. As an ideology, it was closely associated with the political compromise born in the aftermath of the English civil wars of 1640–1660, and cemented by the "Glorious Revolution" of 1688, when the Stuart dynasty (restored in 1660 as part of the original compromise) was finally driven from the British throne once and for all.

In the aftermath of 1688, the Newtonian worldview became deeply entrenched in British educational and cultural institutions, at least in part because its image of a universe governed by laws rather than arbitrary powers served to support the new political ideology of a society governed, at least in theory, on the same basis.[1] Still, even in England, it was not the only game in town, and in the broader context of European thought, the Newtonian synthesis, was only one of many different theories of the nature of the universe. In France, at that time the intellectual center of Europe, Cartesian writers fiercely assailed Newton for allowing "occult properties" such as action at a distance into his system. Paracelsian and other alchemical theories remained prominent in the German-speaking states of central Europe well into the eighteenth century,[2] and the traditional science based on Aristotle's writings remained a major presence in the educational system for many years to come. In addition, new currents in religion interacted freely with the scientific debates of the age.

A hundred years after the "Glorious Revolution," by contrast, this plethora of different approaches had been narrowed down to two. The first of these two was, again, the Newtonian system, increasingly allied with the theological stance known as Deism—the idea of a "clockmaker God" who had created the universe and, so to speak, wound it up, and then let it run by itself without any further divine interference. For all practical purposes, the new science made religion an irrelevancy by denying spiritual beings and forces any power to shape the world, ghettoizing God in an increasingly nebulous Hereafter. The one alternative that retained any public presence at all was an increasingly rigid

and literalistic Christianity, forced into oppositional stances as spokes-
men for scientific ideology claimed more and more of knowledge as its
exclusive preserve.

Historians of science, up until quite recently, typically explained the
shift from the many different worldviews of 1688 to the two of 1788
by way of a triumphalist model that claimed, often in so many words,
that the sheer self-evident truth of the new science drove all other contenders out of existence in short order, except among the ignorant and
superstitious.[3] Some versions of this argument have also pointed to the
technological achievements made possible by science as a reason for the
triumph of the Newtonian paradigm. Unfortunately for such claims,
Newtonian approaches—useful as they were for understanding planetary motion and the like—proved frustratingly hard to apply outside of
a fairly narrow range of phenomena. Magnetism, static electricity, and
combustion, to name only three important topics of scientific discussion
in the eighteenth century, remained areas of controversy all through the
period.[4] Furthermore, the application of science to technology was still
mostly a hopeful fantasy in 1788; it was the middle of the nineteenth
century before scientific research began to have a major impact on the
rate of technological change.

Scientific triumphalism aside, what drove the narrowing of intellectual options in the century after the Glorious Revolution? Few works on
the history of ideas deal with this question with any degree of adequacy.
Fortunately, we have a somewhat comparable set of events within living
memory as a guide to insight. The set of events I have in mind are those
surrounding the development of economic thought in the Western
world in the twentieth century. It's often forgotten that in the first three
decades of this century, the various schools of capitalist and Marxist
economic ideas were only a small part of a much wider spectrum of possibilities. Schools of economic thought such as guild socialism, Social
Credit, distributism, and syndicalism, nearly all of them forgotten now,
were major theoretical forces through the 1930s—and in some cases,
significant political ones as well.[5]

What happened? Here, at least, the answer is clear enough. Two of
the options were taken up as ideological battle flags in the struggle
between the Russian Empire (aka "the Soviet Union") and its client
states, on the one hand, and the Anglo-American alliance and its client
states (aka "the Free World"), on the other. This struggle has sometimes
been portrayed as a matter of cynical power politics, but the Cold War

was at least in part a struggle over ideological issues as such, and there were plenty of people on both sides who believed passionately in the principles at stake.

Whatever the mixture of motives involved, though, the effect was a radical hardening of orthodoxies. "Those who are not with us are against us" was the motto on both sides; to question the claims made for capitalism in Cold War America was to risk being called a Communist subversive, in exactly the same way that those who questioned the claims of Marxist theory in Russia during the same period were assumed to be lackeys of American imperialism. In such an environment, alternative ways of thinking do not flourish.

The eighteenth-century Cold War

It is often forgotten nowadays, though, that this aspect of the Cold War was nothing particularly new. The fusion of ideology with national self-interest that marked the Cold War period is a common feature throughout world history and has had a major impact on the history of ideas. The struggle between Athens and Sparta did much to shape the thought of classical Greece; equally, the history of medieval theology and philosophy was profoundly affected by the struggles between Popes and Holy Roman Emperors.

A similar situation existed in the period after 1688, with Britain and France as the two major contenders. Much of the struggle was a matter of pure economic and political advantage; both nations had major colonial empires in North America, significant commitments in the turbulent politics of Central Europe, and similar ambitions to succeed Spain as the major political and economic power in Europe and the world. Even without ideological differences, a collision was probably inevitable, but ideological differences there were in plenty. Britain was Protestant, France Catholic; the French king could blithely proclaim "I am the State" and by a stroke of his pen revoke the religious freedom granted by one of his predecessors, while the British Parliament had executed one king and driven another from the throne for their attempts at the same sort of absolute rule. Under the circumstances, Europe faced an epic clash. The ensuing struggle unfolded over more than a century, from 1688—when the Stuarts, backed then and later by France, were driven out in favor of William of Orange—until 1815, when Napoleon's Old Guard broke before Wellington's lines at Waterloo. During that time, French and British troops fought each other on four different continents, and the major European wars of the period all pitted Britain and France against each other.[6]

Of the two contenders, Britain was in many ways the underdog: smaller, less populous, poorer in resources and in infrastructure. The French also started out with the advantage of a fifth column inside Britain itself—the Jacobites, supporters of the exiled Stuart dynasty.[7] James Stuart, called the "Old Pretender," and his son Charles were effectively puppets of the French king, maintained and supported by the French royal treasury while their usefulness lasted, and all the major Jacobite risings in Britain were backed by French money and troops. (Romantic historians and novelists have tended to ignore the fact, well-attested in contemporary sources, that the army of "Bonnie Prince Charlie" included a sizable contingent of French soldiers—"technical advisors," as we would now say—who fought in uniform at Culloden.) The status of the Jacobites as French-backed quislings, to put matters in modern language, was well understood in Britain at the time, and goes far to explain the lack of support Jacobite ventures encountered in the Scottish Lowlands and England.

This was the context, then, faced by the new political order in Britain after 1688. The partisans of that order had embraced the Newtonian paradigm and its associated religious and political ideas largely in response to the demands of Britain's internal politics. The fall of the Stuarts, though, made the phrase "Britain's internal politics" an oxymoron. The French connections of the Stuarts, the ambitions of France's "Sun King" Louis XIV, and the role of Britain's new king William (who was also the Dutch head of state) as the central figure in a Protestant coalition opposed to French expansionism, guaranteed that the events of 1688 would have continent-wide implications.

The cultural consequences

It also guaranteed that, for many people in England and elsewhere, questions of the truth or falsehood of the Newtonian approach would be inextricably caught up in the political sphere. Throughout continental Europe, Newtonian science was embraced by those who favored religious toleration or constitutional monarchy on the English model, and it was opposed by those who supported religious uniformity and absolutist monarchy. In England, by contrast, the Newtonian system was backed by those who benefited from the post-1688 settlement, and opposed by those who stood against the existing power structure. It's on this political basis, for example, that Voltaire's support of the Newtonian system and William Blake's rejection of it can best be understood.[8] Both favored liberal political reforms in their respective countries; for Voltaire, Newton was an alternative to the status quo; for Blake, Newton *was* the status quo.

Similar patterns can be traced through many aspects of eighteenth-century history. The development of Freemasonry, for example, was powerfully shaped by these factors.[9] The original "blue lodge" Masonry, comprising the three Degrees of Entered Apprentice, Fellow Craft, and Master Mason, developed out of stoneworkers' craft guilds in the seventeenth century and was enthusiastically taken up by the new English governing elite in the early years of the eighteenth. As it spread to the rest of Europe, it functioned as a forum for British ideas concerning religious tolerance, politics—and Newtonian science. (The Catholic fulminations against Masonry have much of their origin here, since the Catholic hierarchy was consistently on the side of France.) Early Scottish Rite Masonry, by contrast, appears to owe its origin to attempts by Jacobites to co-opt Masonic secrecy and organization in the cause of French absolutism, and thus tended to jettison the egalitarian stance of the blue lodges in favor of an aristocratic, chivalric ethos and a stress on obedience to unknown "Secret Chiefs." M. K. Schuchard, whose works on the history of Western occult traditions are required reading in this context, has built a compelling case for major Masonic involvement on both sides in the Jacobite rising of 1745, with the blue lodges supporting the Hanoverian regime, while the Scottish Rite and the Swedish Rite carried out operations in support of the Stuart cause.

A full account of the twists and turns of the struggle between Britain and France would involve far too much detail to cover here, and may be looked up in any number of good works of eighteenth-century political and intellectual history. For our present purposes, the one crucial point is that Britain won—not only in a political and military context but ideologically as well. In another parallel to the more recent Cold War, the French system collapsed from within. Attacked by ceaseless British propaganda, and undermined by fashions for British cultural imports such as Freemasonry, the ideology of Catholic and monarchical absolutism lost its support even among the French governing classes, and without its ideological backing the French monarchy soon went under.

Ironically, this turn of events led not to peace but, ultimately, to the resumption of the struggle on a far larger scale. Here, at least for the moment, history has not repeated itself; post-communist Russia has yet to find its Bonaparte.

The long-term consequences of this sequence of events, however, are still with us. The two opposing positions formulated in the crucible of eighteenth-century polities remain, in the eyes of many people in the modern West, the only two conceivable stances from which the universe can be faced. Materialist science and traditionalist Christianity continue to be presented as the only real alternatives, and all other viewpoints are consigned—by popular opinion as well as the polemics of the dominant systems—to the lunatic fringe.

The implications of history

One of the things that comes through most clearly from a study of the history of ideas is the extent to which actions and decisions made in one age, sometimes for the most momentary of advantages, have consequences that can echo for centuries. For nearly 2000 years, it has been argued, Christians have been waiting for the end of the world on a day-to-day basis because early Christian writers inserted traditional apocalyptic themes into early "sayings Gospels" to bolster their standing as Jewish patriots in the anti-Roman rebellion of 66 CE.[10] Similarly, modern scholars who state (as a supposedly objective definition) that religion differs from magic in that religion supplicates, while magic seeks to compel, are simply parroting a standard argument of Protestant polemics, directed first against Catholicism, then against the Hermetic tradition, and finally against non-Western religions in general. In this context, it may not be out of place to talk about the implications of the history this article has tried to explore.

The scientific worldview, like the basic reality maps of every culture, has often been presented as something close to self-evident truth, but as we've seen, it emerged—again, like its equivalents in other cultures—out of very specific historical and political circumstances. We've traced the ways in which that worldview and its associated ideology rose to dominance in the Western world, and came to be seen as simple common sense, despite the fact (discussed at length in Part One of this article) that they exclude many aspects of common human experience from the realm of the officially real. To deal with such questions on a purely historical basis, though, is to avoid issues that are far from purely historical at present. The scientific worldview is not simply an intellectual construct; it serves, like all worldviews, to justify certain claims to authority while ruling out others.

Central to this political role is the habit of seeing the value of world-views in purely black-and-white terms. Either a way of understanding the universe is true, according to this way of thinking, or it isn't, and the only available middle ground is that of "partly true and partly false"— a status accorded, in many modern histories of science, to those older teachings posthumously labeled "on the right track." On this basis of "single vision," to borrow Blake's term, the most common argument for the exclusive validity of the scientific worldview is built. Since our modern technology is based on the scientific worldview, the argument typically goes, and since our technology works (much of the time, at least), it is often claimed that the currently accepted version of the scientific model of reality is true, in the most complete and positivistic sense of that word, while all other views are simply false.

The problem with arguments of this sort is that they are based on a very simple-minded approach to questions of knowledge. Implicitly or explicitly, they assume that the human mind can directly experience, and human languages (either verbal or mathematical) exactly express, absolute unmediated truth. Such claims went out the window when epistemology—the branch of philosophy that concerns questions about what can be known—got past the toddler stage in the Western world.[11] In India and other Asian societies, where epistemology has been far more central to religious thought and where it has accordingly reached far greater heights of sophistication, such notions were laughed out of court centuries ago.[12]

It's fairly easy to prove,[13] even without the heavy artillery of Buddhist logic or Vedantist epistemological analyses, that the only things we can actually perceive—the images of the outside world (and our inside world) that are reflected in our consciousness—are at the end of various intricate Rube Goldberg chains of physical, biochemical, neurological and cognitive transformations, playing a game of "telephone" in which the message must not only pass from player to player but, in essence, from language to language as well. The messages passed on via ran-domly bouncing photons, chemical reactions in the retina, electrical charges rushing along neuron axons, and the whole complex hierarchy of cognitive processing that turns the end result of these into what we call visual perception, end up having only the most distant relationship with whatever it is that the photons on the far end of the process are originally hitting.

Equally, it's relatively easy to prove that the theories, categories, and systems we construct to understand our experiences of the world are precisely that—constructions—with no guaranteed relevance to the universe "out there," much less to the system of "natural laws" that modern science invokes as the ultimate foundation of that universe. While Edward Sapir and Benjamin Whorf may have gone too far in their celebrated hypothesis that all human thought consists of manipulations of language, and is thus completely conditioned by linguistic habits, it's clear that verbal or mathematical theories of nature simply provide us with cognitive models that duplicate, with more or less precision, various roughly regular phenomena in the universe of our experience. Einstein's theory of relativity, for instance, simply models the way our experience of light seems to behave; it does so by way of conceptual constructs (such as the term "photon") and mathematical constructs (such as $E=mc^2$) that allow our experience to be grasped in a way that makes sense to the human mind. The bizarrely indeterminate nature of light—it can be made to behave like a wave or like a particle, depending on what kind of experiment you choose—should remind us that while we know plenty about what happens when we make light do different things, we actually know very little about what it *is*, in any deep sense.

The dual nature of our experience of light, as wave or as particle, points to one of the most crucial issues about worldviews. In some practical applications, it's important to think of light as a pattern of waves, so that various kinds of wave-behavior can be put to use. In others, it's important to think of light as a collection of particles, so that various kinds of particle-behavior can be used. Both models of the nature of light, in other words, have their uses. To insist that light is particulate, and that the wave-model is untrue, is to discard a tool that makes it possible to do some extremely useful things; the same is true if the positions are reversed and the particle-model is rejected.

The lesson here is that true and untrue may not be the best categories for understanding our mental models of the universe. More useful and less useful may be more relevant—and it's always worth asking, "More or less useful for what?"

Obviously, for understanding certain common, relatively stable aspects of the universe of our experience—the aspects we normally file under "physics," "chemistry," "engineering," and so on—the world-view that was born in the Scientific Revolution, and reached full maturity in the nineteenth century, has much to recommend it. Many of the publicists of modern institutionalized science, though, go from this valid point to the far more questionable claims that their worldview is true in an absolute sense, that all others are false, and that any phenomenon that doesn't fit within the limits of that worldview must be imaginary or fraudulent. It's as though the partisans of the particle theory of light were to reject the wave-theory unconditionally, and then go on to condemn diffraction and the Doppler effect as rank superstition or fakery.

The question that needs to be debated, then, is not whether the scientific worldview is true—that is ultimately unanswerable—or even whether it is useful—that is unquestionable, at least in certain areas of the universe of human experience. The question that has to be asked, and potentially answered, is whether we benefit from a situation in which that one worldview is entrenched as the only acceptable way of looking at the universe, and in which anything that seems to offer a challenge to it is rejected with an attitude not far from crusading zeal.

It's worth noting in this context that such attitudes are by no means universal among the world's cultures. In many societies, while certain core elements of the common worldview are held inviolable, there is an enormous amount of flexibility at the margins, and intrusions of new or strange ideas are typically handled with a graceful combination of laissez-faire and cultural inertia. Thus, for example, Indian culture was easily able to assimilate Greek astrology and medicine, despite the existence of well-developed native forms of both these sciences; Hindu pandits simply stretched the borders of their own paradigms to embrace the knowledge of the Yavanas.

Furthermore, and critically, the basic worldviews of non-Western cultures rarely if ever exclude any substantial portion of ordinary human experience from their definitions of reality. The phenomena of vital energy, for example, can be described and discussed quite readily within most other worldviews, and in fact vitalistic ideas are extremely common outside the modern West. It is our present culture that is the odd one out, and perhaps—whatever the political implications—it may be high time to reconsider this stance.

Notes to Part Three

1. See Part Two of this article, and particularly notes 1 and 17, for sources on the political character of Newtonian thought.
2. The *Aurea Catena Homeri*, a major work of alchemical theory and practice, was published in Austria as late as 1723. See Kirchweger, A.J., *Aurea Catena Homeri: The Golden Chain of Homer* (Bacstrom, S., trans., Kuntz D. and Greer, J.M., ed., forthcoming). [Note: this was never published.]
3. See the critique of such approaches in Jacobs, M., *The Cultural Meaning of the Scientific Revolution* (Temple University Press, 1988).
4. See, for example, Cohen, I.B., *Franklin and Newton* (American Philosophical Society, 1956), and Conant, J.B., *The Overthrow of the Phlogiston Theory* (Harvard University Press, 1950).
5. For the economic movements mentioned here, see Webb, J., *The Occult Establishment* (Open Court Publishing Company, 1976, pp. 81–114).
6. These were the War of the Grand Alliance (1690–1695), the War of the Spanish Succession (1702–1713), the War of the Austrian Succession (1738–1748), the Seven Years' War (1756–1763) and the Napoleonic Wars (1793–1815).
7. The portrayal of the Jacobite movement here differs, of course, from the romantic version common in all too many histories. For points raised here concerning the Jacobite movement, see especially McLynn, F., *The Jacobites* (Routledge & Kegan Paul, 1985); Speck, W.A., *The Butcher: The Duke of Cumberland and the Suppression of the 45* (Blackwell, 1981); and Szechi, D., *The Jacobites: Britain and Europe 1688–1788* (Manchester University Press, 1994).
8. For Voltaire, see especially *The English Letters*; for Blake, nearly all the late poems, especially *Milton* and *Jerusalem*. A perceptive study of the role of politics in Blake's thought is Erdman, D., *Blake: Prophet Against Empire* (Dover, 1954).
9. For the history of Freemasonry, see Hamill, J., *The Craft* (Crucible, 1986); le Forestier, R., *La Franc-Maçonnerie Ternpliere et Illuministe aux XVIIIe et XIXe Siecles* (Paris, 1970); Schuchard, M.K., "Freemasonry, Secret Societies, and the Continuity of the Occult Traditions in English Literature" (Ph.D. dissertation, Univerisity Texas, 1975); and Stevenson, D., *The Origins of Freemasonry: Scotland's Century* (Cambridge University Press, 1988). For the origins of Masonic Templarism and the chivalric Degrees, see especially Partner, P., *The Murdered Magicians: The Knights Templar and their Myth* (Oxford University Press, 1982). For the role of different Masonic obediences in the 1745 Jacobite insurrection,

see Schuchard, M.K., "Yeats and the 'Unknown Superiors': Swedenborg, Falk, and Cagliostro," in Roberts, M.M., and Ormsby-Lennon, H., *Secret Texts: The Literature of Secret Societies* (AMS Press, 1995). Interestingly, possible links between Masonry and the Jacobite movement have also inspired a recent novel by fantasist Kurtz, K., *Two Crowns for America* (Spectra Books, 1993), although it's worth noting that the actual conspiracies mapped out by Schuchard and others go considerably beyond Kurtz' fictional ones.

10. This is the argument of Davies, S.L., *The Gospel of Thomas and Christian Wisdom* (Seabury: 1983).

11. It's interesting to note that the rise of a fully coherent epistemology in the West took place in Britain in the eighteenth century, during the course of the same events covered in this article. Relevant figures here are John Locke (1638–1704), George Berkeley (1685–1753), and David Hume (1711–1776).

12. The English-language literature on Hindu and Buddhist epistemology is still limited. See Shankaracharya, *Vivekachudamani (Crest-Jewel of Discrimination)* (Advaita Ashrama, 1966), for a classic Hindu work on the subject.

13. This topic is covered in slightly more detail in my book Greer, J.M., *Paths of Wisdom: The Magical Cabala in the Western Tradition* (Lewellyn, 1996), pp. 3–29.

Bibliography

Cohen, I.B., *Franklin and Newton* (American Philosophical Society, 1956).

Conant, J.B., *The Overthrow of the Phlogiston Theory* (Harvard University Press, 1950).

Davies, S.L., *The Gospel of Thomas and Christian Wisdom* (Seabury: 1983).

Erdman, D., *Blake: Prophet Against Empire* (Dover, 1954).

Greer, J.M., *Paths of Wisdom: The Magical Cabala in the Western Tradition* (Lewellyn, 1996), pp. 3–29.

Hamill, J., *The Craft* (Crucible, 1986).

Jacobs, M., *The Cultural Meaning of the Scientific Revolution* (Temple University Press, 1988).

Kirchweger, A.J., *Aurea Catena Homeri: The Golden Chain of Homer* (Bacstrom, S., trans., Kuntz, D. and Greer, J.M., ed., forthcoming).

Kurtz, K., *Two Crowns for America* (Spectra Books, 1993).

le Forestier, R., *La Franc-Maçonnerie Ternpliere et Illuministe aux XVIIIe et XIXe Siecles* (Paris, 1970).

McLynn, F., *The Jacobites* (Routledge & Kegan Paul, 1985).

Partner, P., *The Murdered Magicians: The Knights Templar and their Myth* (Oxford University Press, 1982).

Schuchard, M.K., "Freemasonry, Secret Societies, and the Continuity of the Occult Traditions in English Literature" (Ph.D. dissertation, Univerisity Texas, 1975).

Schuchard, M.K., "Yeats and the 'Unknown Superiors': Swedenborg, Falk, and Cagliostro," in Roberts, M.M., and Ormsby-Lennon, H., *Secret Texts: The Literature of Secret Societies* (AMS Press, 1995).

Shankaracharya, *Vivekachudamani (Crest-Jewel of Discrimination)* (Advaita Ashrama, 1966).

Speck, W.A., *The Butcher: The Duke of Cumberland and the Suppression of the 45* (Blackwell, 1981).

Stevenson, D., *The Origins of Freemasonry: Scotland's Century* (Cambridge University Press, 1988).

Szechi, D., *The Jacobites: Britain and Europe 1688–1788* (Manchester University Press, 1994).

Webb, J., *The Occult Establishment* (Open Court Publishing Company, 1976, pp. 81–114).

The G.D. elemental grades: a new version

The project of building bridges between the modern Hermeticism of the Golden Dawn and the richer and more complete Hermeticism of the Renaissance took me in various directions. One of them was the revision of the original Golden Dawn initiation rituals, which I felt (and still feel) could benefit from extensive reworking. The four rituals that follow were a first attempt at this, aimed at the four Elemental Grades, which many students of the tradition consider the weakest parts of the Golden Dawn ritual system. Looking back on them with another twenty years of experience, these rituals still work, though I would make much more sweeping changes now if I were to revisit the same project. The first three appeared in issues 5, 7, and 8 of Abiegnus; *the last remained unpublished when I closed down* Abiegnus *at the end of 1999.*

Part One: The Zelator Grade

The existing rituals of the Elemental Grades of the Hermetic Order of the Golden Dawn have been harshly criticized down through the years by various people in and out of the Order and its many offshoots. Standard criticisms are that the rituals as given are verbose, repetitive, and tedious and that they lack the strengths that are so evident in the Neophyte, Portal, and Adeptus Minor rituals of the Order.

207

Some Golden Dawn-derived groups have dealt with this problem by scrapping the Elemental Grades altogether. Others slog through them as written and try to put up with the limitations. There is at least one other option. This is to revise them. The following Grade ritual, for the Zelator or 1=10 Grade, is the first of four such revisions, which will be issued here in *Abiegnus*.

The principles guiding the construction of these revised rituals are as follows:

First, excess verbiage has been trimmed, sometimes brutally.

Second, some of the symbolism has been replaced with other, equivalent material from the Hermetic tradition in one or another of its branches, where the replacement results in clearer symbolism or simply pleases the revisers more than the original set. (Part of the subtext to this is that such alterations can be made without ill effect if done intelligently.)

Third, two unnecessary officers (the Stolistes and Dadouchos) have been cut and their actions given to other officers, so that Temples with fewer members can carry out the rituals effectively. All four of these revised grade ceremonies can be performed with a total of four officers: Hierophant, Hiereus, Hegemon, and Kerux. These are stationed in the four quarters of the temple, and correspond with the four elements— the Hierophant in the east to air, the Hegemon in the south to fire, the Hiereus in the west to water, and the Kerux in the north to earth. Certain changes in the symbolism and actions of the officers follow from these changes.

Fourth, the practice of taking candidates out of the hall into the ante-chamber at intervals during the ritual—a habit that, in my experience, leads to a significant lessening of energy—has been removed. In all four of these rituals, the candidate enters once, passes through the whole ceremony, and leaves before the closing.

Fifth, the overelaborate Victorian hardware of the original Order has been trimmed somewhat. Specifically, the officers carry plain staves, painted red for Hierophant, black for Hiereus, white for Hegemon, and yellow for Kerux, and other aspects of the symbolism have been left up to the individual Temple. Thus, for example, the Emblem of Earth which allows the candidate to enter the hail may or may not be the Fylfot Cross used in the traditional Golden Dawn Zelator Grade.

The Temple for this ritual is set up exactly the same as that for the standard Golden Dawn Zelator Grade in the first part, except that an altar diagram (as described below) placed on a stand or easel to the east of the altar. The Temple may be decorated as the members see fit. Simplicity usually works as well or better than the more ornate arrangements used in the past.

Several specific changes made in this ritual deserve comment. The most important of them is the replacement of the material from the Sepher Yetzirah and the Temple of Solomon in the Second Point of the old ritual with material about Hermes' sacred city of Adocentyn from the *Picatrix*, which can be found quoted in Frances Yates' *Giordano Bruno and the Hermetic Tradition*. This replacement has been made partly to show that such changes can be appropriate, and partly because the material from the *Picatrix* is more interesting and less familiar, and thus produces less of a ho-hum reaction from initiates. Attentive readers will notice that the same symbolism of Three, Seven and Twelve is central to both versions.

Like the other three rituals, this one also stresses the elemental nature of the work more than the older ritual does. The idea of changing the name of the ritual altogether to "the Grade of Earth" was considered, and while the traditional name was kept for the sake of clear communication, the alternative does have some merit. The relation of the Golden Dawn grades to the Tree of Life is in some ways overstated—neither the Neophyte nor the Portal grades fit well in that framework—and a different concept of the grades might be worth exploring.

As a final practical note, an exclamation point—!—stands for one rap made with an officer's staff.

Grade of Zelator

Opening of the grade of Zelator

Hierophant: Fratres and Sorores, you will assist me to open this Temple in the grade of Zelator. Frater Kerux, see that the Temple is properly guarded.

Kerux: (*Knocks without opening door; Sentinel knocks in answer*). Very Honored Hierophant, the Temple is properly guarded.

Hierophant: Honored Hiereus, see that none below the grade of Zelator is present.

Hiereus: Fratres and Sorores, give the Sign of the grade of Zelator. (*All give sign to Hiereus, who responds with the same sign.*)

Very Honored Hierophant, no one below the Grade of Zelator is now present. *(Hiereus gives the Sign to Hierophant, who responds with the same sign.)*

Hierophant: Purify and consecrate the temple with water and with fire. *(Kerux advances between the pillars. Hegemon and Hiereus take up censer and cup, respectively, and stand to either side of pillars facing East. Each in turn makes a cross in the air to the East with the implement, sprinkles or censes thrice to the East, and says:)*

Hegemon: I consecrate with Fire.

Hiereus: I purify with Water.

(All three make Zelator sign and return to places.)

Hierophant: Let the element of this grade be named that it may be awakened in the spheres of those present and the sphere of the Order.

Hegemon: The element of Earth.

Hierophant: Let us adore the Lord and King of Earth. *(All face east.)* Adonai ha-Aretz, Adonai Malakh, *(traces Qabalistic Cross on self while saying the following)* unto thee be the Kingdom, the Power, and the Glory, the rose of Sharon and the lily of the valley. Amen. *(All make sign of Earth.)* *(Hierophant leaves the East, goes with Sun around lodge one full circuit and then continues around to North. Kerux, Hiereus, and Hegemon fall in from their stations as Hierophant first passes them, Kerux before Hierophant, Hiereus, and Hegemon in that order behind. At the end of the movement, officers fan out: Hierophant stands before northern altar, Hegemon to left and behind, Kerux to right and behind, Hiereus directly behind and further back; the four officers form a diamond-shape, as shown in diagram. All face north.)*

Hierophant: *(traces an invoking pentagram of Earth to the north).* And the Elohim said, Let us make Adam in our own image, after our likeness, and let him have dominion over every creeping thing which creepeth over the Earth. In the Name of Adonai Malakh and of the Bride and Queen of the Kingdom, spirits of Earth, adore your Creator! *(Hierophant traces the symbol of Taurus in the center of the pentagram.)*

Hegemon: In the name of Auriel, great archangel of Earth, and in the sign of the head of the ox, spirits of Earth, adore your Creator!
(Hierophant traces an equal-armed cross over the pentagram.)

Kerux: In the names and letters of the great northern quadrangle, spirits of Earth, adore your Creator!
(Hierophant holds the head of his scepter at the center of the pentagram.)

Hiereus: In the three great secret Names of God borne upon the banners of the north, EMOR DIAL HECTEGA, spirits of Earth, adore your Creator!

Hierophant: In the name of ICZODHICIAL, great king of the north, spirits of Earth, adore your Creator!
(Officers face east, fall into line as Kerux begins moving, and move around hall with Sun. They complete one full circuit from north to north and then go on, falling out as they reach their stations.)

Hierophant: In the Name of Adonai ha-Aretz, I declare this Temple duly opened in the 1=10 grade of Zelator.

Hierophant: !!!! !!! !!!
Hegemon: !!!! !!! !!!
Hiereus: !!!! !!! !!!

Introduction of the candidate

Hierophant: Fratres and Sorores, our Frater/Soror, having been proved in the work of the Neophyte Grade, is now eligible for advancement to the Grade of Zelator, and I have received a dispensation from the Chiefs to admit him/her in due form. Honored Hiereus, see that the hall is prepared.
(Hiereus sees that salt is placed at his/her station, that a cushion for kneeling is before the pillars, and that all furniture is in place.)

Hiereus: Very Honored Hierophant, the hall is prepared.

Hierophant: Honored Hegemon, you will see to the preparation of the candidate, and give the alarm. Kerux, you will guard the door.

(Hegemon makes Zelator Sign, goes to door and leaves hall; Kerux follows and stands by door. Hegemon blindfolds candidate, makes sure he/she has the Emblem of Earth, and instructs him/her in the knock !!!! !!! !!! Candidate then gives knock at door, and Kerux opens door slightly.)

Hegemon: Let me enter the Portal of wisdom.

Kerux: I will. *(Door is opened, and Hegemon brings candidate into the lodge, placing him/her West of the Pillars, facing East. Kerux closes door and then goes to stand in front of candidate.)*

Hierophant: Except Adonai build the house, their labor is but lost that build it. Except Adonai keep the city, the watchman waketh in vain. Frater/Soror Neophyte, by what powers do you seek admission to the Grade of Zelator?

Hegemon **(for candidate):** By the guidance of Adonai; by the completion of the work of the Neophyte Grade; by the permission of the Chiefs; by the signs and tokens of the Zelator Grade; and by this Emblem of Earth.

(Kerux takes Emblem, and steps out of way.)

Hierophant: Give the step and signs of a Neophyte.

(Candidate gives them.)

Hierophant: Kerux, receive from the candidate the Token, Grand Word and Word of the Neophyte Grade.

(Kerux steps back in front of candidate and receives them.)

Kerux: Very Honored Hierophant, I have received them.

Hierophant: Lead the Neophyte to the West and set him/her between the Pillars, with his/her face toward the East. *(This is done; Hegemon stands behind candidate.)* Frater/Soror N., will you pledge yourself to maintain the same secrecy and diligence in the mysteries of this Grade as you are pledged to maintain for those of the Neophyte Grade?

(Candidate answers.)

Hierophant: Then you will kneel on both your knees. *(This is done, Hegemon helping. Meanwhile, Kerux goes to north, leaves Emblem on Earth altar, takes salt, continues around lodge to west with Sun and stands before candidate.)* Place your right palm upon the ground and say, "I pledge by the Earth on which I kneel."

(Candidate does so.)

Hierophant: Let the symbol of blindness be removed.
(This is done by Hegemon. Hegemon and Hiereus then both go with sun around the lodge, take the censer and cup from their stations, and return, Hegemon standing by White Pillar, Hiereus by Black. Hegemon leaves hoodwink at his/her station.)

Hierophant: Take salt with your left hand and cast it to the north, and say, "Let the powers of Earth witness my pledge."
(Candidate does so. Kerux then takes salt back to Hiereus's station and returns to the Pillars by the circle.)

Hierophant: Let the Neophyte rise, and let him/her be purified with Water and consecrated with Fire in confirmation of this pledge, and in the name of the Lord of the Universe, who works in silence and whom nothing but silence can express.

Hegemon: I consecrate with Fire. *(Censes candidate thrice, and traces cross before candidate with censer.)*

Hiereus: I purify with Water. *(Sprinkles candidate thrice, and traces cross before candidate with cup.)*
(Hiereus and Hegemon then move in diagonal lines straight to their stations and put down cup and censer, then take up their staffs and stand halfway between stations and central altar, facing candidate. Kerux moves cushion out of the way, and goes to stand near Candidate's right.)

Advancement of the candidate

Hierophant: Initiation into the Neophyte Grade is a preparation for our work; it is the threshold of our discipline, and its imagery shows forth the light of the Secret Wisdom dawning in the darkness of the outer life. You are now to begin to analyze and comprehend the nature of that light. To this end, you stand between the Pillars, in that gateway where the secrets of the Neophyte Grade were communicated to you.

Prepare to enter the immeasurable region.

And Tetragrammaton Elohim planted a garden eastward in Eden, and out of the ground made he to grow every tree that is pleasant in the sight and good for food; the Tree of Life also, in the midst of the garden, and the Tree of Knowledge of Good and of Evil. This is the Tree that has two paths, and it is the tenth Sephirah Malkuth, and it has about it seven columns, and the four splendors whirl around it as in the vision of Ezekiel; and from Gedulah it receives Mercy, and from Geburah Severity, and the Tree of the Knowledge of Good and of Evil shall it be until it is united with the Supernais in Daath.

But the good which is under it is called the Archangel Metatron, and the evil is called the Archangel Samael, and between them lies the strait and narrow way where the Archangel Sandalphon keeps watch. The souls and angels are above its branches, and the fallen powers of the Kingdom of Shells are beneath its roots.

Let the candidate enter the Path of Evil.

(Kerux leads candidate from between Pillars toward the Hiereus, who bars way with staff.)

Hiereus: Whence come you?

Kerux: I come from between the two Pillars, and I seek the light of the hidden knowledge in the Name of Adonai.

Hiereus: And the great angel Samael answered and said: I am the prince of darkness and of night. The ignorant gaze on the face of the created world and find there nothing but terror and obscurity. It is to them the terror of darkness and they are as drunken men stumbling in the darkness. Return, for you cannot pass by.

(Kerux leads candidate back between the Pillars.)

Hierophant: Let the candidate enter the Path of Good.

(Kerux leads candidate from between Pillars toward the Hegemon, who bars way with staff.)

Hegemon: Whence come you?

Kerux: I come from between the two Pillars, and I seek the light of the hidden knowledge in the Name of Adonai.

Hegemon: And the great angel Metatron answered and said: I am the angel of the divine presence. The wise gaze on the face of the created world and behold there the dazzling image of the Creator. Not yet can your eyes bear that dazzling image. Return, for you cannot pass by.

(Kerux leads candidate back between the Pillars.)

Hierophant: Let the candidate enter that Path which turns neither to the right hand nor to the left.
(Kerux leads candidate from between Pillars to the altar. Hiereus and Hegemon come to altar and cross staves in front of the candidate, barring the way.)

Hiereus and Hegemon *(together):* Whence come you?

Kerux: I come from between the two Pillars, and I seek the light of the hidden knowledge in the Name of Adonai.

Hierophant: *(advances to east of altar, thrusts his staff beneath the others and raises it to a 45 degree angle).* But the great angel Sandalphon answered and said: I am the reconciler for earth and the celestial soul therein. Form is invisible alike in darkness and in blinding light. I am the left hand Kerub of the Ark and the feminine power, as Metatron is the right hand Kerub and the masculine power; and I prepare the way to the celestial light.
(Hiereus, Hegemon, and Kerux return to their stations. Hierophant takes candidate by the right hand with his left, and brings him/her around the altar to the diagram. This is closed, showing the diagram of the Tree of Life.)

Hierophant: And Tetragrammaton Elohim placed Kerubim in the east of the Garden of Eden, and a flaming sword which turned every way to keep the paths of the Tree of Life. You now stand in the Garden of Eden, which is also the garden of yourself. But, in the mysteries of our tradition, this garden is also a City.

Hegemon: It was Hermes who, in the east of Egypt, built a city twelve miles long, and in it a castle which had four gates. On the eastern gate he placed the image of an Eagle; on the western gate, the image of a Bull; on the southern gate, the image of a Lion, and on the northern gate, the image of a Dog. In these images, he placed spirits who spoke with voices, and no one could enter the gates of the city except by their leave.

Kerux: Atop the castle, he raised a tower thirty cubits high with a beacon at its summit. The color of the beacon changed every day until the seventh day, when it returned to the first color, and so the city was illuminated.

Hiereus: In the city, he planted trees and in the midst of them a great tree which bore the fruit of all generation. Near the city was an abundance of waters in which were many kinds of fish. And around its outer wall, he placed engraved images, and ordered them in such a way that by their influence the inhabitants were made virtuous and delivered from all wickedness and harm.

Hierophant: The name of the city was Adocentyn. *(Hierophant opens the altar diagram.)*

Here is the secret meaning of that City. The twelve miles of the city's measure, and the four gates guarded by four guardians, represent the mystery of the Dodecad of Creation. The twelve miles are the twelve signs of the Zodiac, and the four guardians are the four elemental triplicities of those signs, and the four archangels and four kerubim ruling over the four quarters of the world. These twelve miles are also the twelve single letters of the Hebrew alphabet, the twelve loaves of the table of shewbread and the twelve foundation stones of the city of Revelation. They are the outer petals of the Rose.

The seven colors of the beacon represent the mystery of the Elohim, the Heptad of Creation. They are the seven planets and the seven palaces of Assiah, the material world; the seven double letters of the Hebrew alphabet, and the seven lamps before the Throne. They are the middle petals of the Rose.

The Tree in the midst of the City which bore the fruit of all generation is the Tree of Life, which has three pillars. It represents the mystery of the Triad of Creation, and the secret of balance between contending opposites, which was shown to you in the Neophyte Grade. These three pillars are the three mother letters of the Hebrew alphabet; they are Mercy, Severity, and Balance; and they are the inner petals of the Rose.

Reception of the candidate

Hierophant: The work before you is to build this City, in yourself and of yourself, to bring the Three, the Seven and the Twelve into the perfect harmony of the Garden of Eden and the petals of the Rose. I ask you, therefore: Are you willing to take up this work?

(Candidate answers.)

Hierophant: Then I confer on you the secrets of this grade. The Sign of the grade is given thus: *(does so)* and represents the staff of Sandalphon, interposed for you between the Light and the Darkness. The symbol of the grade is ARETZ, Aleph, Resh, Tzaddi, the Hebrew word for Earth.

I also confer upon you the title Periclinus de Faustis, which signifies that you are a wanderer upon this Earth, far from the garden of the happy.

Kerux, you will proclaim that our Frater/Soror has been duly admitted to the grade of Zelator.

Kerux: In the Name of Adonai Malakh, and by the command of the Very Honored Hierophant, I proclaim that Frater/Soror N. has been admitted to the 1=10 grade of Zelator, and that he/she has obtained the Mystic Title of Pereclinus de Faustis and the symbol of Aretz.

(Kerux comes forward and leads candidate to a seat in the southeast of the hail. Hierophant returns to place.)

Hierophant: The grade of Zelator is the first of four steps which lie between the Neophyte Grade, where you first saw the Light shining in darkness, and the Portal Grade, where that Light will be resumed in the living Stone of yourself. Each of these four steps corresponds to one of the four elements, and it is fitting that you begin this part of your pilgrimage in the dense and unyielding element of Earth.

In the course of your work as a Frater/Soror of our Order, the virtue of Earth, prudence—with its companion virtues, patience, persistence, and the capacity for hard work—will be required of you again and again. Practice them in your daily life as well as in your magical work, for like the Earth itself, these things reward labor with a rich harvest.

The grade of Zelator is the grade of the Builder. It is for this reason that the symbolism of the City of Adocentyn is shown therein. In your studies in this grade, let the patience and self-discipline of the builder guide you as you begin to work upon the uncarved stone you saw in the Neophyte Grade to build the temple that is yourself.

I present you, therefore, with the working tool of this grade, the Pentacle. *(He shows it.)* The Pentacle is a disk which bears, in symbolic form, the image of the universe. Like the tracing boards used by ancient builders, it provides the pattern for the work before you—for the image of yourself and the image of the universe are one. You will make such a Pentacle for yourself as part of the work of this grade; think well upon the designs you place upon it.

Another of the principal emblems of this grade is the Great Watchtower of the North, the third Tablet of the Angelic or Enochian system *(points to tablet on north altar)*. The letters on it spell out Names of Power. From it are drawn the Three Holy Secret Names of God EMOR DIAL HECTEGA, which are borne upon the banners of the north, and there are also numberless names of angels, archangels and spirits ruling the element of Earth.

Before you will be eligible to enter into the next grade of our Order, you must master certain further portions of our ancient wisdom, and you must continue to take an active part in the work of this Temple and our Order. A syllabus of the work required will be provided to you.

Closing of the Zelator Grade

Hierophant: ! Fratres and Sorores, you will assist me to close this lodge in the grade of Zelator. Let us adore the Lord and King of Earth. !!! *(All rise and face East.)* Adonai ha-Aretz, Adonai Malakh, blessed be thy name to the countless ages, Amen. *(All give sign and face as usual.)*

(Hierophant then goes around lodge one full circuit against Sun and then continues around to north. Kerux, Hiereus, and Hegemon fall in as Hierophant passes their stations, Kerux in front, Hiereus and Hegemon behind him in that order. In the north, they form the diamond facing north as before, except that the Hegemon is at the right and the Kerux at the left:)

Hierophant: Let us rehearse the prayer of the Earth Spirits.

O Invisible King who, taking the earth for foundation, did hollow its depths to fill them with thy almighty power; thou whose name shaketh the arches of the world, thou who causest the seven metals to flow in the veins of the rocks, king of the seven lights, rewarder of the subterranean workers, lead us into the desirable air and into the realm of splendor. We watch and we labor unceasingly, we seek, and we hope, by the twelve stones of the holy city, by the buried talismans, by the axis of the lodestone which passes through the center of the earth—O Lord, O Lord, O Lord! Have pity on those who suffer. Expand our hearts, unbind and upraise our minds, enlarge our natures.

O stability in motion! O darkness veiled in brilliance! O day clothed in night! O master who never withholds the wages of thy workmen! O silver whiteness! O golden splendor! O crown of living and harmonious diamond! Thou who wearest the heavens on thy finger like a ring of sapphire! Thou who hidest beneath the earth in the kingdom of the gems, the marvelous seed of the stars! Live, reign, and be thou the eternal dispenser of the treasures whereof thou hast made us the wardens.

Depart now in peace to your habitations, *(traces banishing pentagram of Earth)* and peace be between us.
(Officers face west, fall in line behind Kerux, and move around hail against sun one circuit, then fall out as they reach their stations.)

Hierophant: In the Name of Adonai Melekh, I declare this Temple closed in the 1=10 grade of Zelator.

Hierophant: !!!! !!! !!!

Hiereus: !!!! !!! !!!

Hegemon: !!!! !!! !!!

Hierophant: ! (All are seated.)

Part Two: The Theoricus Grade

This second installment of "The G.D. Elemental Grades: A New Version" introduces the first thoroughly reworked ritual of the set. The first of the revised Grade rituals, the 1=10 Zelator, required mostly cosmetic alterations in the course of this project. The Grades that follow it needed a good deal more.

The verboseness of these Grades, their repetitiousness, and the general tedium that greets the candidate as he begins yet another circumambulation, accompanied by yet another recitation from an obscure Hermetic text, are symptoms of a deeper problem that had to be fixed. That problem is a certain lack of imagination that pervades the design of these Grade rituals.

Imagination is one thing that the founders of the G.D. rarely lacked. The rituals they designed on their own are on the whole vivid, creative and impressive. But the Cipher Manuscripts that inspired the whole affair were the work of a less creative mind, and the elemental grades were taken more or less intact from the Cipher Manuscripts.

In the Cipher Manuscripts and the traditional Golden Dawn grades based on them, the Theoricus, Practicus, and Philosophus rituals all involved symbolically climbing the paths of the Tree of Life. Each of these grades is assigned to a Sephirah, and the ritual of each grade involved reaching that Sephirah by each of the paths leading up to it from below. This was an interesting idea, but only the first of these (the Path of Tau, in the Theoricus Grade) is handled in a really effective manner, with banners, challenges, and other dramatic elements.

The remaining path journeys follow a rigid framework that grows increasingly dull as the paths to be traversed in each ritual increase. The candidate is brought into the hall carrying an admission badge. He or she circumambulates the hall while various officers recite passages corresponding to the path symbolism, and then sits down and listens to further verbiage of the same sort. He or she then approaches the Hierophant, who explains the symbolism of the path's admission badge and Tarot Trump, proclaims the candidate Lord of the fill-in-the-blank Path, and sends him or her out of the hail to allow for the next scene change.

One option I considered was trying to expand and develop the journeys on the paths in the existing Grades, so that each of them presented an effective and meaningful experience to the candidate. The drawback was that the rituals where multiple paths had to be covered would have gone on for hours.

Another drawback is that it would be all but impossible to do this without taking the candidate out of the hall at intervals and dissipating energy. Removing this bad habit of the original Grades was one of the original goals of the revision effort.

The alternative—and the choice I finally made—was to retain the journeys on the paths in a simplified form but shift the major focus of the Grade Ritual to the elemental symbolism. The result is a distinctly different ritual set in a similar structure.

The one really effective path journey in the original grades was retained but in a different way. It consists of four stages, corresponding to the four elements of Malkuth and the four elemental Kerubim of the 32nd Path. Since the elemental grades—"which in one sense quitteth not Malkuth," as the Portal Grade reminds us—correspond to these four stages as well, this part of the older Theoricus ritual has been used to frame the symbolic path journeys all through this new version.

The first stage alone is used in the new Theoricus ritual, corresponding to the ascent of the 32nd Path; the first and second appear in the Practicus, corresponding to the 31st and 30th; the first, second, and third appear in the Phiiosophus, corresponding to the 29th, 28th, and 27th; while all four stages were intended to appear in the revised Portal Grade, corresponding to the four paths essayed but not taken in that rite, as well as the four elements resolved into spirit.

Two other changes should be mentioned. First, the purification and consecration of the candidate by water and fire are repeated once in each of the four elemental grades. This is a repetition and recollection of the four purifications and consecrations performed in the Neophyte Grade. Second, the two pillars are placed west of the altar in all four grades, forming the portal through which the candidate passes to begin each of the four elemental journeys. The implications of this latter change will become clearer later.

Opening of the grade of Theoricus

Hierophant: Fratres and Sorores, you will assist me to open this Temple in the grade of Theoricus. Frater Kerux, see that the Temple is properly guarded.

Kerux:	*(Knocks without opening the door; Sentinel knocks).* Very Honored Hierophant, the Temple is properly guarded.
Hierophant:	Honored Hiereus, see that none below the grade of Theoricus is present.
Hiereus:	Fratres and Sorores, give the sign of the Theoricus Grade. *(All give sign to Hiereus, who responds with the same sign.)* Very Honored Hierophant, all present have attained the grade of Theoricus. *(Hiereus gives the Sign to Hierophant, who responds with the same sign.)*
Hierophant:	Honored Hegemon, to what element is this grade attributed?
Hegemon:	To the element of Air.
Hierophant:	Honored Hiereus, to what planet does this grade especially refer?
Hiereus:	To the Moon.
Hierophant:	Honored Hegemon, what path is attached to this grade?
Hegemon:	The 32nd Path of Tau.
Hierophant:	! *(Knocks.)* Let us adore the Lord and King of Air. *(All rise and face east.)* Shaddai El Chai, almighty and everlasting—ever-living be thy Name, ever magnified in the life of all. Amen. *(All make sign of Air.)* *(Hierophant leaves the East, goes with Sun around lodge once to East. Kerux, Hiereus, and Hegemon fall in from their Outer stations as Hierophant circumambulates, Kerux before Hierophant, Hiereus, and Hegemon in that order behind. At the end of the movement, officers fan out: Hierophant stands before eastern altar, Hegemon to left and behind, Kerux to right and behind, Hiereus directly behind and further back; the four officers form a diamond-shape. All face east.)*
Hierophant:	*(traces an invoking pentagram of Air to the east).* And the Elohim said: Let us make Adam in our own image, after our likeness, and let him have dominion over the birds of the Air. In the Name YHVH, Tetragrammaton, and in the Name Shaddai El Chai, spirits of Air, adore your Creator! *(Hierophant traces the symbol of Aquarius in the center of the pentagram.)*
Hegemon:	In the name of Raphael, great archangel of Air, and in the sign of the head of the Man, spirits of Air, adore your Creator! *(Hierophant traces an equal-armed cross over the pentagram.)*

Kerux:	In the names and letters of the great eastern quadrangle, spirits of Air, adore your Creator!
	(Hierophant holds the head of his staff at the center of the pentagram.)
Hiereus:	In the three great secret Names of God borne upon the banners of the east, ORO IBAH AOZPI, spirits of Air, adore your Creator!
Hierophant:	In the name of BATAIVAH, great king of the east, spirits of Air, adore your Creator!
	(Officers face east, fall into line as Kerux begins moving, and move around hail with Sun. They complete one circuit from east to east and then fall out as they reach their stations, taking their places for this Grade.)
Hierophant:	In the Name of Shaddai El Chai, I declare this Temple opened in the 2=9 Grade of Theoricus.
Hierophant:	!!! !!! !!!
Hiereus:	!!! !!! !!!
Hegemon:	!!! !!! !!!
Kerux:	!!! !!! !!!
Hierophant:	! *(Knocks; all are seated.)*

Introduction of the candidate

Hierophant:	Fratres et Sorores, our Frater/Soror N, having been proved in the work of the Zelator Grade, is now eligible for advancement to the grade of Theoricus, and I have received a dispensation from the Chiefs to admit him/her in due form. Honored Hegemon, superintend the preparation of the Zelator and give the customary alarm.
	(Hegemon goes to door and leaves hall; Kerux makes sure bindings for candidate's hands and cushion for kneeling are in place and stands by door. Hegemon blindfolds candidate, gives him/her the Emblem of Air, and instructs him/her in the knock !!! !!! !!! Candidate then gives knock at door, and Kerux opens door slightly.)
Kerux:	Quit the material and seek the spiritual. *(Door is opened; and Hegemon brings candidate into the lodge, facing him/her East. Kerux follows, and stands by candidate.)*

Hierophant:	Frater/Soror Periclinus de Faustis, by what emblem do you seek admission to this hail of the rushing winds?
Hegemon *(for candidate)*:	By this Emblem of Air.
Hierophant:	Give me the Sign of a Zelator. *(Candidate gives it.)*
Hierophant:	Frater/Soror Kerux, receive from the candidate the Symbol of the Zelator Grade. *(Candidate gives word to Kerux.)*
Kerux:	Greatly Honored Hierophant, I have received it.
Hierophant:	Let our Frater/Soror be placed between the Pillars, with his/her face toward the East. *(This is done; Hegemon stands behind candidate.)* Frater/Soror Periclinus de Faustis, will you pledge yourself to maintain the same secrecy and diligence in the mysteries of this grade as you are pledged to maintain for those of the preceding grades? *(Candidate answers.)*
Hierophant:	Then you will stretch out your hand, holding the Emblem of Air toward heaven, and say: "I pledge by the firmament of Heaven." *(Candidate does so.)*
Hierophant:	Let the symbol of blindness be removed. *(This is done by Hegemon. At this point Hegemon and Hiereus both go sunwise around the lodge, take the censer and cup from their places, and return to candidate, Hegemon standing by White Pillar, Hiereus by Black.)* Stretch forth your right hand, holding the Emblem of Air toward the east in the position of the Zelator Sign, and say: "Let the powers of Air witness my pledge." *(Candidate does so. Kerux then takes Emblem to station and returns.)*
Hierophant:	Let our Frater/Soror be purified with Water and consecrated with Fire in confirmation of this pledge, and in the name of the Lord of the Universe, who works in silence and whom nothing but silence can express.
Hiereus:	I purify with Water. *(Sprinkles candidate thrice, and traces cross before candidate with cup.)*
Hegemon:	I consecrate with Fire. *(Censes candidate thrice, and traces cross before candidate with censer.)* *(Hiereus and Hegemon return to stations, moving sunwise.)*

Advancement of the candidate

Hierophant: Frater/Soror Periclinus de Faustis, as a member of the Zelator Grade, you stand symbolically in Malkuth, the tenth Sephirah. Before you are the Portals of the 31st, 32nd, and 29th Paths, leading from the Grade of Zelator to the three other grades which are beyond. The Path now open to you is the 32nd, which leads to the grade of Theoricus. Follow now your guide, Anubis the Guardian, who leads you from the material to the spiritual.

Kerux: Let us enter into the presence of the Lord of Truth. Arise and follow me.

(Kerux leads Candidate forward from between pillars and once around the lodge with Sun, stopping just west of pillars. Meanwhile Hegemon reads, slowly:)

Hegemon: The Sphinx of Egypt spoke and said: I am the synthesis of the elemental forces. I am also the symbol of Humanity. I am life and I am death. I am the Child of the Night of Time.

(During this reading, Hiereus leaves station and goes to stand between altar and pillars.)

Hierophant: *(as candidate returns to west).* Let the candidate be placed between the pillars, that he/she may stand in the gateway of the realm of Air.

(This is done. Kerux stands behind candidate.)

Hierophant: Let the candidate's hands be bound.

(Kerux does so, tying them behind candidate's back. Hiereus draws sword. As candidate is placed between pillars, Hiereus extends sword so that its point is a foot or so from candidate's heart.)

Hiereus: Frater/Soror Periclinus de Faustis, the lessons you learned in the Grade of Earth will not by themselves bring you to the high and hidden places of the secret wisdom. Not prudence alone, but courage as well will be asked of you. Behold this naked sword barring your path into the realm of Air! If you would enter that realm, and go in quest of the Mysteries, step boldly forward and face the test of steel.

(Candidate, prompted if necessary by Kerux, steps forward. As the sword comes into contact with candidate, Hiereus

allows it to be pushed back, so that candidate is not harmed. Hiereus then draws back the sword and reverses it.)

Hierophant: Well done. Let the candidate's hands be unbound. *(Done. Kerux takes bindings away and returns.)*

Hiereus: *(Hands candidate the sword.)* Take this sword, and remember the words spoken to you in the Neophyte Grade: "Courage is the beginning of all virtue." Enter now into the realm of Air, and learn the wisdom of Air from the rushing winds of heaven. The sword in your hand is the key to many of the mysteries of Air, and of our secret wisdom— for this is the Sword which was drawn from the Stone.

(Hiereus returns to place. Hierophant leaves station and stands before altar diagram; candidate and Kerux remain in position.)

Hegemon: And when morning was come, there was seen in the churchyard, against the high altar, a great stone four square, like unto a marble stone, and in the midst thereof was like an anvil of steel a foot on high, and therein stuck a fair sword naked by the point, and letters there were written in gold about the sword that said thus: who so pulleth this sword out of this stone and anvil is rightwise born king.

Hiereus: And at the feast of Pentecost all manner of men assayed to pull at the sword that would, but none might prevail but Arthur, and pulled it out before all the lords and commons that were there. And therewithal they kneeled at once, both rich and poor, and Arthur took the sword between both his hands and offered it upon the altar, and so he was made Knight.

Hierophant: Bring the Frater/Soror to the east of the Altar. *(Done. Hierophant points to one side of the closed diagram.)* Here is the image of that Sword which was drawn from the stone, formed of the ten Spheres of the Tree of Life in their descending order. The sword is the Lightning Flash, the current of power that shattered the darkness at the dawn of Creation; the anvil is the Sphere Tiphareth, the central station of the descending light; while the stone, in which the point of the sword comes to rest, is Malkuth, the tenth Sphere, the world of matter.

Here *(Hierophant points to the other side of the closed diagram)* is the image of that other sword, Excalibur, which rose up from the deep waters. This sword is formed of the ten Spheres of the Tree in their ascending order, from Malkuth to Kether. The one is the descent of power from the divine to the world, the other the ascent of power from the world to the divine; the one is creation, the other is redemption; the one is grace, the other is will.

But every sword is drawn forth from the stone, and every sword rises up from the water. The steel of the blade you hold was smelted with fire out of the stony ore and was quenched in water to be tempered and to come to its perfection. Even so, you must pass through water and fire to achieve the perfection of the First Degree—and you must pass through a deeper Water and a greater Fire to achieve the perfection of yourself.

(Hierophant opens diagram.)

Before you stands the Tree of Life formed of the Spheres and their connecting Paths. With its complete symbolism, it is the key of all things when properly understood. As you see, the sequence of the Paths forms the symbol of the Serpent of Wisdom, while the natural succession of the Spheres forms the Flaming Sword and the course of the Lightning Flash. The Sword and the Serpent between them resume the whole of our secret wisdom.

The two pillars, right and left of the Tree, are the symbols of active and passive, male and female, Adam and Eve. They also allude to the Pillars of Fire and Cloud. The pillars further represent the two kerubim of the Ark—the right, Metatron, male, and the left, Sandalphon, female. Above them ever burn the lamps of their spiritual essence, of which they are partakers in the eternal, uncreated One.

Reception of the candidate

Hierophant: Frater/Soror Periclinus de Faustis, the peaceful work of the builder is one image of the path we travel as Fratres et Sorores of the Golden Dawn; the way of the knight upon the field of battle is another, and it is this image that corresponds to the grade of Theoricus. Thus, you have been called upon to show that courage which is the heart of knighthood, as it is the beginning of every virtue.

The work before you is to face the perils and the challenges of our quest with courage—to draw this sword from the living stone of yourself, and to wield it in the service of Light against all the inner enemies of Wisdom. I ask you, therefore: Are you willing to take up this work? *(Candidate answers.)*

Hierophant: Then you will kneel on both your knees.
(Candidate does so. Hierophant dubs him on right shoulder, left shoulder and top of head.)

Hierophant: Arise, my Frater/Soror. Take this sword and place it upon the altar, as Arthur placed the Sword drawn from the Stone, remembering that every power you have is given you to be set upon the altar of the Infinite.
(Candidate takes sword and puts it on the altar.)

Hierophant: I now confer on you the secrets of this grade. The Sign of this grade is given thus: *(does so)* and represents you holding the Pillars of Mercy and Severity in balance. It is the Sign made by the Titan Atlas, who supported the universe on his shoulders. It is the Isis of Nature, supporting the heavens.

I also confer upon you the title Poraios de Rejectis, which means "brought from among the rejected," and I give you the symbol RUACH, which is the Hebrew word for Air. It is spelled Resh, Vau, Cheth.

Frater/Soror Kerux, you will announce that our Frater/Soror has been duly admitted to the Grade of Theoricus.

Kerux: In the Great Name Shaddai El Chai, and by command of the Very Honored Hierophant, I proclaim that our Frater/Soror has been duly advanced to the 2=9 Grade of Theoricus, and that he/she has received the Mystic Title of Poraios de Rejectis and the Symbol of Ruach.
(Kerux leads candidate to a seat in the southeast of the hail and goes to station. Hierophant returns to station.)

Hierophant: The grade of Theoricus is the second of four steps which lie between the Neophyte and Portal Grades—between the first glimpse of the Light, and the door to its full manifestation. Each of these four steps corresponds to one of the four elements, and just as the first step of your pilgrimage rested on the dense and unyielding element of Earth, the second passes through the turbulent element of Air, the realm of storm and cloud—but also of clarity, for Air is also the medium of Light.

The Grade of Theoricus is the Grade of the Knight. It is for this reason that in your passage between the pillars, you were met by an adversary who barred your path with steel. There are many adversaries to be faced and vanquished as you travel the path that leads to wisdom; in your studies in this grade, let the courage of the warrior guide you as you strive against them.

I present you, therefore, with the working tool of this grade, the Dagger. *(He shows it.)* You will prepare such a dagger for yourself as part of the work of this grade. As you fashion it and wield it, remember the lesson you learned when you faced the guardian of the Portal of this Grade; and also remember that, like any instrument of power, it has two edges, and can cut and wound the one who holds it if it is used without proper skill.

Another of the principal emblems of this grade is the Great Watchtower of the East, the first Tablet of the Angelic or Enochian system (points to tablet on east altar). The letters on it spell out Names of Power. From it are drawn the Three Holy Secret Names of God ORO IBAH AOZPI, which are borne upon the banners of the east, and there are also numberless names of angels, archangels and spirits ruling the element of Air.

Before you will be eligible to enter into the next Grade, the Grade of Practicus, you must master certain further portions of our ancient wisdom, and you must continue to take an active part in the work of your lodge and our Order. A syllabus of the work required will be provided to you.

Closing of the Theoricus Grade

Hierophant: ! *(knocks).* Assist me to close the Temple in the grade of Theoricus. Let us adore the Lord and King of Air.!!!

(All rise and face East.) Shaddai El Chai, almighty and ever-living, blessed be thy name to the countless ages, Amen. *(All give sign, then face as usual.)*

(Hierophant then goes around lodge once against sun and then to east. Kerux falls in before Hierophant as he begins; Hiereus and Hegemon fall in behind him as he passes their stations. In the east, they form the diamond facing east as before, except that Hegemon is to the right and Kerux to the left.)

Hierophant: Let us rehearse the prayer of the Air Spirits.

Spirit of life, spirit of wisdom, whose breath giveth forth and withdraweth the form of all things; thou, before whom the life of beings is but a shadow which changeth, and a vapor which passeth; thou, who mountest upon the clouds, and waikest on the wings of the wind; thou, who breathest forth thy breath, and endless space is peopled; Thou, who drawest in thy breath, and all that cometh from thee, returneth unto thee.

Ceaseless motion in eternal stability, be thou eternally blessed! We bless thee and we praise thee in the changeless empire of created light, of shades, of reflections and of images, and we aspire without cessation to thy immutable and imperishable brilliance.

Let the ray of thy intelligence and the warmth of thy love penetrate even unto us. Then that which is volatile shall be fixed; the shadow shall be a body; the spirit of air shall be a soul; the dream shall be a thought; and no more shall we be swept away by the tempest, but we shall hold the bridles of the winged steeds of dawn, and we shall direct the course of the evening breeze to fly before thee.

O spirit of spirits, O eternal soul of souls, O imperishable breath of life, O creative sigh, O mouth which breathest forth and withdrawest the life of all beings, in the flux and reflux of thy eternal word, which is the divine ocean of movement and of truth.

Depart now in peace to your habitations, *(traces banishing pentagram of Air)* and peace be between us.

(Officers turn left, fall in line behind Kerux, and move around hail against sun one circuit, then fall out as they reach their stations.)

Hierophant: In the Name Shaddai El Chai, I declare this Temple closed in the 2=9 Grade of Theoricus.

Hierophant: !!! !!! !!!

Hiereus: !!! !!! !!!

Hegemon: !!! !!! !!!

Hierophant: ! (All are seated.)

Part Three: The Practicus Grade

This third installment of "The G.D. Elemental Grades: A New Version" continues along the lines of the two already published. As with the earlier Grades, the Practicus Grade has been streamlined and refocused. The old format of climbing the Tree of Life one Path at a time according to a fixed (and often monotonous) formula has been replaced, the elemental aspect of the Grades amplified, and new material substituted for some of the old.

The source of some of this new material is worth a word or two. Gareth Knight's book *The Secret Tradition in Arthurian Legend* is a neglected classic that deserves a lot more attention than it has received on this side of the Atlantic. Knight's interpretation of the Arthurian mythos draws deeply on Qabalistic sources and lends itself readily to the sort of ritual work presented here. The references to the Sword in the Stone in the Theoricus Grade, and to the Holy Grail in the Practicus, link into this source. At the same time, they provide symbolic links to the elements of Air and Water—the governing elements of these two grades.

Most of the other changes have been discussed in the introductions to the first two installments of this series.

Opening of the grade of Practicus

Hierophant:	Fratres and Sorores, you will assist me to open this Temple in the grade of Practicus. Frater Hegemon, see that the Temple is properly guarded.
Hegemon:	*(Knocks without opening the door; Sentinel knocks).* Very Honored Hierophant, the Temple is properly guarded.
Hierophant:	Honored Hiereus, see that none below the grade of Practicus is present.
Hiereus:	Fratres and Sorores, give the sign of the Practicus Grade. *(All give sign to Hiereus, who responds with the same sign.)* Very Honored Hierophant, all present have attained the Three equals Eight Grade. *(Hiereus gives the sign to Hierophant, who responds with the same sign.)*
Hierophant:	Honored Hegemon, to what element is this grade attributed?
Hegemon:	To the element of Water.
Hierophant:	Honored Hiereus, to what planet does this grade especially refer?

Hiereus:	To the Planet Mercury.
Hierophant:	Honored Hegemon, what paths are attached to this grade?
Hegemon:	The 31st and 30th Paths of Shin and Resh.
Hierophant:	! *(Knocks.)* Let us adore the Lord and King of Water. *(All rise and face east.)* Elohim Tzabaoth—Elohim of Hosts! Glory be to the Ruach Elohim who moved upon the face of the Waters of Creation! Amen. *(All make sign of Water.)* *(Hierophant leaves the east, goes with sun around lodge once to east. Hiereus and Hegemon fall in as Hierophant circumambulates, Hiereus before Hierophant, Hegemon behind. At the end of the movement, officers fan out: Hierophant stands before western altar, Hegemon to left and behind, Hiereus to right and behind; the three officers form a triangle. All face west.)*
Hierophant:	*(traces an invoking pentagram of Water to the east)*. And the Elohim said, Let us make Adam in our own image, after our likeness, and let him have dominion over the Fish of the Sea. In the Name EL, and in the name ELOHIM TZABAOTH, spirits of Water, adore your Creator! *(Hierophant traces the symbol of the Eagle's Head in the center of the pentagram.)*
Hegemon:	In the name of Gabriel, great archangel of Water, and in the sign of the head of the Eagle, spirits of Water, adore your Creator! *(Hierophant traces an equal-armed cross over the pentagram.)*
Hiereus:	In the names and letters of the great western quadrangle, spirits of Water, adore your Creator! *(Hierophant holds the head of his staff at the center of the pentagram.)*
Hierophant:	In the three great secret Names of God borne upon the banners of the west, MPH ARSL GAIOL, spirits of Water, adore your Creator! In the name of RA AGIOSEL, great king of the west, spirits of Water, adore your Creator! *(Officers face north, fall into line as Hiereus begins moving, and move around hail with Sun. They complete one circuit from west to west and then fall out as they reach their stations, taking their places for this Grade.)*
Hierophant:	In the Name of Elohim Tzabaoth, I declare this Temple opened in the 3=8 grade of Practicus.
Hierophant:	! !!! ! !!!
Hiereus:	! !!! ! !!!

Hegemon: ! !!! ! !!!
Hierophant: ! *(All are seated.)*

Introduction of the candidate

Hierophant: Fratres and Sorores, our Frater/Soror N., having been proved in the work of the Theoricus Grade, is now eligible for advancement to the grade of Practicus, and I have received a dispensation from the Chiefs to admit him/her in due form. Honored Hegemon, superintend the preparation of the Theoricus and give the customary alarm.
(Hiereus sees that white cloth, cups for the three major officers, and salt-water cup are placed on the appropriate altars. Hegemon goes to door and leaves hall; Hiereus stands by door. Hegemon blindfolds candidate, gives him/her the Emblem of Water, and instructs him/her in the knock ! !!! ! !!! and the words he/she is to say later on in the ceremony. Candidate then gives knock at door, and Hiereus opens door slightly.)

Hiereus: And the Ruach Elohim moved on the face of the Waters. *(Door is opened, and Hegemon brings candidate to west of pillars, facing him/her east.)*

Hierophant: Frater/Soror Poraios de Rejectis, by what emblem do you seek to enter this hall of the mighty waters?

Hegemon   By this Emblem of Water.
(for candidate):

Hierophant: Give the sign of a Theoricus.
(Candidate gives it.)

Hierophant: Frater Hiereus, receive from the candidate the Grand Word of the Theoricus Grade.
(Candidate gives word to Hiereus.)

Hiereus: Greatly Honored Hierophant, I have received it.

Hierophant: Let our Frater/Soror be placed between the Pillars, with his/her face toward the east. *(This is done; Hegemon stands behind candidate.)* Frater/Soror Poraios de Rejectis, will you pledge yourself to maintain the same secrecy and diligence in the mysteries of this Grade as you are pledged to maintain for those of the preceding grades? *(Candidate answers.)*

Hierophant: Then you will stretch forth your right hand in the position of the Sign of the Enterer, and say: "I pledge by the Abyss of the Waters."
(Candidate does so.)

Hierophant: Let the symbol of blindness be removed. *(This is done by Hegemon. At this point Hegemon and Hiereus both go with sun around the lodge, take the censer and cup from their altars, and return, Hegemon standing by White Pillar, Hiereus by Black. Hegemon turns candidate around to face west, puts down cup, and brings salt-water cup.)* Sprinkle with your hand a few drops of water to the West, and say, "Let the powers of Water witness my pledge."
(Candidate does so. Hegemon takes salt-water cup back to its altar and returns, turning candidate to face east.)

Hierophant: Let our Frater be purified with Water and consecrated with Fire in confirmation of this pledge, and in the name of the Lord of the Universe, who works in silence and whom nothing but silence can express.

Hiereus: I purify with Water. *(Sprinkles candidate thrice, and traces cross before candidate with cup.)*

Hegemon: I consecrate with Fire. *(Censes candidate thrice, and traces cross before candidate with censer.)*
(Hiereus returns to station by the circle; Hegemon returns cup to station by the circle and then returns to candidate.)

Advancement of the candidate

Hierophant: Frater/Soror Poraios de Rejectis, before you are the Portals of the 31st, 32nd, and 29th Paths. Of these, as you know, the central one leads to the grade of Theoricus from that of Zelator, and from that standpoint, the Portals of the 30th, 25th, and 28th Paths stand before you. Of these, the 31st Path of Shin and the 30th Path of Resh are now open to you. Take in your right hand the Emblem of Water, and follow your guide, Anubis the Guardian, who leads you through the Paths of Fire and the Sun.
(Hegemon leads Candidate forward from between pillars and twice around the lodge with Sun, stopping just west of pillars. Meanwhile Hiereus reads, slowly:)

Hiereus: *(first circumambulation).* The Sphinx of Egypt spoke and said: I am the synthesis of the elemental forces. I am also the symbol of Humanity. I am life and I am death. I am the Child of the Night of Time.

Hiereus: *(second circumambulation).* I am the soul in twin aspect, united to the Higher by purification, perfected by suffering, glorified by trial. I have come where the great gods are through the power of the mighty Name.

Hierophant: *(as candidate returns to west).* Let the candidate be placed between the pillars, so that he/she stands in the gateway of the realm of Water.

(Candidate is placed between pillars. Hegemon returns to station. Then Hierophant, Hegemon, and Hiereus all leave their stations, taking cups with them, and go around the hall with sun. Hegemon goes around to north and then goes between the altar and the pillars, facing candidate; Hiereus and Hierophant, in that order, do the same, timing their movement so that each one arrives as the previous officer leaves.)

Hegemon: I am water, motionless and still, reflecting all, concealing all. I am the past; I am the inundation. He who rises from the great waters is my name. Hail unto ye, dwellers of the Land of Night! For the rending of the darkness is near.

Candidate: *(prompted).* I seek light in the darkness.

Hegemon: Before all things are the waters and the darkness and the gates of the land of night. From the father of waters went forth the spirit, rending asunder the veils of darkness. And there was but a vastness of silence and of depth in the place of the gathering waters. Terrible was the silence of that uncreated world, immeasurable the depth of that abyss.

(Hegemon returns to station directly. Hiereus faces candidate.)

Hiereus: I am water, turbid and troubled. I am the banisher of peace in the abode of the Waters. None is so strong as to withstand the power of the great Waters and the roar of their thundering voice. I am the future, shrouded in mist and gloom; I am the drawing back of the torrent. The storm clad in terror is my name. Hail unto ye, dwellers of the whirling storm! For the rending of the darkness is upon you.

Candidate: *(prompted).* I seek light in the darkness.

Hiereus: The countenances of darkness arose half-formed; they abode not; they hastened away, and in the darkness of vacancy, the Spirit moved, and the lightbearers existed for a space. I have said darkness of darkness—are not the countenances of darkness fallen with kings? Do the children of the night of time last forever, and have they not yet passed away?

(Hiereus returns to station with sun. Hierophant faces candidate.)

Hierophant: I am water, pure and shining, ever flowing on toward the sea. I am the ever-passing present that stands between past and future; I am the fertilized land. The traveler through the gates of the darkness is my name. Hail unto ye, dwellers of the wings of the morning! For the rending of the darkness is done.

Candidate: *(prompted).* I seek light in the darkness.

Hierophant: And the chaos cried aloud for the unity of form, and the face of the Eternal arose. Before the glory of that countenance, the night rolled back and the darkness hastened away. In the waters beneath was that face reflected, in the formless abyss of the Void. Its brow and its eyes formed the triangle of the measureless heavens—and their reflections formed the triangle of the measureless waters. Thus, was formulated the eternal hexad, the number of the dawning creation.

(Hierophant returns to station with sun. Hegemon returns to candidate.)

Hegemon: The river Kishon swept them away, that ancient river, the river Kishon. O my soul, you have trodden down strength!

Hierophant: Let the Candidate enter into the realm of Water, and hear the wisdom of Water from the voices of the sea. The Grade of Practicus has as its chief symbol the Cup, and in the traditions of our secret wisdom that Cup has always, as its archetype, the Grail.

(Hegemon leads Candidate to the altar and reads:)

Hegemon: And then the king and all estates went home to Camelot, and so went to evensong to the great minster, and so after upon that to supper, and every knight sat in his own place. Then anon they heard cracking and crying of thunder, so that they thought the place should all be to drive. In the midst of this blast entered a sunbeam more clear by seven times than ever they saw day, and they were all alighted by the grace of the spirit. Then began every knight to behold the others by their seeming fairer then ever they saw before. Yet among them, there was no knight might speak one word a great while, and so they looked every one on other as they had been dumb. Then there entered the hall the Holy Grail covered with white samite, but there was none might see it, nor who bare it. And there was all the hall fulfilled with good odors, and every knight had such meats and drinks as he best loved in this world. And when the Grail had been borne through the hall, then the holy vessel departed suddenly, that they wist not where it became.

(While Hegemon reads, Hiereus veils the Cup with a white cloth and leaves station. At the words "Then there entered the hall ..." above, Hiereus goes with Sun around to east and crosses in front of diagram, bearing the veiled Cup in both hands, so that it passes before the candidate. Hiereus then proceeds with Sun back to station. Hierophant goes from station to stand between altar and diagram.)

Hierophant: Enter now into the presence of the Grail. *(Hegemon leads candidate around altar to east; Hierophant points to diagram.)* On the Tree of Life, the Grail embraces nine of the Spheres, while Kether, the first and highest Sphere, is that which descends into the Grail. The Grail further contains within it the symbolism of the three elements Water, Air, and Fire, which in their combination make Earth. On another and a more secret level, however, the crescent is the Moon; the sphere is the Sun; and the triangle is another, Secret Fire, the nature of which will be shown in a higher Grade.

The hiding place of the Grail is called Sarras, in the spiritual realm—that place which, in another symbolism, is called Eden. *(Hierophant opens diagram.)*

Before you is represented the symbolism of the Garden of Eden. At the summit is the Supernal Eden, containing the three Supernal Sephiroth, summed up and contained in Aima Elohim, the Mother Supernal, the woman of the Apocalypse, clothed with the Sun, with the Moon beneath her feet, and upon her head the crown of twelve stars, Kether; this represents the Father joined to the Mother in the glory of the Ancient of Days. And in. the Garden was the Tree of the Knowledge of Good and Evil, which is from Malkuth; and below that Tree is the dragon having seven heads and ten horns, the presence of the Kingdom of Shells.

And a river went forth out of the Supernal Eden to water the rest of the Garden, and from thence it was divided into four heads in Daath, whence it is said, "In Daath the depths are broken up, and the clouds drop down dew." The first head is PISON, the river of fire, which flows into Geburah. The second is GIHON, the river of waters, flowing into Chesed. The third is HID-DEKEL, the river of air, flowing into Tiphareth, and the fourth, which receives the virtues of the other three, is PHRATH, which floweth down upon the Earth.

This river going forth out of Eden is the river of the Apocalypse, the Waters of Life. Thus, the waters of Eden form a cross, and upon that cross ADAM, humanity, who was to rule the nations with a rod of iron, is extended from Tiphareth and his arms stretch out to Chesed and Geburah. In Malkuth is EVE, Nature, mother of all and completion of all, and above the universe she supports with her hands the eternal pillars of the Sephiroth.

Reception of the candidate

Hierophant: As the grade of Zelator has for its model the builder who works in stone, and the grade of Theoricus the knight on the field of battle, so the grade of Practicus is the special grade of the Seer, the visionary who enters into contact with the Unseen in search of the healing and transforming Light therein. The Grail is a symbol of that Light, and the quest for the Grail a symbol of that search.

The work before you is to set out in search of the Grail, to receive the descending current of the Waters of Life, those waters which make fruitful the Garden of Eden and fill the Holy Grail. I ask you, therefore: Are you willing to take up this work?

(Candidate answers.)

Hierophant: Then I confer on you the secrets of this grade. The Sign of the grade is given thus: *(does so)* and represents the triangle of the Waters. The Symbol of the grade is MAYIM, Mem, Aleph, Yod, Mem, the Hebrew word for Water. I also confer upon you the title Monocris de Astris, the Unicorn of the Starry Heavens.

(Hegemon leads candidate to a seat in the southeast of the hail. Hierophant and Hegemon return to place.)

Hierophant: The grade of Practicus is the third of four steps between the Neophyte and Portal Grades—between the first glimpse of the Light, and the door to its full manifestation. In your progress among us, you have passed from the depths of the Earth, through the winds of heaven, to the shores of the Great Sea.

As the grade of Earth is the grade of the Builder, and the grade of Air that of the Knight, this grade is the Grade of the Seer. It is for this reason among others that the symbolism of the Grail is central in it, for the Grail is among the highest symbols of the visionary life in the secret traditions of the Western world. The virtue of this grade is, therefore, temperance, for temperance is a necessity to all who would venture into the visionary realm.

It is written that of four who entered Paradise, one died, one went mad, and one became obsessed with strange doctrines; only one entered in peace and left in peace. In the same way, when Lancelot tried, unpurified, to enter the Chapel of the Grail he was struck down. Remember this, and as you work with the lessons of this grade, learn to approach the powers of the spiritual realm in a temperate manner, balancing the transforming experiences of the Magic of Light with the material, the practical and the mundane.

I now present you with the working tool of this grade, the Cup. *(He shows it.)* The Cup is a receptacle both for physical Water and for those subtle energies our tradition assigns to that element. Its power and its worth come not from what it is in itself, but from that which it bears, from that which enters it from outside. You will prepare such a cup for yourself in the work of this grade; let it teach you the value of the passive, the receptive and the responsive in our work.

Another of the principal emblems of this grade is the Great Watchtower of the West, the third Tablet of the Angelic or Enochian system (points to tablet on west altar). The letters on it spell out Names of Power. From it are drawn the Three Holy Secret Names of God MPH ARSL GAIOL, which are borne upon the banners of the west, and there are also numberless names of angels, archangels and spirits ruling the element of Water.

Before you will be eligible to enter into the next grade, the grade of Philosophus, you must master certain further portions of our ancient wisdom, and you must continue to take an active part in the work of your lodge and our Order. A syllabus of the work required will be provided to you.

Closing of the Practicus Grade

Hierophant: ! *(knocks)* Assist me to close this lodge in the Three equals Eight grade of Practicus. Let us adore the Lord and King of Water. !!! *(All rise and face east.)* Let Blohim Tzabaoth be praised unto the countless ages of time, Amen. *(All give Practicus sign, then face as usual.)*

(Hierophant then goes around lodge once against sun and then to west. Hiereus falls in before Hierophant, and Hegemon falls in behind him as he posses their stations. In the west, they form the triangle facing west as before, except that Hegemon is to the right and Hiereus to the left.)

Hierophant: Let us rehearse the prayer of the Water Spirits.

Terrible king of the sea, who holds the keys of the cataracts of heaven, and who encloses the subterranean waters in the cavernous hollows of earth; king of the deluge and of the rains of Spring; who opens the sources of the rivers and the fountains; who commands moisture, which is the blood of the earth, to become the sap of the plants; we adore you, and we invoke you. Speak to us, your mobile and changeful creatures, in the great tempests, and we will tremble before you. Speak to us also in the murmur of the clear waters, and we will desire your love.

O vastness in which all the rivers of being seek to lose themselves, which renew themselves ever in thee! O thou ocean of infinite perfection! O height that reflects itself in the depths! O depth that exhales to the heights! Lead us into the true life, through intelligence, through love! Lead us into immortality through sacrifice, that we may be found worthy to offer one day unto you the water, the blood and the tears for the remission of sins. Amen.

Depart now in peace to your habitations, *(traces banishing pentagram of Water)* and peace be between us. *(Officers face south, fall in line behind Hiereus, and move around hall against sun one circuit, then fall out as they reach their stations.)*

Hierophant: ! !!! ! !!!
Hiereus: ! !!! ! !!!
Hegemon: ! !!! ! !!!
Hierophant: ! *(All are seated.)*

Part Four: The Philosophus Grade

(Abiegnus ceased publication before this final part could be published. It appears here in print for the first time.)

Opening of the grade of Philosophus

Hierophant: Fratres and Sorores, you will assist me to open this Temple in the grade of Philosophus. Frater Hegemon, see that the Temple is properly guarded.

Hegemon: *(Knocks without opening the door; Sentinel knocks).* Very Honored Hierophant, the Temple is properly guarded.

Hierophant: Honored Hiereus, see that none below the grade of Philosophus is present.

Hiereus: Fratres and Sorores, give the sign of the Philosophus Grade. *(All give sign to Hiereus, who responds with the same sign.)* Very Honored Hierophant, all present have attained the Four equals Seven Grade. *(Hiereus gives the sign to Hierophant, who responds with the same sign.)*

Hierophant: Honored Hegemon, to what element is this grade attributed?

Hegemon: To the element of Fire.

Hierophant: Honored Hiereus, to what planet does this grade especially refer?

Hiereus: To the Planet Venus.

Hierophant: Honored Hegemon, what paths are attached to this grade?

Hegemon: The 29th, 28th, and 27th Paths of Qoph, Tzaddi, and Peh.

Hierophant: ! *(Knocks.)* Let us adore the Lord and King of Fire. *(All rise and face east.)* Yod Heh Vau Heh Tzabaoth—Blessed be thou. Leader of armies is thy name! Amen. *(All make sign of Fire.)*

(Hierophant leaves the east, goes with sun around lodge once to east. Hiereus and Hegemon fall in as Hierophant circumambulates, Hiereus before Hierophant, Hegemon behind. At the end of the movement, officers fan out: Hierophant stands before southern altar, Hegemon to left and behind, Hiereus to right and behind; the three officers form a triangle. All face south.)

Hierophant:	*(traces an invoking pentagram of Fire to the east).* And the Elohim said, Let us make Adam in our own image, after our likeness, and let him have dominion over the beasts of the field. In the Name of Elohim, mighty and ruling, and in the name of Tetragrammaton Tzabaoth, spirits of Fire, adore your Creator! *(Hierophant traces the symbol of Leo in the center of the pentagram.)*
Hegemon:	In the name of Michael, great archangel of Fire, and in the sign of the head of the Lion, spirits of Fire, adore your Creator! *(Hierophant traces an equal-armed cross over the pentagram.)*
Hiereus:	In the names and letters of the great southern quadrangle, spirits of Fire, adore your Creator! *(Hierophant holds the head of his staff at the center of the pentagram.)*
Hierophant:	In the three great secret Names of God borne upon the banners of the south, OIP TEAA PDOCE, spirits of Fire, adore your Creator! In the name of EDEL PRNAA, great king of the south, spirits of Fire, adore your Creator! *(Officers face north, fall into line as Hiereus begins moving, and move around hail with Sun. They complete one circuit from south to south and then fall out as they reach their stations, taking their places for this Grade.)*
Hierophant:	In the Name of Yod Heh Vau Heh Tzabaoth, I declare this Temple opened in the 4=7 grade of Philosophus.
Hierophant:	!!! !!! !
Hiereus:	!!! !!! !
Hegemon:	!!! !!! !
Hierophant:	! *(All are seated.)*

Introduction of the candidate

Hierophant:	Fratres and Sorores, our Frater/Soror N., having been proved in the work of the Practiicus Grade, is now eligible for advancement to the grade of Philosophus, and I have received a dispensation from the Chiefs to admit him/her in due form. Honored Hegemon, superintend the preparation of the Practicus and give the customary alarm.

(Hiereus sees that lamps for the three major officers and fire incense are placed on the altars. Hegemon goes to door and leaves hail; Kerux stands by door. Hegemon blindfolds candidate, gives him/her the Emblem of Fire, and instructs him/her in the knock !!! !!! ! and in the words he/she will be expected to say. Candidate then gives knock at door, and Kerux opens door slightly.)

Kerux: All things shall be tested by the Fire. *(Door is opened, and Hegemon brings candidate to West of the pillars, facing him/her east.)*

Hierophant: Frater/Soror Monocris de Astris, by what emblem have you entered this hall of living flame?

Hegemon **(for candidate):** By this Emblem of Fire. *(Kerux takes Emblem.)*

Hierophant: Frater/Soror, give the sign of the Grade of Water. *(Candidate gives it.)*

Hierophant: Companion Kerux, receive from the candidate the Word of the Grade of Water.
(Candidate gives word to Kerux.)

Kerux: Greatly Honored Hierophant, I have received it.

Hierophant: Let our Frater/Soror be placed between the Pillars, with his/her face toward the east. *(This is done; Hegemon stands behind candidate, and Kerux goes with sun to Fire altar, leaves Emblem, gets incense, and returns.)* Frater/Soror Monocris de Astris, will you pledge yourself to maintain the same secrecy and diligence in the mysteries of this grade as you are pledged to maintain for those of the previous grades?
(Candidate answers.)

Hierophant: Then you will stretch your arms above your head to their full limit and say: "I pledg by the torrent of Fire."
(Candidate does so.)

Hierophant: Let the symbol of blindness be removed. *(This is done by Hegemon. At this point Hegemon and Hiereus both go with Sun around the lodge, take. the censer and cup from their altars, and return, Hegemon standing by White Pillar, Hiereus by Black.)* Take the incense in your right hand and wave it to the south, and say: "Let the powers of Fire witness my pledge."

(Candidate does so. Kerux takes incense back to its altar and returns with sun.)

Hierophant: Let the candidate be purified with Water and consecrated with Fire in confirmation of this pledge, and in the name of the Lord of the Universe, who works in silence and whom nothing but silence can express.

Hiereus: I purify with Water. *(Sprinkles candidate thrice, and traces cross before candidate with cup.)*

Hegemon: I consecrate with Fire. *(Censes candidate thrice, and traces cross before candidate with censer.)*

(Hiereus and Hegemon go back to their stations with Sun when done.)

Advancement of the candidate

Hierophant: Frater/Soror Monocris de Astris, before you are the Portals of the 31st, 32nd, and 29th Paths. Of these, as you know, the central one leads to the grade of Theoricus from that of Zelator, and from that standpoint the Portals of the 30th, 25th, and 28th Paths stand before you. From both these two Grades, the Path to the left leads to the Grade of Practicus, and from that further standpoint the Portals of the 27th, 26th, and 23rd Paths stand before you. Of all these, the 29th Path of Qoph, the 28th Path of Tzaddi, and the 27th Path of Peh are now open to you. Take in your right hand the Emblem of Fire, and follow your guide, Anubis the Guardian, who leads you through the Paths of Pisces, Aquarius, and Mars.

Kerux: Let us enter into the presence of the Lord of Truth. Arise and follow me.

(Kerux leads Candidate forward from between pillars and once around the lodge with Sun, stopping just west of pillars. Meanwhile the following passages are read, slowly:)

Hiereus: *(first circumambulation).* The Sphinx of Egypt spoke and said: I am the synthesis of the elemental forces. I am also the symbol of Humanity. I am life and I am death. I am the Child of the Night of Time.

Hegemon: *(second circumambulation).* I am the soul in twin aspect, united to the Higher by purification, perfected by suffering, glorified by trial. I have come where the great gods are, through the power of the mighty Name.

Hiereus: *(third circumambulation)*. I have passed through the gates of the firmament. Give me your hands, for I am made as you, O Lords of Truth! For you are the formers of the soul.

Hierophant: *(as candidate returns to west)*. Let the candidate be placed between the pillars, that he/she may stand in the gateway of the realm of Fire.

(Candidate is placed between pillars. At this point Hierophant, Hegemon, and Hiereus all leave their stations, taking lamps with them, and go around the hall with sun. Hierophant goes directly to south and then goes between the altar and the pillars, facing candidate; Hiereus and Hegemon, in that order, do the same, timing their movement so that each one arrives as the previous officer leaves.)

Hierophant: I am the apex of the pyramid of flame. I am the solar fire pouring forth its beams on the lower world, life-giving, light-producing. By what sign do you seek to pass by?

Candidate: *(prompted)*. By the sign of the pyramid of flame.

Hierophant: Stoop not down into that darkly splendid world, wherein lieth a faithless depth and Hades wrapped in gloom, delighting in unintelligible images, precipitous, winding, a black ever-rolling abyss ever espousing a body unluminous, formless, and void. Stoop not down, for a precipice lies beneath the earth, a descent of seven steps, and therein is established the throne of an evil and fatal force. Stoop not down, for there is a place for your image in a realm ever splendid.

(Hierophant returns to station with Sun. Hiereus faces candidate.)

Hiereus: I am the left basal angle of the triangle of flame. I am fire volcanic and terrestrial, flaming through abysses of earth, rending, penetrating, tearing asunder the curtain of matter. I am fire constrained and tormented, whirling in storm. By what sign do you seek to pass by?

Candidate: *(prompted)*. By the sign of the pyramid of flame.

Hiereus: Nature persuades us that there are pure spirits, and that even the lowest seeds of matter can become useful and good. But these are mysteries which are evolved in the profound abysses of the mind. So therefore first that priest who governs the works of fire must sprinkle with the lustral water of the loud-resounding sea.

(Hiereus returns to station with sun. Hegemon faces candidate.)

Hegemon: I am the right basal angle of the triangle of flame. I am the fire astral and fluid, winding and coruscating through the firmament. I am the life of beings, the vital heat of existence. By what sign do you seek to pass by?

Candidate: *(prompted).* By the sign of the pyramid of fire.

Hegemon: Such a fire exists, extending throughout the rushings of air, or even a formless fire whence comes the image of a voice, or even a flashing light, abounding, revolving, whirling forth, crying aloud. Also, there is the vision of the fire-flashing courser of light, or of a child borne aloft on the shoulders of the celestial steed, fiery or clothed in gold, or naked and shooting shafts of light with a bow. But if your meditation prolongs itself, you shall unite all these symbols in the form of a lion.

(Hegemon returns to station with sun.)

Kerux: And when, after all the phantoms are banished, you shall see that holy and formless fire—that fire which darts and flashes through the hidden depths of the universe—hear the voice of Fire.

Hierophant: Let the candidate enter into the realm of fire, and learn the mysteries of fire in the midst of the purifying flame. Those mysteries are of the high wisdom of alchemy, passed down to us in the words of the Emerald Tablet.

(Candidate is brought forward to altar, and Kerux gestures at the flame of the lamp.)

Hiereus: True, without error, certain and most true: that which is above is as that which is below, and that which is below is as that which is above, to perform the miracles of the One Thing. And as all things were from One, by the meditation of One, so from this One Thing come all things by adaptation. Its father is the Sun; its mother is the Moon, the wind carried it in its belly, the nurse thereof is the Earth.

Hegemon: It is the father of all perfection and the consummation of the whole world. Its power is integral if it be turned to Earth. Thou shalt separate the Earth from the Fire, the subtle from the coarse, gently and with much ingenuity.

It ascends from Earth to Heaven and descends again to Earth, and receives the power of the superiors and the inferiors.

Hierophant: Thus, thou hast the glory of the whole world; therefore, let all obscurity flee before thee. This is the strong fortitude of all fortitude, overcoming every subtle and penetrating every solid thing. Thus, the world was created. Hence are all wonderful adaptations, of which this is the manner. Therefore, am I called Hermes the Thrice Great, having the three parts of the philosophy of the whole world. That is finished which I have to say concerning the operation of the Sun.

(Hierophant leaves station and goes between altar and diagram.)

The Hieroglyphic Monad, like the Emerald Tablet, resumes the whole mystery of the alchemical work. *(Hierophant points to Monad on closed diagram.)* It is composed of the circle of the Sun; the crescent of the Moon; the cross of the four elements—Earth, Air, Water, and Fire—and the sign of Aries, representing another Fire, the Secret Fire of transmutation, which is present in all material things and which descends in a hidden manner in the Spring of the year.

The Monad also comprises the signs of the seven planets: Sun; Moon; Mercury; Venus; Mars; Jupiter; Saturn. *(Hierophant traces out signs as he names them.)* It is also, in its simplest meaning, Mercury, the First Matter of the alchemists, heated by the alchemical fire of Aries.

The work of alchemy is a work of the redemption of matter, for it is an axiom of the Great Art that Nature, unaided, fails. The natural mineral in the Earth too rarely achieves the perfection of gold; the natural man or woman in the world too rarely achieves the perfection of humanity. It is for this reason that in the secret wisdom, the world we know is said to be a fallen world.

(Hierophant opens the altar diagram.)

This is the symbolic representation of the Fall. For the great goddess EVE, Nature, who in the Grade of Water supported the columns of the Sephiroth, was tempted by the tree of knowledge whose branches reach upward into the seven lower Sephiroth, but also downward into the Kingdom of Shells. She reached down unto the Qlippoth, and the columns were unsupported; the system of the Sephiroth was shattered and with it fell ADAM, Humanity, the Lesser Countenance.

Then arose the great dragon with seven heads and ten horns, and the garden was made desolate, and Malkuth was cut off from the Sephiroth by the coils of the dragon and linked to the Kingdom of Shells. And the seven lower Sephiroth were cut off from the three Supernals in Daath, at the feet of Aima Elohim.

And on the heads of the dragon are the crowns of the Kings of Edom. And since the greatest rise of the Serpent was in Daath; therefore, there is, as it were, another Sephirah, making for the averse Tree, eleven Spheres rather than ten. Thus, were the rivers of Eden desecrated, and from the mouth of the dragon rushed the infernal waters in Daath. This is Leviathan, the Crooked Serpent.

But between the devastated garden and the Supernal Eden, Tetragrammaton Elohim placed the letters of the Name and the Flaming Sword, that the uppermost part of the Tree of Life might not be involved in the Fall. And thence it is necessary that the BEN ADAM shall descend to Malkuth and from thence rise up, to cast down the dragon, purify the celestial rivers and make all things new.

This same renewal is the goal of the transmuting art of the alchemists.

Reception of the candidate

Hierophant: The work before you is to make the radiant gold of the perfected self from the cold and corruptible lead of the natural self—to achieve the Great Work of alchemy in yourself, with yourself as both the *prima materia* and the transmuting Stone. I ask you, therefore: Are you willing to take up this work?
(*Candidate answers.*)

Hierophant: Then I confer on you the secrets of this grade. The step of this grade is the same as that of the other elemental grades. The sign of the grade is given thus: *(does so)* and represents the triangle of Fire. The Word of the grade is AESH, Aleph, Shin, the Hebrew word for Fire.

I also confer upon you the title Pharos Illuminans, which means Illuminating Tower of Light. And as you have now attained to the highest of the elemental grades of our Order, I further give you the Word which completes the First Degree: PHRATH, the Fourth River of Eden. It is spelled Peh, Resh, Tau. Remember it well, for it will become a key to further mysteries.

(Kerux leads candidate to a seat in the southeast of the hall. Hierophant returns to place.)

Hierophant: The grade of Philosophus is the last of the four steps which lie between the Neophyte and Portal Grades— between the first glimpse of the Light, and the door to its full manifestation. In your progress among us, you have passed from the depths of the Earth, through the winds of Heaven, along the shores of the Great Sea, to the realms of Fire.

The grade of Earth, as you have seen, is the grade of the Builder; the grade of Air, that of the Knight; the grade of Water, that of the Seer. The grade of Fire, in turn, is the grade of the Alchemist, and in it the symbolism of alchemy is central. As you continue on the quest of the Companions, however, you will learn that the four ways symbolized in these four grades are ultimately one. Similarly, the four tasks you have taken upon yourself—the building of the city of Adocentyn, the struggle against the inner enemies of wisdom, the quest for the light of the Grail, and the work of alchemical transmutation—are, in the final analysis, the same. It is because of this that the virtue of this grade is Justice, which balances and comprises all the other virtues.

Therefore, be prompt and active as the sylphs, but avoid frivolity and caprice. Be energetic and strong as the salamanders, but avoid irritability and ferocity. Be flexible and attentive to images, like the undines, but avoid idleness and changeability. Be laborious and patient like the gnomes, but avoid grossness and avarice. So shall you develop the powers inherent in yourself, and make yourself fit to command the spirits of the elements.

I now present you with the working tool of this grade, the Wand. *(He shows it.)* You will prepare such a wand for yourself as part of the work of this grade. It is not an accident that this is closely akin to the pilgrim's staff. Wand and staff alike represent unity, but where the staff symbolizes the unity of will that alone can control the powers of magic, the wand signifies that deeper unity of self toward which you must always. strive.

Another of the principal emblems of this grade is the Great Watchtower of the South, the third Tablet of the Angelic or Enochian system. *(Points to tablet on south altar)* The letters on it spell out Names of Power. From it are drawn the Three Holy Secret Names of God OIP TEAA PDOCE, which are borne upon the banners of the south, and there are also numberless names of angels, archangels and spirits ruling the element of Fire.

Beyond the elemental grades lies the Portal Grade, to which you are now eligible to aspire. In order to receive this, you must prove yourself in the lore and the disciplines of our ancient wisdom, and you must continue to take an active part in the work of your lodge and our Order. A syllabus of the work required will be provided to you.

Closing of the Philosophus Grade

Hierophant: ! *(knocks).* Companions, you will assist me to close this lodge in the Four equals Seven grade of Philosophus. Let us adore the Lord and King of Fire. !!! *(All rise and face East.)* Elohim, blessed be thy name to the countless ages, Amen. *(All give sign, then face as usual.)*

(Hierophant then goes around lodge once against sun and then to south. Hiereus falls in before Hierophant, and Hegemon falls in behind him as he possess their stations. In the west, they form the triangle facing south as before, except that Hegemon is to the right and Hiereus to the left.)

Hierophant: Let us rehearse the prayer of the Fire Spirits.

Immortal, eternal, ineffable and uncreated father of all, borne upon the chariot of worlds which ever roll in ceaseless motion; ruler over the ethereal vastness where the throne of your power is raised, from the summit of which your eyes behold all, and your pure and holy ears hear all—help us, your children, whom you have loved since the birth of the ages of time! Your majesty, golden, vast, and eternal, shines above the heaven of stars. Above them are you exalted.

O flashing fire, there you illuminate all things with your insupportable glory, whence flow those ceaseless streams of splendor that nourish your infinite spirit. This infinite spirit nourishes all and makes that inexhaustible treasure of generation which ever encompasses you, replete with the numberless forms with which you have filled it from the beginning.

From this spirit arise those most holy kings who are around your throne and who compose your court. O universal father, one and alone! Father alike of immortals and mortals, you have specially created powers similar to your eternal thought and to your venerable essence. You have established them above the angels who announce your will to the world.

Lastly, you have created us as a third order in our elemental empire. There our continual exercise is to praise and to adore your desires; there we burn in eternal aspiration unto you, O father! O mother of mothers, archetype eternal of maternity and love! O child, flower of all children! Form of all forms! Soul, spirit, harmony and numeral of all things. Amen.

Depart now in peace to your habitations, *(traces banishing pentagram of Fire)* and peace be between us.
(Officers face south, fall in line behind Hiereus, and move around hall against sun one circuit, then fall out as they reach their stations.)

Hierophant: !!! !!! !
Hiereus: !!! !!! !
Hegemon: !!! !!! !
Hierophant: ! *(All are seated.)*

Swordsmanship and esoteric spirituality: an introduction to Gerard Thibault's Academie de l'Espee

This introductory essay discussing The Academy of the Sword *was penned for the* Journal of Asian Martial Arts, *a peer-reviewed journal of martial arts studies, and was published in 2000. Different audiences have different interests, and this article thus focused on the technical side of Thibault's work. It was no more successful in attracting interest to Thibault's remarkable work than "Geometries of the Sword," my earlier article for* Gnosis, *and thus makes a suitable conclusion for a decade of frustrations and incomplete achievements. While this article was in press, I decided to turn my attention primarily to the nature spirituality of the Druid Revival, and it would be many years before I returned to the themes discussed in this volume.*

The relation between Asian martial arts and Western combat systems has been understood in sharply different ways over the last century or so. In 1887, Arthur Conan Doyle could simply describe a derivative of jujutsu as "Japanese wrestling," implying that whatever the differences in technique, Asian and European fighting methods could still be placed in same general categories (Tracy, 1977: 25; Barton-Wright, 1899: 268–275, 402–410).[1] By contrast, toward the middle of the twentieth century, Asian combat systems came to be seen in the West as a set of exotic practices somehow connected to the "Eastern wisdom" of Asian spiritual traditions, and thus radically different from anything Western cultures had to offer. The term "martial art" itself came into common use on the wings of this perception; until quite recently it was rare to see the phrase used for any combat system originating outside East Asia.

More recently the pendulum has moved back the other way to some degree. Much of the hype and confusion surrounding Asian martial arts, not to mention Asian spiritual traditions, has been cleared away as these have become more familiar in the West. Equally, it has become increasingly clear that Western combat systems in the Middle Ages, Renaissance, and early modern periods had much in common with their Asian equivalents.

One distinction between East and West that has seemed solid up to the present, though, has to do with the presence of systems of combat rooted in philosophical and spiritual traditions of inner development. Hype or no hype, many Asian martial arts do fall into this category, some (for example, taijiquan and other Chinese arts of the neijia or Inner School) deriving much of their theory and practice from spiritual teachings (Schipper, 1993).[2] In the Western world, by contrast, connections of this sort have been thought to be absent.

This situation has recently been transformed by the discovery that at least one European combat system had deep connections to mystical and occult teachings. This recognition was the work of Joy Hancox (1992: 46–48, 203–205), whose study of a tradition of mystical geometry led her to the inner basis of the most enigmatic text in the history of Western swordsmanship, Gerard Thibault's *Academie de l'Espee* ("Academy of the Sword"), originally published in 1630.[3] The present author's research has confirmed and expanded Hancox' original insight. In the course of translating Thibault's text and putting his methods into practice, it has become clear that his system—which has called forth baffled responses from many modern historians of fencing—makes sense only if it is understood as a martial art rooted in Western esoteric spirituality (Castle, 1969: 67–73).

The rediscovery of this dimension of Thibault's system has relevance to the scholarly study of martial arts generally (as well as to the study of Western esoteric traditions), but it also has a special relevance to students of Asian martial arts. Up to the present, East Asian traditions have provided the only known examples of deep interconnection between the martial arts and esoteric spirituality, and those examples are inevitably colored by the distinctive cultural patterns of mysticism and combat in China, Japan, and other Asian societies. Coming as it does from the very different setting of Renaissance Europe, Thibault's swordsmanship system embodies radically different assumptions about spirituality, combat, and their potential connections. It, therefore, casts a new light on the entire range of issues implied by the spiritual dimensions of the martial arts.

Western and Eastern esotericism

Several factors have played a role in obscuring the inner side of Thibault's swordsmanship. One of these is a tendency, pervasive in Western cultures since the Scientific Revolution, to dismiss the esoteric spirituality of the West as a body of superstitions unworthy of serious study. It is still common to find scholars with solid backgrounds in comparative religion, who are highly familiar with Buddhist, Daoist, and other non-Western traditions of inner transformation, but have never heard of equivalent Western systems such as Neo-Platonism or Cabala (Faivre, 1994).

However, another obscuring factor is more central to the present study. While there are important similarities between the esoteric traditions of Asia and Western Europe, the differences are also significant. One crucial distinction is found in the relative importance of ideas of intrinsic or subtle energy. Concepts of this sort are central to many Asian spiritual traditions, and thus play an equally central role in many Asian martial arts.[4] While the idea of subtle energy does occur in European thought, it has typically had a much less central place—particularly in the traditions of spiritual practice that form the bridge between esoteric philosophy and the martial arts.[5]

For example, many Asian methods of meditation give a great deal of attention to issues of posture, breathing, and the flow of subtle energies through the body. In some traditions (for example, Daoist "breath circulation"), subtle energy work is the primary focus of meditative practice. By contrast, few European methods of meditation paid more than cursory attention to such issues until quite recent times. Typically, the major focus of older Western meditative methods was on perceiving and understanding aspects of existence beyond the material. The standard methods included contemplation of symbolic images and training in philosophic modes of thought. The body and its subtle energies played little if any role in this work.[6]

This difference in focus must be grasped to make sense of the corresponding difference between Gerard Thibault's swordsmanship and Asian martial arts. The primary esoteric element in Thibault's system is not energetic but conceptual. Like many Asian martial arts, it bases itself on teachings concerning the hidden reality that underlies ordinary experience. However, in the West, that reality was not generally understood in terms of interactions of subtle energies. Rather, in the teachings from which Thibault's fencing derived, it was seen as a structure of transcendent ideas or patterns—a structure traditionally expressed in terms of geometry.

Geometry has had a place in Western esoteric traditions since the time of Pythagoras, who taught a doctrine of mystical mathematics in the late seventh century BCE (Guthrie, 1988; Burkert, 1972). At various points in the history of Western esoteric spirituality, the Pythagorean tradition has played a significant role, but never so centrally as in the Renaissance.

Pythagorean geometry was one of the few branches of ancient Greek and Roman mystical tradition that the Christian Church accepted and incorporated into its own synthesis, with results that can be seen in the magnificent Gothic cathedrals of medieval Europe (Flint, 1991; Lesser, 1957). To this medieval heritage was added a substantial body of teaching rediscovered with the resurgence of classical learning at the beginning of the Renaissance. As a result, Pythagorean ideas came to be part of the common currency of thought all through Renaissance Europe (Hersey, 1976; Yates, 1969). At the same time, the importance of geometry to architects and engineers during the same period meant that geometrical ideas formed an obvious bridge between the esoteric and the practical—a bridge that architects, in particular, used constantly all through the Renaissance (Hersey, 1976).

Gerard Thibault and Academie de l'Espee

Gerard Thibault d'Anvers, painter, physician, and architect as well as master swordsman—the phrase "Renaissance man" comes irresistibly to mind—was born in 1574 in Antwerp. The names of his fencing teachers have not been preserved, as European martial traditions paid less attention to issues of lineage than their Asian equivalents, but he would have had the opportunity to study with masters of the Spanish school of fencing; Spain at that time ruled the Netherlands, and Spanish fencers had a continent-wide reputation as lethal duelists. Certainly, the approach to fencing preserved in Thibault's book bears many similarities to the Spanish style, with the upright stance and the use of a circle to govern footwork being only the most obvious connections.[7]

The Spanish style was one of several new schools of fencing that had arisen out of a revolution in the arts of combat then underway in Europe. Central to that revolution was the abandonment of the heavy medieval broadsword and shield for a new style of weapon, the rapier, with a lighter, longer blade and a set of metal bars around the hilt to protect hand and wrist. The new rapier swordsmanship relied far more on thrusts than on cutting blows; and, in the Spanish school and some others, drew heavily on geometry as a theoretical basis. It is not hard to see why: the rapier is the most geometrical of weapons, a straight line moved through space to intersect another line or to penetrate the surface of the opponent's body. It was in this context, certainly, that Thibault himself came to understand the art of fencing.

In 1611, Thibault presented himself before the acknowledged Dutch fencing masters in a competition in Antwerp and took first prize. Summoned before Prince Maurice of Nassau to demonstrate his skill, he defeated all corners in a famous exhibition that lasted several days. The resulting reputation and financial support enabled him to begin work on a systematic manual of his approach to swordsmanship. *Academie de l'Espee*, produced with the support of the Holy Roman Emperor, the King of France, and a galaxy of lesser notables, was more than a decade in production and was finally published one year after Thibault's death in 1629 (de la Fontaine de Verwey, 1978).

Nearly 400 folio pages long, illustrated with forty-nine double-page engravings each showing a dozen or more images of fencing technique, the original edition of *Academie de l'Espee* may well be the largest and most ornate book on swordsmanship ever written. It was republished once, in a much less lavish form, in 1660. By that time, however, the Spanish school had begun to wane in popularity; the Italian school, ancestral to modern sport fencing, was well on its way to dominance. At the same time, Renaissance traditions of mystical geometry were of increasingly little interest to a society whose attention had been caught by the successes of the Scientific Revolution (Yates, 1964). While esoteric spiritual traditions played an important role all through Renaissance culture, they were thrust to the intellectual and cultural fringes of the Western world as the modern period dawned. Correspondingly, Thibault's work was entirely forgotten except by a few historians of the literature of swordsmanship until quite recent times.

Elements of Thibault's method

Trying to reconstruct an extinct martial art from a written descrip- tion is a difficult task. In the present case, that task is made easier by the extraordinary level of detail in Thibault's book. The techniques in *Academie de l'Espee* are presented with a thoroughness unmatched by other contemporary fencing manuals; positions and movements are marked against an intricate geometric pattern, and such details as shifts of body weight from leg to leg and the relative pressure of one sword against the other are covered wherever relevant. It is thus possible not only to describe but also to practice most of Thibault's techniques with some assurance.

Summary of the basic principles of Thibault's approach to swordsmanship

1. Geometrical proportion

"[A]ll the measures and stances to be observed in this practice," Thibault proclaims near the beginning of his book, "proceed from the proportions of the human body" (Thibault, 1998: 10). These proportions give rise to the "mysterious circle," the complex geometrical pattern used to teach swordsmanship; to the proper length of the sword; to the three Instances, or combat distances; and even to such apparently minor details as the design of the hanger and cincture that support the rapier from the sword belt. In Thibault's system, each fencer uses his own height as the basic unit of measure, with every other factor unfold- ing from this by way of a series of geometrical operations.

2. Natural posture and movement

Thibault criticized the fencing styles of his day for a reliance on unnatural stances. "I have seen that people are accustomed by all of these styles to strange postures: the body bent in several angles with feet and legs put out of their natural proportion, and in postures wholly repugnant to the ordinary way one walks or stands. Instead of showing any great courage by these postures, in fact, those who use them inconvenience themselves and lessen their own force" (Thibault, 1998: 17). Thibault's own posture, based on that of the Spanish school, is an upright stance with the feet one foot-length apart, the toes slightly angled outward, and the sword and arm extended straight out toward the opponent. All his footwork, similarly, is based on the ordinary walking pace.

3. Use of sentiment

In fencing, the French word *sentiment* ("awareness" or "sensitivity"), implies a fine degree of sensitivity to the pressure of one blade against the other. To Thibault, sentiment is the key to all close combat. Accordingly, and in flat contradiction to contemporary practice, he instructs the student to keep his blade in contact with the opponent's, using the second "weight"—that is, the lightest possible degree of pressure—to maintain contact. "Once we have contact between the blades, we are able to make our approaches against the adversary with assurance, since we are certain always to know in time the designs which he makes against us; no sooner are these begun than we have already prepared ourselves against them" (Thibault, 1630: Ch. 9, p. 12). Mastery of sentiment makes it possible to "subject" the opponent's blade, controlling its movements. In turn, the key to sentiment is a matter of footwork and the proper position of the body.

4. Unity of attack and defense

Like most early fencing manuals, Thibault's book teaches few purely defensive techniques. Instead, nearly all of his techniques combine attack and defense: thrusts are made at angles that simultaneously ward off the adversary's attacks, and footwork is designed to move the body out of danger and create openings for an immediate response at the same time. In some of Thibault's most typical techniques, an attack is deflected and the attacker cut down in a single motion. Similarly, in the last or "execution" stage of most techniques the opponent's sword is forced out of line by the same movement that delivers the final killing thrust, making it impossible for him to counterattack even in his death throes.

5. Constant motion

Static postures play a role in training, but Thibault cautions that they are not to be used in actual combat: "Let [the student] continue always to move, using a free and natural pace, toward one or the other of the two sides... [a]s soon as he comes into measure, let him assure himself of his

262   THE CITY OF HERMES

opponent's sword, by attacking it to subject it, or by binding it, or by covering it, or by carrying out an estocade of first intention along it, if this is convenient, continuing to move always without interruption" (Thibault, 1998: 49). Constant movement was also one of the most noted features of the Spanish school from which Thibault's system was derived.

6. Control of the centerline

One of the major strategic issues in Thibault's fencing was the center-line—the "Straight Line," in his terminology—measuring the shortest distance between the two opponents. To hold the centerline is to close it against the opponent's attacks, forcing him to use slower, more round-about trajectories that can more easily be countered or forestalled. Should the opponent leave the centerline unguarded, at least two immediate options present themselves: first, "entering within the angle," a movement similar to the *irimi* technique of aikido, which slips past his point and permits a variety of attacks, including grappling moves that seize or pin the hilt of his sword; and second, an "estocade [straight thrust] of first intention," which strikes along the open centerline to a vital target.

7. Alternation of line and circle

Like the geometry on which it is based, Thibault's fencing system relies on a combination of straight lines and circular movements. Most of the attacks are made along straight lines of least distance, and the basic posture extends the sword straight out toward the opponent along the centerline: still, circular attacks and a variety of cuts also play a significant role. In the same way, footwork includes both linear and circular movements: for example, it is very common for a fencer using Thibault's system to step straight with one leg and bring the other one after it along an arc, shifting to a more advantageous angle.

8. Predominance of the mind

In many ways, the most important feature of Thibault's method, and the one that links it most closely to Western esoteric traditions, is its reliance on the mental dimension. Thibault dismissed the purely physical approach to fencing as inadequate: "It is hardly surprising that those who do not aspire to any science of arms, but try to succeed solely by long and continual exercises in quickness of the body and of the arm, by which they are able to prevail by forestalling and taking advantage of opponents rather than by compelling them, do not comprehend the secrets of so noble a weapon" (Thibault, 1998: 49). From his standpoint, strength and speed are of small importance, and the fencer who relies on either one is likely to come to grief. In fact, Thibault cautions the student against "wasting his movements by an ill-advised quickness" (Thibault, 1630: Ch. II, p. 5), and provides plenty of counters to use against those who try to force their way out of a situation by simple strength. In the Pythagorean teachings of Renaissance esoteric spirituality, the realm of matter is passive, shaped and governed by the realm of Nous, the transcendent Mind. In the same way, in Thibault's system of swordsmanship, the opponent is first conquered mentally, and his physical defeat follows inevitably after.

Notes

1. The art of baritsu, "the Japanese system of wrestling," is mentioned in one of Doyle's Sherlock Holmes stories as a skill possessed by the great detective. Doyle derived this from "bartitsu," a version of jujutsu developed by (and named after) the Englishman E. W. Barton-Wright, and introduced to England in 1899.
2. The English-language literature on the interface between Asian martial arts and esoteric spirituality is immense, though dwarfed by that in several other languages. For the relation between Daoism and Chinese martial arts, see especially Schipper, K., *The Taoist Bod* (University of California Press, 1993).
3. The first eight chapters have been published in an English translation by the present author in Greer, J.M., *Academy of the Sword: A Renaissance Handbook of Hermetic Swordsmanship, Part One: Philosophy and Practice* (Fir Mountain Press, 1998), and the remainder will be published in three additional volumes by the same press. All quotes from the first eight chapters are from the published translation, cited as Thibault, 1998; all quotes from the remainder of the text are original translations made for this article and cited as Thibault d'Anvers, G., *Academie de l'Espee* (Elzevier, 1630).
4. The Chinese term *qi*, its Japanese cognate *ki*, and its partial Sanskrit equivalent *prana* are typical.
5. The Latin word *spiritus*, "spirit" or "breath," was the standard term for intrinsic energy in European medieval and Renaissance sources. More recent traditions in the West have made use of coined words such as *od* or *vril*, relied on transliterated Asian terms, or borrowed words such as "ether" and "magnetism" from the terminology of contemporary science.

6. Classic accounts of Western meditative practice may be found in the writings of Neoplatonist philosophers such as Plotinus (204–270 CE) and Iamblichus (c. 250–c. 325 CE) and in early Cabalistic works such as the anonymous *Sepher Yetzirah*. For modern accounts of Western esoteric meditative traditions, see Greer, J.M., *Paths of Wisdom* (Llewellyn, 1996), Bardon, F., *Initiation into Hermetics* (Kettig uber Koblenz, Osiris, 1962), Kaplan, A., *Meditation and Kabbalah* (Weiser, 1982), and Knight, G., *Experience of the Inner Worlds* (Weiser, 1995).

7. The question of an esoteric dimension to the Spanish school as a whole must be left open at this time. Spain was as influenced by the Pythagorean revival of the Renaissance as any other European country, but the constant presence of the Inquisition made Spanish practitioners of esoteric spirituality more than usually interested in keeping out of sight. A translation of *De la Filosofia de las Armas* (1582), the major work by the Spanish fencing master Jeronimo de Carranza, is reportedly in preparation and may shed light on this issue.

Bibliography

Bardon, F., *Initiation into Hermetics* (Kettig uber Koblenz, Osiris, 1962).

Barton-Wright, E., "The New Art of Self-Defence." *Pearson's Magazine* (1899, 7, pp. 268–275, pp. 402–410).

Burkert, W., *Lore and Science in Early Pythagoreanism* (Harvard University Press, 1972).

Castle, E., *Schools and Masters of Fence* (Shumway, 1969).

De la Fontaine de Verrwey, H., "Gerard Thibault and his *Academie de l'Espee*." In, *Quaerendo VIII*. (EJ. Brill, 1978).

Faivre, A., *Access to Western Esotericism* (State University of New York Press, 1994).

Flint, V., *The Rise of Magic in Early Medieval Europe* (Princeton University Press, 1991).

Greer, J.M., *Paths of Wisdom* (Llewellyn, 1996).

Greer, J.M., *Academy of the Sword: A Renaissance Handbook of Hermetic Swordsmanship, Part One: Philosophy and Practice* (Fir Mountain Press, 1998).

Guthrie, W., ed., *The Pythagorean Sourcebook and Library* (Phanes, 1988).

Hancox, J., *The Byrom Collection* (Jonathan Cape, 1992).

Hersey, G., (1976). *Pythagorean Palaces: Magic and Architecture in the Italian Renaissance* (Cornell University Press, 1976).

Kaplan, A., *Meditation and Kabbalah* (Weiser, 1982).

Knight, G., *Experience of the Inner Worlds* (Weiser, 1995).

Larocca, D., *The Academy of the Sword: Illustrating Fencing Books 1500–1800* (The Metropolitan Museum of Art, 1998).

Lesser, G., *Gothic Cathedrals and Sacred Geometry* (Alec Tiranti, 1975).

Schipper, K., *The Taoist Bod* (University of California Press, 1993).

Thibault d'Anvers, G., *Academie de l'Espee* (Elzevier, 1630).

Tracy, J., *Encyclopedia Sherlockiana* (Doubleday, 1977).

Yates, F., *Giordano Bruno and the Hermetic Tradition* (University of Chicago Press, 1964).

Yates, F., *Theatre of the World* (Chicago University Press, 1969).

INDEX